The Multilingual City

Full details of all our publications can be found at http://www.multilingual-matters.com, or by writing to Multilingual Matters, St Nicholas House, 31–34 High Street, Bristol BS1 2AW, UK.

This project has been funded with support from the European Commission. This publication reflects the views only of the authors, and the Commission cannot be held responsible for any use which may be made of the information contained therein.

 Lifelong Learning Programme

The Multilingual City

Vitality, Conflict and Change

Edited by
Lid King and Lorna Carson

MULTILINGUAL MATTERS
Bristol • Buffalo • Toronto

Library of Congress Cataloging in Publication Data
The Multilingual City: Vitality, Conflict and Change/Edited by Lid King and Lorna Carson.
Includes bibliographical references and index.
ISBN 978-1-78309-477-6 (hbk : alk. paper) — ISBN 978-1-78309-476-9 (pbk : alk. paper) — ISBN 978-1-78309-478-3 (ebook) 1. Multilingualism–Social aspects. 2. Urban dialects–Social aspects. 3. Linguistic change. I. King, Lid, editor. II. Carson, Lorna.
P115.45.M55 2016
306.44'6–dc23 2015029087

British Library Cataloguing in Publication Data
A catalogue entry for this book is available from the British Library.

ISBN-13: 978-1-78309-477-6 (hbk)
ISBN-13: 978-1-78309-476-9 (pbk)

Multilingual Matters
UK: St Nicholas House, 31–34 High Street, Bristol BS1 2AW, UK.
USA: UTP, 2250 Military Road, Tonawanda, NY 14150, USA.
Canada: UTP, 5201 Dufferin Street, North York, Ontario M3H 5T8, Canada.

Website: www.multilingual-matters.com
Twitter: Multi_Ling_Mat
Facebook: https://www.facebook.com/multilingualmatters
Blog: www.channelviewpublications.wordpress.com

Copyright © 2016 Lid King, Lorna Carson and the authors of individual chapters.

All rights reserved. No part of this work may be reproduced in any form or by any means without permission in writing from the publisher.

The policy of Multilingual Matters/Channel View Publications is to use papers that are natural, renewable and recyclable products, made from wood grown in sustainable forests. In the manufacturing process of our books, and to further support our policy, preference is given to printers that have FSC and PEFC Chain of Custody certification. The FSC and/or PEFC logos will appear on those books where full certification has been granted to the printer concerned.

Typeset by Techset Composition India (P) Ltd, Bangalore and Chennai, India.

Contents

Contributors	vii
Foreword	ix
Introduction: 'Multilingualism is Lived Here'	1
Lorna Carson and Lid King	
Investigating the City	1
New Patterns of Living, Working, Communicating and Belonging	2
The Study of Urban Multilingualism	3
Stories from the LUCIDE Cities	5
The Aims of the LUCIDE Consortium	5
LUCIDE's Research on Urban Multilingualism	7
Defining the Parameters of this Volume	8
The Vitality of Multilingualism	9
The Structure of this Volume	12
1 The Vitality of Urban Multilingualism	17
Itesh Sachdev and Sarah Cartwright	
From Antiquity to the 21st Century	18
The LUCIDE Cities	22
The Vitality of Urban Multilingualism across LUCIDE	41
The Increasing Vitality of Urban Multilingualism	46
2 The Sights and Sounds of the Multilingual City	49
Lorna Carson	
Investigating Multilingual Cityscapes	51
A Snapshot of LUCIDE Cityscapes	54
Views from Three LUCIDE Cityscapes	58
Some Visible Features of Multilingual Cityscapes	65
The Sounds of the Cityscape	73
Ordinary Multilingualism	80

3	Urban Multilingualism: Bond or Barrier? *Maria Stoicheva*	85
	The Image and Identity of the City and Why It Matters	86
	City Linguistic Diversity as a Social Fact	88
	The Linguistic Legibility of the Cityscape	93
	Languages and City Places	105
4	Language Policies and the Politics of Urban Multilingualism *Peter Skrandies*	115
	Public Policy and Urban Linguistic Diversity	115
	Language Policy and Planning and Urban Linguistic Diversity	119
	Evidence from the LUCIDE Cities	126
	The Politics of Urban Linguistic Diversity	142
5	Languages at School: A Challenge for Multilingual Cities *David Little*	149
	The Language of Schooling	150
	Integrating Minority Language Pupils	153
	Minority Languages in Education	160
	Foreign Language Learning	168
	Towards Integrated Plurilingual Repertoires	171
6	Multilingual Cities and the Future: Vitality or Decline? *Lid King*	179
	City and Hinterland: A More Historical Perspective	179
	Our City Stories: Some Conclusions From the Reports	184
	Some Reflections on the Future of our Cities	197
	LUCIDE City Reports	203
	References	204
	Index	218

Contributors

Lorna Carson is Assistant Professor in Applied Linguistics and Director of the Trinity Centre for Asian Studies at Trinity College Dublin, Ireland. She was the founding director of Trinity College's English for Academic Purposes programme (now the Centre for English Language Learning and Teaching) as well as the university's Japanese, Korean and Chinese Studies programmes. Her research focuses on multilingualism and language learning.

Sarah Cartwright read modern languages at university before going on to study for an MA in French at Pennsylvania State University, USA. After a long career as a languages teacher and manager in the 16–19 state sector, she joined London Metropolitan University in 2001 as Senior Lecturer in Education/PGCE Course Leader for Modern Languages. She subsequently worked for CILT, the National Centre for Languages, from 2006 until 2011, where she led a UK government project, 'Our Languages', supporting the teaching of community languages through partnerships between complementary and mainstream schools.

Lid King was a teacher of languages for 15 years. He worked for the Centre for Information on Language Teaching and Research (CILT) between 1989 and 2003 (for 11 years as Director) and was the National Director for Languages for England between 2003 and 2011. His early research interests were in modern Greek language and culture. He has also given courses and written on many aspects of language teaching and learning. For the last decade his main work has been in language policy development, not only in England but also in France, Eastern Europe and on behalf of the Council of Europe.

David Little retired in 2008 as Associate Professor of Applied Linguistics and Head of the School of Linguistic, Speech and Communication Sciences at Trinity College Dublin. His principal research interests are the theory and practice of learner autonomy in second language education, the exploitation of linguistic diversity in schools and classrooms, and the use of the *Common European Framework of Reference for Languages* to support the design of second language curricula, teaching and assessment.

Itesh Sachdev is Emeritus Professor of Language and Communication in the Department of Linguistics at the School of Oriental and African Studies, University of London. His research foci include ethnolinguistic vitality and identity in relations between members of minority and majority groups, multilingualism and multiculturalism, the role of attitudes and motivation in language teaching and learning, and intercultural communication.

Peter Skrandies is Coordinator for German and Sociolinguistics at the Language Centre of the London School of Economics and Political Science. Before joining LSE he worked as a language tutor, lexicographer, translator and lecturer in the Czech Republic, Germany and the UK. He studied English language and literature, history and British studies at the University of Hannover and Humboldt University, Berlin and completed a PhD in German and translation studies at the University of Manchester.

Maria Stoicheva is Jean Monnet Chair at Sofia University, St Kliment Ohridski, Bulgaria, where she also serves as Vice Dean of the Faculty of Philosophy and Associate Professor at the Department of European Studies. She studied at Sofia University and received a PhD in history of philosophy and habilitation in the philosophy of politics and culture from the same university. Her research concerns language policy, multilingualism, European identity and education policy.

Foreword

As the title suggests, this book is an exploration both of the vitality of multilingualism and of its critical importance in and for contemporary cities. It focuses mainly on Europe, not only because the initial research was carried out in the context of a European network, but also in light of the particularities of the European urban experience. In addition to stories about multilingualism from European cities, the authors include examples from Australia and Canada, drawn from cities which share something of the European experience but which are rather different in a number of ways. The book examines how the city has emerged as a key driver of the multilingual future, a concentration of different, changing cultures that somehow, together, manage to create a new identity. Through a network of multilingual cities, part-funded by the European Union Lifelong Learning programme, we have been able to analyse these phenomena more closely in 18 cities (13 in Europe and five in Canada and Australia). The LUCIDE network (*Languages in Urban Communities: Integration and Diversity for Europe*) is composed of university and civic partners, and represents the following 18 cities: Athens, Dublin, Hamburg, Limassol, London, Madrid, Melbourne, Montreal, Osijek, Oslo, Ottawa, Rome, Sofia, Strasbourg, Toronto, Utrecht, Vancouver, Varna.

The aims of our network are to depict how communication occurs in multilingual cities and to develop ideas about how to manage multilingual citizen communities.

Our network of multilingual cities is interested in the real-life complexities faced in various spheres and aspects of city life, guided by five overarching topics:

(1) *Good practice in the provision of language learning opportunities for immigrants.* How do immigrants learn the language of the host country and how are they helped to maintain their own languages? What happens in schools and also in adult education?
(2) *Social inclusion.* How do cities support social inclusion through linguistic support in social services, health, etc., and what kind of training is desirable in these areas? What happens about translation and interpreting?

(3) *Neighbouring languages*. How do cities provide for communication and cultural exchange with 'neighbouring languages'? What do we mean by neighbouring languages in a city context?

(4) *Intercultural dialogue*. How do cities promote intercultural dialogue and understanding by celebrating community cultures in common spaces? What is the culture of a multilingual city?

(5) *New patterns of migration*. Do particular challenges confront cities in countries that have traditionally been countries of emigration but are now receiving many immigrants? How do they respond to this changed perspective and what is the impact on civil society?

Our consortium has engaged in a variety of research and outreach activities designed to make connections with stakeholders in our partner cities, and to share our findings about good practice in managing multilingual citizen communities.

A series of stakeholder workshops were held in 2013, in Rome, Osijek, Athens, Dublin and Hamburg. The workshops were well attended by different stakeholders, including business people, community groups, public health representatives, researchers in the multilingual cities field and other interested parties, as well as project partners. City partners also organised site visits to community projects and languages schools for immigrants to see the multilingual city in action. We held three academic seminars between 2012 and 2014 in Utrecht, Varna and Madrid, and a major international conference was held at the London School of Economics and Political Science in the autumn of 2014.

LUCIDE published a series of Multilingual City Reports, described in the first chapter of this book, and a set of toolkits containing recommendations for decision makers on how to make the most of the multilingual resources represented in a city. The LUCIDE toolkits and City Reports are freely available on the consortium's website: www.urbanlanguages.eu.

This book, which takes these City Reports as a springboard for discussion and analysis, is organised into five central chapters. Taken together, these provide a narrative (the 'story' of the vital multilingual city), bookended by an introductory chapter which lays out some of the key concepts, and a concluding chapter which provides a *quo vadis* – a future vision of how a multilingual city may look and sound.

Nick Byrne
Language Centre Director, London School of
Economics and Political Science

The Multilingual City xi

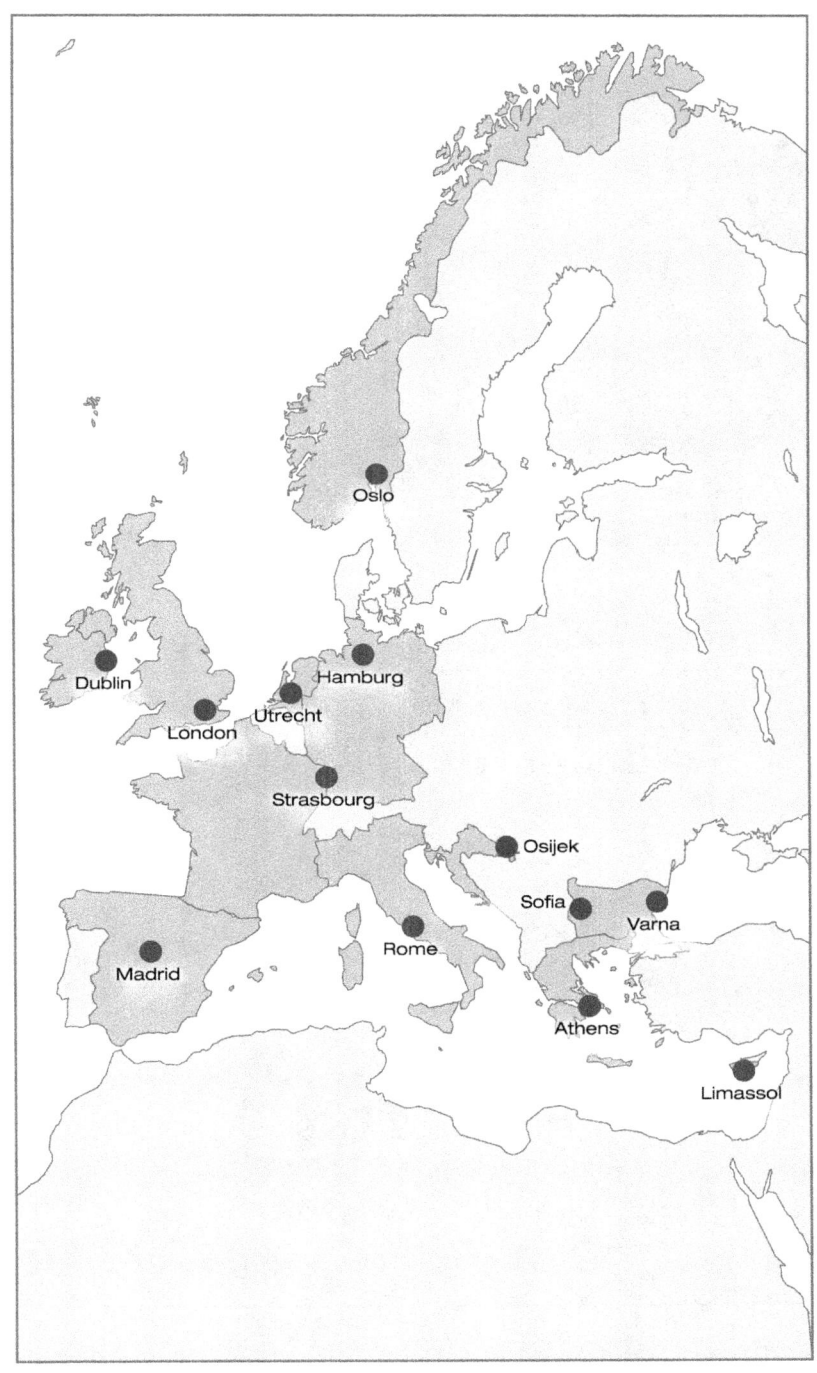

xii The Multilingual City

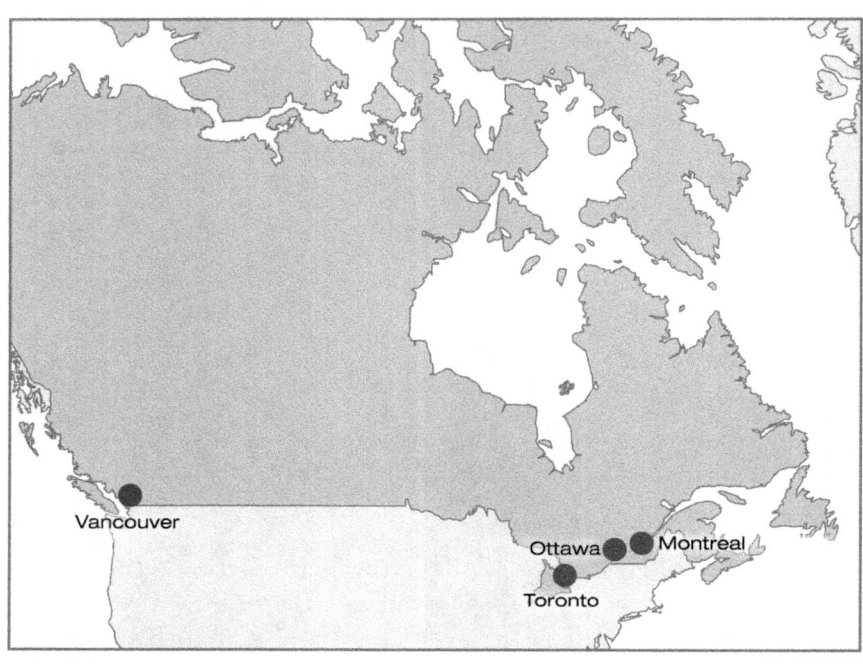

Introduction: 'Multilingualism is Lived Here'

Lorna Carson and Lid King

> *The city blew the windows of my brain wide open. But being in a place so bright, fast and brilliant made you vertiginous with possibility: it didn't necessarily help you grasp those possibilities. I still had no idea what I was going to do. I felt directionless and lost in the crowd. I couldn't yet see how the city worked, but I began to find out.*
> Hanif Kureishi, *The Buddha of Suburbia*

Investigating the City

In literature and lore, cities are viewed with varying degrees of wonder and suspicion as centres of political power, of trade and capital, of information and of consumption, of luxury and of decline. Indeed, there is nothing new in the attraction that urban life exudes: cities have always been sites of power and potential prosperity for their inhabitants. The ancient Greek city state, *polis*, provided protected space for the religious and trading activities of citizens through an *agora* (marketplace) and an *acropolis* (citadel) located on high ground. In medieval European cities, palaces and cathedrals dominated the cityscape, along with universities, hospitals and guildhalls. Contemporary, globalised cities are focal points for flows of capital and intellectual property, and continue to attract new urbanites in search of employment, opportunities and excitement as in ancient and medieval times. The city has also long been a topic of academic, policy and development discourse (Sassen, 2005; Simmel, 1903; Wirth, 1938), investigated as a site where identities are created and recognition claims are raised. Historically dominant themes in urban studies include poverty and wealth, enlightenment and darkness, crime and revolution, inclusion and exclusion (Marcuse & van Kempen, 2002; Sibley, 1995).

We live in an increasingly urbanised world. The United Nations' Population Division (UN, 2014) estimates that 54% of the world – or 3.9 billion people – lived in cities in 2014, and predicts that this figure will increase to 66% by 2050. While there are 28 mega-cities in the world with more than

10 million inhabitants, the most rapid population growth is in fact in small urban settlements with fewer than 500,000 inhabitants. In light of these figures, and the languages necessarily represented, cities are therefore now the primary spaces where policymakers engage with the multilingualism that is an inevitable consequence of a multiplicity of ethnicities and cultures. Recently, global cities have been positioned in the context of the weakening of the national as a 'spatial unit' (Sassen, 2006). In this paradigm, urban centres are viewed as sites of governance where the constraints of national policies and national discourse can be modified or overcome, not least because urban prosperity allows pressing problems to be addressed more quickly and substantially than in rural areas.

New Patterns of Living, Working, Communicating and Belonging

Scholars from a wide range of disciplines have studied cities and city life through their own particular lens – as architects, urban geographers, sociologists or historians. Contemporary urbanism locates the study of the city within a social framework, where the nature of city living is scrutinised, and issues of justice, equity and wellbeing are at the heart of understanding what cities are and can become. In other words, cities are understood as spaces within which intense human interaction occurs, often fleeting yet always constant (Simmel, 1903: 15). This social approach to studies of urbanism can be understood in light of the substantial changes in the way we now work and live. For instance, the exponential growth in mobility patterns, both within Europe and beyond, means that we are all more than ever likely to settle somewhere new. The point of arrival for most migrants, whether elite professionals benefiting from international job markets or labourers in search of a higher wage than at home, is the city. This mobility is multidirectional in terms of destinations and occurs among all ages of people (Castles *et al.*, 2013). The impact of technology and new forms of work in which economic processes generate and depend on the exchange of information is carried out on a global scale (Castells, 2000). The phenomenon of globalisation is built on the premise that there will be a steady flow of potential workers to meet the demands of economic growth at each stage of the supply chain. While international supply chains, in terms of production, distribution and sales, are geographically and linguistically diverse, two major communication phenomena affect this diversity in sometimes counterbalancing ways. English is increasingly used as a lingua franca throughout the globe, with an impact on communication choices, language diversity and maintenance, while there is also a remarkable growth in new communications technologies such as voice recognition and synthesis, and increasingly viable machine translation, digital networked technology and social media.

Figure 0.1 London newspapers (LUCIDE network, 2014)

Together, these factors have a significant impact not just on how we work, but also on how our identities and communities are formed, our patterns of belonging. It is now possible to be based in one location, and to work for a company elsewhere, or to live in one city while maintaining a close social and familial network via communication technology and social media. One of the stakeholders interviewed by the Hamburg research team during the preparation of their City Report described how '[i]n the house where the Turkish community of Hamburg is located there is also a meeting point for Italians and sometimes we all meet on the first level at the bar, drink Italian espresso together and chat in German'. This context represents a new paradigm for understanding multilingualism, what Aronin and Singleton (2012: 1) describe as the new global linguistic dispensation – a qualitatively different version of multilingualism that permeates all aspects of contemporary life. This book is not a paean to linguistic diversity, but rather starts from the assumption that urban multilingualism is an underexploited and under-researched reality.

The Study of Urban Multilingualism

This book is motivated therefore by our belief that the multilingual aspect of city life and urbanism, in terms of intense interaction between citizens from multiple backgrounds, has not been sufficiently explored. Research on urbanism, urban politics and urban planning by sociologists, geographers and political scientists tends either to overlook multilingualism or to focus on aspects of identity/ethnicity without mentioning how inextricably languages are bound up with these concepts. Language matters may be addressed under the headings of migration and cultural or ethnic diversity (see, for example, Cochrane, 2006; Gottdiener & Budd, 2005), but usually rather cursorily and often as a problem to be addressed. While state and institutional responses to the ethnic and cultural mix of cities are discussed extensively, the linguistic mix of cities is rarely mentioned (Mac Giolla Chríost & Thomas, 2008). The *Encyclopedia of Urban Studies* (Hutchinson, 2010), for example, has no entries for 'multilingualism' or 'language', and its article on 'ethnic enclaves' discusses the formation of transnational and diasporic neighbourhoods in global cities without referring to the crucial role that language plays in their development. In other words, there is a lack of serious and sustained research on the relationship between the languages spoken by citizens and the city itself.

Kraus (2011: 25) points out that even when researchers analyse cultural diversity, they do not devote much attention to the effects of linguistic diversity in urban contexts. Some recent studies do indeed focus on the multilingual character of today's cities and add to the recognition of the topic as worth exploring, but they are relatively few in number (Clément & Andrew, 2012; Extra & Yağmur, 2004, 2011; Kraus, 2011). In the context of such research, older essentialist notions of bounded languages linked to stable national or ethnic communities have been challenged and a dynamic picture is emerging of ubiquitous, everyday multilingualism which resists clear-cut classifications and has become part of (post)modern city life (Cadier & Mar-Molinero, 2012; Otsuji & Pennycook, 2010).

In non-academic public debates and discourses, urban linguistic diversity is often viewed from a multilingual skills perspective that stresses the underused 'linguistic capital' of urban populations and the importance of the multilingual repertoires of individuals in terms of employability (Butter, 2013). Alternatively, it is problematised in terms of integration or cost when politicians and mainstream media focus on a perceived lack of proficiency in majority national languages among linguistic minorities or play off the acquisition of majority national languages against the maintenance of minority languages and criticise public spending on translation and interpreting (Collins, 2010; Schäffner, 2008).

The multilingual city provides a test bed for understanding social diversity and complexity. It is not that multilingualism does not exist elsewhere – many rural areas are affected by immigration and mobility – but the city is a particularly concentrated version of this new dispensation, so the LUCIDE cities represent a valuable, distributed 'laboratory space' to help us understand how the needs and wants of diverse communities may interrelate. This convergence of globalisation, technology and urbanism means that, in the words of one of the LUCIDE stakeholders from Hamburg, '[m]ultilingualism is lived here'.

Stories from the LUCIDE Cities

As outlined in the preface, the LUCIDE consortium comprises a network of 18 cities in Europe, Canada and Australia, used as a laboratory to investigate the new paradigm of urban multilingualism. Ranging from Dublin to Varna, from Oslo to Limassol and from Vancouver to Melbourne, this international network of cities includes cities where many national groups have traditionally co-existed, as well as places where multilingualism is a relatively recent phenomenon.

For many people, a 'multilingual city' refers to a metropolis such as New York, Paris or Berlin, where people of many different ethnic and national backgrounds live. But this is not necessarily the case. Utrecht is a relatively small city and yet very multilingual; one in three of the city's population comes from a non-Dutch background, and the city strives to be a European hotspot and laboratory for multilingualism. Although linguistic diversity may be limited or reduced by the 'language regime' in which cities function (the 'public face' of the city, which may be officially monolingual in the case of London and Varna, or bilingual in Dublin or Montreal), the availability of different and diverse languages form an environment in which a particular role can be ascribed to each language in the expression and formation of an individual's identity. Mac Giolla Chríost (2007: 202–203) describes how 'the city and language shape and are shaped by one another' and how multilingual repertoires have become central to 'the multiple, everyday social practices that are necessary to the mundane negotiation of being in the city' (Mac Giolla Chríost, 2007). Together the research conducted in these LUCIDE cities demonstrates that the city is becoming part of networked new identity spaces where the meaning of 'here' is changing because it relates less to national hinterlands and more to preference networks, where the meaning of 'neighbour' has expanded from a pre-industrial definition of the next village and a 20th-century definition of the bordering country to a global definition determined by air routes, migration patterns and digital communication tools. As we will explore in Chapters 2 and 3, multilingual language use is simply part of the social fabric of everyday life in the city environment.

The Aims of the LUCIDE Consortium

The LUCIDE consortium set out to examine the realities of the multilingual city in terms of city policies and the attitudes and behaviour of citizens.

This publication draws together three years of research into a single narrative and explores some of the real-life complexities faced in various spheres and aspects of multilingual city life. Given LUCIDE's concern with contemporary European multilingualism, much of this book shares stories from LUCIDE's European partner cities, although the inclusion of external partners from Australia and Canada allowed us to locate our research within a wider network of global cities. Nevertheless, much of this volume relates specifically to mobility, migration and multilingualism in Europe.

In order to ensure a comprehensive and systematic exploration of how languages are encountered, used and learned, the project focused on five spheres of city life. These spheres – which are not mutually exclusive and inevitably overlap in some ways – comprised the public sphere, education, economic life, the private lives of citizens, and urban spaces or the 'cityscape'. The educational sphere embraces education and language learning for children and adults: language diversity across education systems and sectors (primary, secondary and tertiary, public, private and complementary/voluntary), language learning for immigrants (host languages and home languages), foreign and heritage language learning, and bilingual and multilingual education.

The public sphere refers to measures taken by public authorities and city actors (for instance, municipalities, public transport, the media) regarding the management of diverse citizen communities, in relation to interpretation/translation, arrangements in healthcare and the law, how social inclusion is supported by linguistic measures, and what kind of training and provision is seen as desirable or necessary in these areas of city life.

Our research on multilingualism in the economic life of a city examined the role of language skills in different parts of the labour market, the types of jobs (or job shortages) linked to language skills, measures to support and provide language learning, whether language policies are in place in companies, and whether economic competitiveness is perceived by stakeholders in this sphere to be strengthened through language learning.

We also turned our attention to multilingualism in the everyday lives of citizens – the 'private' sphere. City partners recorded the various migrant support organisations and local neighbourhood associations as well as types of citywide or neighbourhood festivals and celebrations. In this sphere, we also examined the role of language in arts and cultural organisations and language clubs, and multilingualism in religious life and places of worship.

The final sphere of interest was 'urban spaces', which included the publicly visible and audible languages of a city's shared spaces: public signage, shop fronts, and the particularities of certain districts as well as official and unofficial street signage. In this sphere, LUCIDE's research teams focused on what locals and tourists notice about the cityscape, and recorded how the cultures of city communities are celebrated in common spaces.

LUCIDE's Research on Urban Multilingualism

LUCIDE's research activities occurred in two stages: a phase of secondary data collection, followed by primary data collection. These two phases were designed to feed into LUCIDE's events (seminars, workshops and a conference) and publications (City Reports, toolkits and this book). The first phase of data collection involved meta-surveys of recent secondary data on multilingualism in the network's cities. As well as academic or policy documents on multilingualism, research teams collected practical examples of multilingual practices. These varied in each sphere, but included artefacts (printed/visual/digital) which illustrated the multilingual reality of the city, such as websites, advertising campaigns, public or private documents (biographies, diaries, official correspondence). The secondary research phase yielded a considerable quantity of data which allowed the consortium to generate hypotheses regarding language visibility and audibility), affordances and challenges:

- *Visibility/audibility*: that some languages are more visible/audible than others in city life, and that this visibility (invisibility)/audibility (inaudibility) is meaningful; that sometimes, when languages are visible/audible, the visibility/audibility operates at a symbolic level.
- *Affordances at the level of governance/policy*: that when cities want to encourage multilingualism, meaningful linguistic diversity (projects, examples of languages in use) will emerge.
- *Challenges/obstacles*: that costs/inconvenience/lack of political will/prejudices can inhibit good communication between people in multilingual cities; that there is sometimes a mismatch between policy and practice in daily reality; that language is sometimes understood to represent only cultural/economic capital.

In the second phase of data collection, LUCIDE's research teams in each partner city recruited a sample of stakeholders from the five key spheres of city life, and interviewed them about the reality of multilingualism in their city. A series of semi-structured interviews were organised, using a semi-standardised interview template adapted to local circumstances. Stakeholders were asked about the visibility of different languages, about the challenges involved in creating and managing multilingualism in an urban context, and about some of the difficulties faced by individual city dwellers. As well as underpinning the individual City Reports, the outcomes from the secondary and primary data collection phases contributed to a set of toolkits designed to promote multilingualism and provided a springboard for discussions with city stakeholders about pressing local issues.

The City Reports form the basis of the present volume. Designed for a general readership and reporting on contemporary multilingualism in the cities under scrutiny, the reports are freely available on the LUCIDE website. Authored by the research teams named at the end of this volume, they offer unique insights into how national governments, local policymakers, civic institutions, groups of activists, and individuals are engaging in the development and implementation of language policy in urban multilingual settings. Most give examples of language diversity that existed prior to recent incoming populations. While the languages represented might be different from today, the City Reports confirm that urban multilingualism is not a new phenomenon but has always been a reality, only now intensified by the effects of large-scale mobility and globalisation. Some of the City Reports demonstrate how power is exerted through language policy, for instance the rise and fall of German in Osijek before and after World War II, and the attempts to render Croatian and Serbian as a single language variety. In many cities, language proficiency in the majority language for second-generation migrants is often comparable to that of native speakers of the majority language. This belies the general idea that people from migrant backgrounds fail to learn the majority language adequately. Yet support for majority language learning in cities varies considerably from city to city. It is evident from the City Reports that 'foreign' (German, French, Spanish) languages enjoy higher status than migrant languages, and that the role of English can be described as 'hypercentral' (de Swaan, 2001).

Defining the Parameters of this Volume

This volume draws the City Reports together and explores issues and challenges common to the European, Australian and Canadian partner cities as well as locating the outcomes of the LUCIDE consortium's research within an overarching framework of multilingual vitality. We note that in such a large consortium, composed of many researchers from different traditions spread over three continents, problems inevitably arise when data collected by different teams under different circumstances (e.g. variations in the numbers of interviewees and the type of stakeholders) are subjected to comparative analysis. For instance, collecting reliable information on the population diversity in multilingual cities is not easy. While some comparative information can be found within the European Union, it is difficult to compare cities in Canada and Australia. Reliable and comparable demographic information on immigrant minority groups is almost impossible to obtain. In some cities, no demolinguistic data were included, often because they were not available; posing questions about ethnicity in a survey, for instance, is prohibited in some contexts. Nevertheless, the data from these reports depict a rich variety of multilingual contexts and practices. This book picks out some of the most salient themes that help us understand the vitality of contemporary urban multilingualism from a variety of disciplinary perspectives.

It is important to address two key points that arise in our study of urban multilingualism. One is terminological, the other contextual, and both must be considered before attempting to draw any meaningful comparisons between cities. First, in order to investigate multilingualism in any serious way, its parameters have to be pinned down. It is an extraordinarily complex notion to capture, not least because there are many competing lay and academic understandings of what it means to be multilingual. At the very least, multilingualism can be generally understood in everyday life as the inclusion of, or the ability to use, several languages. It can be used to describe both the capacities of speakers and the languages that co-exist in a geographical location; in other words, it refers to both speakers and communities that use a number of languages. The LUCIDE consortium adopted a distinction made in the work of the Council of Europe between 'multilingualism' as the co-existence of many languages in a society and 'plurilingualism' as the capacity of an individual to communicate in two or more languages. It is important to note that plurilingual individuals may not demonstrate a balanced or native-life proficiency in all the languages in their repertoire, and language proficiency and use vary greatly according to the background and context of the speaker.

Secondly, within the geographical spread of LUCIDE cities, most are located within a centralised legislative framework where decisions are made nationally rather than locally, excluding city governments from the formulation of policy. In fact, there are only a few cities or city states in the world with a plenipotentiary governance structure; most urban governments are subject to higher tiers of regional or national governance. In the LUCIDE consortium, a city such as Hamburg, a federal state in its own right with absolute control of educational policy and its implementation, evidently has a much greater level of self-governance than the city of Strasbourg, subject to France's centralised policy framework. Hamburg can therefore adapt more quickly and flexibly to the changing needs of its citizens, for instance with regard to the provision of public services, the subject of Chapter 4 of this volume, or multilingual education policy, explored in Chapter 5.

The Vitality of Multilingualism

In this volume, we take the notion of ethnolinguistic vitality, usually applied to individual languages and speech communities as an indicator of their long-term viability, and extend it to the complex interrelationships between languages and speakers: visibility and demographic features, status, and aspects which support or control societal multilingualism. Despite surface indicators that may seem to point to a densely multilingual environment, some city spaces may in fact be populated by speech communities composed of speakers from a multilingual background but who are de facto monolingual speakers in their daily lives. In this type of situation, the vitality of multilingualism is threatened, leading towards what Joshua Fishman (1991) describes as language shift, towards monolingualism in the dominant language of the city, usually the national language variety. When the many languages of a city are equally accepted, valued and welcomed, and indeed recognised as apt for use in all kinds of situations with other speakers of the same languages, we recognise something of the European ideal of 'unity in diversity'. We argue that these are the cities that succeed in capturing and distilling the social and linguistic capital, creativity and culture embodied by vital multilingualism. Therefore, we are not so much interested in the number of languages present in a city, because these figures are constantly shifting, but in how the many languages of citizens interrelate in city contexts, and how these languages are learned, used and maintained in their daily lives.

We also focus on the diagnostic aspect: 'the social, cultural and political *structures*' (Blommaert, 2013: 3, original italics) that allow multilingualism to survive and flourish, and any evidence that may point to its future viability. As explored in Chapters 3 and 4, the visibility of a city's languages in various spheres of city life and the self-image of a city point not just to the relative health of the languages themselves, but also to the status of their citizens: included or excluded, empowered or disempowered. Blommaert describes the physical space of the city as:

Figure 0.2 Vancouver Chinese Lutheran church (LUCIDE network, 2014)

also social, cultural and political space: a space that offers, enables, triggers, invites, prescribes, proscribes, polices or enforces certain patterns of social behaviour; a space that is never no-man's-land, but always, somebody's space; a *historical* space, therefore, full of codes, expectations, norms and traditions; and a space of *power* controlled by, as well as controlling, people. (Blommaert, 2013: 3, original italics)

For Plato, the ideal *polis* or city state in *The Republic* was founded on justice and virtue. Its power structures were designed to allow individuals to maximise their potential through specific functions, to serve others through duty, and to display wisdom, courage, temperance and justice. Injustice and inequity form a counterpoint in the dialogue: the same city state could be a site of tyranny, corruption and exploitation. In our multidisciplinary examination of contemporary cities, power structures and policies can create conditions where multilingualism is controlled and excluded – both explicitly and implicitly, or where individual and societal language diversity is encouraged and integrated in the various functions of city life.

In the following chapters, our common point of departure is that multilingualism in its many forms is a resource to be cultivated, rather than a deficit to be addressed or a hurdle to be cleared. However, the data of the LUCIDE consortium suggest that in each of the cities investigated, some languages are much less visible than others, and therefore less valued according to Blommaert's argument. And while the authors of the LUCIDE City Reports describe, in various ways, accepted attitudes to what can be described as prestigious versions of multilingualism, typically comprising a constellation of powerful world languages, they also share vivid stories from speakers whose languages are hidden, unrecognised or stigmatised.

The social and cultural changes represented by population diversity bring tensions and prompt questions about how best to manage city life. Large-scale mobility – and, more specifically, immigration – is a major area of political controversy in Europe and beyond. Discussions regarding integration and multiculturalism have become politically embroiled, arguing for a strong assimilationist approach to belonging and citizenship. Many accepted liberal consensual views about multiculturalism – the co-existence of multiple cultures and the possibility of adhering to more than one set of cultural norms or allowing room for overlapping identities – are being called into question. For instance, access to education which provides support for learning 'mother tongues' is no longer the norm in countries where this was previously a tradition, and together the LUCIDE City Reports suggest that there has been a move at both national and European levels away from valuing, respecting and supporting immigrant languages towards more single-minded concentration on learning the national language of the various states (King *et al.*, 2011: 29). Many governments are leaning towards policies based on the assumption that diversity represents a threat to social cohesion rather than

Figure 0.3 Oslo restaurant (LUCIDE network, 2014)

a means of allowing citizens to flourish in their private and public lives, to maintain and develop their personal language repertoires, and to fulfil their full potential as citizens in the complex, heterogeneous space that is the multilingual city.

The Structure of this Volume

In the following six chapters, we use the LUCIDE City Reports as a way of sharing stories about some specific aspects of multilingual city life. The authors of our volume approach multilingualism from diverse academic disciplines (applied linguistics, sociolinguistics, psychology, philosophy, education, language teaching, policy), bringing distinct but often interlocking perspectives on the multilingual city. Chapter 1 explores some of the historical aspects of multilingual cities, where linguistic diversity was regarded as a norm. Against this backdrop, the authors provide an overview of the data from the LUCIDE City Reports, framed in this chapter by the notion of the vitality of multilingualism. This construct can be understood as the conditions within which both individual and societal multilingualism can thrive and flourish in an urban setting, particularly in terms of demography, status, institutional support and control. In Chapter 2 we explore some of the physical evidence of multilingualism – indeed the new varieties that seem to be emerging in cities as a result of close language contact. The written languages visible in a city are all indicators of its diverse speech communities and visitors. However, it is important to note that most city dwellers do not pay much attention to the languages they see and hear around them, and the chapter argues that the languages we see (or do not see) reflect the power and social relations in a city – inclusion or exclusion, solidarity and belonging. Chapter 3 moves on from the sights and sounds of the multilingual city to the image and representations of the city, including how people position themselves vis-à-vis the urban multilingual environment in terms of affiliation and new identities. It offers thoughts on how we can read city multilingualism in relation to the shifting identities of 'city-zens'. Chapter 4 focuses on language policies and the politics of multilingualism, especially in terms of how civic institutions respond to the challenges of governing increasingly multilingual urban communities. The reality of urban multilingualism is shaped by a variety of political and institutional instruments from above as well as by activism and initiatives from below. This chapter explores the public use and status of languages, including policies designed to facilitate language learning and maintain languages as well as the use of public service translation and interpreting. In Chapter 5, we turn to the specific case of multilingualism and education. While many policies designed to respond to multilingualism are determined by national or regional governments, cities often have a direct impact on the provision of public education. The chapter addresses key dimensions of language education from the perspective of plurilingual repertoires, taking into account the languages of schooling, home languages and foreign language learning. The concluding chapter provides a recapitulation of the book's key themes, and explores the possible future of the multilingual city.

This has been a collective endeavour, but one which we have hoped to shape into a coherent narrative. The editors are grateful to the many

Figure 0.4 Rome sign (LUCIDE network, 2014)

contributors who have made this possible. Most obviously these are the chapter authors whose ideas were sharpened through our debates and discussions, in Sofia, and later in Dublin where the main arguments were refined. We are grateful in this context to the Jean Monnet Chair Programme which supported our work in Sofia. Many other individuals have also participated in the narrative – the LUCIDE partners, in particular the writers of the City Reports, who are listed at the end of this book, the many stakeholders with whom we discussed in each of our cities and in the LUCIDE workshops, seminars and conference, events which took place in nine countries. We are grateful to them all, unfortunately too numerous to name here individually. Particular mention should, however, be made of Ingrid Gogolin, Richard Clément and Joe Lo Bianco who have commented critically on our ideas and texts and inspired us with their experience and insights. Of course, in the final analysis none of this would have happened without the meticulous work of Sarah McMonagle and Philip Harding-Esch, in checking texts, references and illustrations.

Multilingualism is not a new phenomenon. It was a common feature of the empires and cities of ancient times. Very often such multilingualism was regarded as normal and non-controversial, and this remained so until the growth of modern nationalism, when the link between nation and language came to be a guiding principle, challenging extant multilingualism. Exponential increases in mobility, especially to urban centres, amid the systematic lowering of economic boundaries in the European Union, combined with globalisation and technological advances over the last two decades, are beginning to bring welcome attention to urban multilingualism. An overview of data on multilingualism from the LUCIDE City Reports is framed in this chapter by the notion of the vitality of urban multilingualism (VUM), defined as the degree to which societal multilingualism and individual plurilingualism are able to thrive and flourish in an urban conglomeration and discussed in LUCIDE cities with reference to three main factors: demography, status and institutional support (and control).

1 The Vitality of Urban Multilingualism

Itesh Sachdev and Sarah Cartwright

> *And the whole earth was of one language, and of one speech. [...] And the Lord came down to see the city and the tower, which the children of men builded. And the Lord said, Behold, the people is one, and they have all one language; and this they begin to do: and now nothing will be restrained from them, which they have imagined to do. Go to, let us go down, and there confound their language, that they may not understand one another's speech. So the Lord scattered them abroad from thence upon the face of all the earth: and they left off to build the city. Therefore is the name of it called Babel; because the Lord did there confound the language of all the earth: and from thence did the Lord scatter them abroad upon the face of all the earth.*
> Book of Genesis, Chapter 11, Verses 1, 5–9 (King James Translation)

The Biblical Babel myth is frequently used to illustrate the historical desirability of monolingualism and conversely the confusions caused by the existence of many languages. In fact, as Blanc (2008) argued in using the quotation above, multilingualism (and plurilingualism) were widely accepted and enriching aspects of ancient societies. Indeed there is a large amount of research suggesting that not only is the vitality of multilingualism high in the ever-expanding urban centres of the world today (Edwards, 1994), but that multilingualism has been normative for millennia (Adams, 2003; Blanc, 2008; Mullen & James, 2012).

In recent years we have become used to a rather different, celebratory discourse countering the 'monolingual conservatism' of the past, with increasing references to the large number of languages spoken in urban localities as an important resource:

> 200 languages: Manchester revealed as most linguistically diverse city in western Europe. (Brown, 2013)

> Home to around 800 different languages, New York is a delight for linguists. (Turin, 2012)

In fact, although useful for headlines, the overall number of languages spoken is a somewhat blunt measure of the vitality of multilingualism in

Figure 1.1 Rome guide books (LUCIDE network, 2014)

urban contexts. A more systematic and nuanced characterisation is attempted in this chapter by introducing the notion of the *vitality of urban multilingualism* (VUM). It is defined as the degree to which multilingualism and plurilingualism are able to thrive and flourish in an urban conglomeration. Based on the notion of ethnolinguistic vitality (Giles *et al.*, 1977; Sachdev & Bourhis, 1993; Sachdev *et al.*, 2012) and considered under factors of demography, status and institutional support (and control), the vitality of urban multilingualism may serve as a useful heuristic to frame data obtained from the LUCIDE cities in Europe, Australia and Canada.

This chapter charts evidence for the vitality of multilingualism in antiquity to the relatively recent 18th-century 'one language: one nation' ideology that has left such a lasting legacy into the 21st century. The second section provides an introduction to the LUCIDE cities as portrayed by the City Reports and is followed by an analysis of vitality under the subheadings of demography, status and institutional support and control. The chapter concludes with some notes, including a reminder about the intergroup nature of multilingual communication in modern urban contexts.

From Antiquity to the 21st Century

Turning once more to the Babel myth, Blanc (2008) began his essay on multilingualism in the Ancient Near East with the reference to the City of Babel, where multiple languages were introduced and dispersed from the tower city of monolingualism: the vitality of urban multilingualism in antiquity. The existence of multilingualism has been attributed to intergroup contact, interaction, co-existence and conflict leading to integration, assimilation and/or exclusion in societies. Contacts between those who spoke different languages from varied social, cultural, religious, ethnic and economic backgrounds and aspirations, coupled with trade and commerce, exchanges (cultural, educational and diplomatic), migration and exogamy, invasion and colonisation, have all been described as contributors to the vitality of multilingualism in ancient times.

Having credited the Sumerians with the invention of irrigation, urbanisation, and writing, Blanc (2008) discusses evidence for multilingualism found on a variety of materials including tablets (clay, stone), obelisks, rock faces, copper, coins, papyrus and parchment. He charts the evolution of ancient multilingualism over several thousand years in Europe and the Middle East from the Proto-Elamite period of the 3rd millennium BC through Egyptian, Sumerian, Persian and Aramaic, up to the Hellenistic Greek (BC 331–323) and Roman periods. He correlates the rise and fall of empires, commerce and trade with material evidence for multilingualism in ancient Greek, Egyptian and Roman times, including languages such as Hebrew, Aramaic, Egyptian, Lycian, Greek and Latin. For instance, he cites the Rosetta Stone, written in two languages and three scripts, as evidence for multilingualism during the Ptolemaic period, and refers to the emergence of a class of bilingual officials needed to mediate between the local Egyptian-speaking population and the Greek-speaking administration and immigrants.

Archival evidence in material written form arguably underestimates the degree, function and spread of spoken multilingualism although there are some edicts as well as liturgical and epistolary correspondence that are closer to spoken forms. According to Blanc:

> On rather rare occasions we catch a glimpse of the spoken language, even of pronunciation, as in the Book of Judges (12:6), where the Gileadites challenged their Ephremite enemies to say the pass-word 'shibboleth', which they could only pronounce 'sibboleth'. 42,000 of them failed to pass the first phonetic test in recorded history and were put to death. (Blanc, 2008: 3)

Rochette (2011) provides a detailed account of Latin in the Roman Empire. Internal governmental communications from the Emperor and other official documents were in Latin. It was also the language of the army (until the beginning of the 7th century), although, unlike in the Hellenistic period (Billows, 2005), the Romans did not aim to impose their language. In the eastern Roman Empire, laws and official documents were regularly translated into Greek from Latin. Latin–Greek bilingualism has been noted among Roman and Greek intellectual elites and both languages were in active use by government officials and the Church during the 5th century. From the 6th century, Greek culture was studied in the West almost exclusively through Latin translation.

Bilingualism and trilingualism were probably common among educated people and others (e.g. army officers) in regions where languages other than Latin or Greek were spoken, such as the western (Gaulish, Brittonic), eastern (Aramaic), northern (Germanic) and southern (Punic, Coptic) parts of the empire. A remarkable piece of multilingual evidence discovered in northeast England on a 2nd-century epitaph has the inscription written in Aramaic and Latin-in-Honorific-Greek style, to 'Regina' – a name that could be either Latin or Celtic (Mullen & James, 2012).

Given that cultures within the Roman Empire were largely oral, evidence for elite and literate multilingualism provides only a small part of the picture concerning the actual vitality of multilingualism across the vast empire. In the western part, Latin in spoken form ('Vulgar Latin') began to dominate Celtic and other languages over time as local populations adopted it. As the empire grew, considerable political power was transferred to the regions from the centre. Following the spectacular fall of the western Roman Empire in the 4th to 5th centuries, and the ongoing transfer of political power away from the centre, Latinate/Romance language varieties such as Spanish, Portuguese, French, Italian, Romanian and Romansch emerged in their local multilingual contexts. The main exception to this seems to be Basque. Elite bilingualism preserved Latin as the international language of learning, intellectual progress and literature up to the 17th century in western Europe, and for the Roman Catholic Church to the present day.

The empowerment of vernaculars in Europe facilitated by the invention of the printing press by Gutenberg in 1439 and the diversification of the linguistic and cultural landscapes of Europe has a long, often violent history, leading to the beginnings of nation states from the 15th to the 17th centuries. Until the turn of the 19th century, however, a dominant form of political entity in much of Europe was the multi-ethnic and multilingual monarchic empires such as the Austro-Hungarian Empire, the Russian Empire and the Ottoman Empire. These empires were ruled by one ethnic (often dynastic) group, but were generally characterised by ethnic, religious and linguistic tolerance. Much of the administration of the Ottoman Empire, for example, was in the hands of the Greek-speaking Phanariots (Stavrianos, 1958: 270). The 18th and 19th centuries were particularly important in Western nation-state formation, beginning with the French Revolution in 1789 which not only led to the creation of the modern French state but also catalysed nationalism across Europe, often in conflict with the great empires and eventually leading to the unification of Germany and Italy in the 19th century. In the 20th century, this process continued after WWI across central and Eastern Europe and more recently with the formation of several nation states in the Balkans following the breakup of the former Yugoslavia.

Nationalist rhetoric and policy, consonant with Herder's 18th-century 'one language-one nation' philosophy, has left a strong and lasting legacy of ideological monolingualism in Europe and elsewhere (Blackledge, 2000). Anderson (1983) suggests that the construction of nations ('imagined communities') in the 19th and early 20th centuries, in combination with the emergence of capitalism, led to linguistic hegemonies: 'Thus English elbowed Gaelic out of Ireland, French pushed aside Breton, and Castilian marginalised Catalan' (Anderson, 1983: 78). This 'monolingual conservatism' (Redder, 2013) promoted by dominant groups and elite minorities has posed the greatest challenge to the languages of indigenous, regional, local and immigrant minorities worldwide. Following two World Wars and subsequently the end of the Cold War in the 20th century, Edwards (1994) reports that the vast majority of countries (up to 75%) still recognise only one language for legal and official purposes, even though there exist several thousand languages across almost 200 countries in the world. Moreover, where several languages are officially recognised, one is usually dominant, carrying 'disproportionate amounts of social, economic and political power' (Edwards, 1994: 2).

It is important to note that in Canada and Australia (home to some of the LUCIDE cities), multilingualism was also the norm among indigenous peoples before colonisation (Elwell, 1982; Sachdev, 1995). Colonisation promoted systematic and vigorous eradication of indigenous cultures and languages, and many languages have died or are in precarious stages of endangerment in Canada and Australia (Austin & Sallabank, 2011; see also LUCIDE City Reports from Canada and Australia). From the middle of the 20th century, with the exception of the Cold War and the conflict in the Balkans, relative post-World War peace has reigned in Europe with unprecedented levels of cooperation in economic and social security combined with rapid technological advance. The postwar influence of the Soviet Union in promoting 'Russification' in culture and language (Kreindler, 1982) in countries allied to it was considerable, but there were also opposing tendencies – especially in the 1920s and 1930s – towards 'indigenisation' and 'institutionalised multi-nationalism' (Martin, 2001) which were important in the creation of terminology banks, dictionaries and textbooks for minority languages, thus promoting multilingual vitality.

The end of the Cold War augmented globalisation processes which were already in motion in the latter part of the 20th century. Central to these processes are increased mobility and the exchange of ideas, people and capital facilitated by revolutionary advances in communication technology, taking place across an ever wider set of national borders and affecting especially urban agglomerations. They are further catalysed by the loosening of rules for movement across EU countries. The increase in intergroup contact and urban living is deemed inexorable and worldwide, with predictions suggesting that the vast majority of humanity will be living in urban contexts by the middle of the 21st century (UN, 2014).

Cities are not only reactive to circumstances (for instance, the switch from wood to stone in the rebuilding of London after the Great Fire in 1666), but they are also the drivers of change in society. In ancient times individual cities rather than nations played a leading innovative role in society as the social mix of trades and professions sparked invention and the creation of wealth. Athens, Harappa, Persepolis, Ur, Babylon, Rome, Carthage, Cusco – all gave rise to flourishing ancient civilisations at the cutting edge of learning and change. Likewise, many centuries later, Italian cities gave rise to the explosion of creativity known as the Renaissance. Today some urban societal developments can seem trivial and fashion led, as in the case of the spread of cafe culture, where even in Dublin coffee outlets are beginning to rival pubs as social spaces. In terms of multilingualism, however, we see emerging a new urban landscape which is multi-textured: a new era of linguistic and cultural co-existence in which value is determined not only on economic criteria but also by the personal values of the plurilingual city dweller able to access language communities worldwide through social media.

Languages spoken, heard, seen and used in the modern cities of the EU originate not only from the EU member states but also from most others around the world (including ex-colonies such as those in the Indian sub-continent or North Africa). Such has been the impact of globalisation (migration, exchange) and rapid technological progress that some modern cities in Europe (and also North America and Australia) are characterised today in terms of their 'super-diversity' (Vertovec, 2007) or 'hyper-diversity' (Tasan-Kok et al., 2013). In all likelihood, therefore, we have 'crossed the Rubicon' for multilingualism: communication in the cities of today (real and virtual, institutional and individual, public and private) involves multi-layered complexities along dimensions of language, religion, ethnicity, culture, class and generation that are unparalleled in human history.

We will next give an overview of the LUCIDE cities as a prelude to an exploratory discussion of the vitality of urban multilingualism today.

The LUCIDE Cities

There is no accepted typology for characterising the multilingualism of the diverse LUCIDE cities. One might, for example, consider relative size, geographical position or historical antecedents as possible indicators of similarity and difference. Any one solution, however, is unlikely to be completely satisfactory given the complexity of the issues and the different contexts of each city. With this caveat we have nonetheless chosen to discuss the LUCIDE cities under four broad categories (as presented also in the final LUCIDE conference), which in some senses reflect their prevalent relationship to multilingualism and to the vitality of multilingualism. There are, for example, cities with long multilingual histories, in some cases dating from

Figure 1.2 Oslo shop (LUCIDE network, 2014)

antiquity, where this sense of historical place still has an impact on current realities; included in this group are Rome, Utrecht and Varna. An even more clear-cut category is the group of cities which are not only multilingual but which have actually been built on and prospered as a result of (multilingual) immigration. These 'immigration cities' include Madrid, Hamburg, London and, outside Europe, Melbourne, Toronto and Vancouver. Then there are cities for which multilingualism, as we have described it (see the Introduction), is a new phenomenon. Even though they may have some historical multilingual precedents, as is the case with Athens and Sofia, their modern history has been one of emigration and only in recent years have the challenges of diversity figured more prominently. As well as Athens and Sofia we include Oslo and Dublin in this group. Finally we include a group of cities which are officially or overtly bilingual, or which occupy border regions including more than one language group: Limassol, Osijek, Strasbourg, Ottawa and Montreal.

Multilingual historicities

Rome, founded in BC 753, the Mediterranean capital city of an ancient empire and civilisation, is distinguished by its long history of tolerant multilingualism according to the City Report. It sits poised between Eastern and Western Europe, yet in distance it is closer to Africa than to much of Europe. Its population in the metropolitan area stands at about 4 million, making it one of the largest cities in the EU. Italian is the official language; however, it is in fact a very young national language based on the Florentine dialect and adopted with the emergence of Italy as a nation state in the 19th century, a process which was completed by 1871. Subsequently, as Italian was diffused by modern media, the multilingual preference for the various dialects of Italy diminished.

Latin, however, the source of all Romance languages, survives as a lingua franca and world faith language within the Roman Catholic Church. Christianity was already established as the state religion by the fall of the Roman Empire. Over the ages the Roman Catholic Church has had a huge impact on the multilingual character of Rome, as the Vatican City established itself not only as the centre of a major religion but also as a political player both within and far beyond Italy. Thus Rome is known as the 'capital of two states' – national and transnational, *urbs et orbis*. In 2011, it was the 18th most-visited city in the world, and the third most-visited in the EU according to the City Report.

In addition to tourists and other temporary visitors, Rome also has a history of permanent settlers from afar. For instance, in the 15th century Sephardic Jews fleeing from religious persecution in Spain and Portugal settled in Rome. Today it remains an important destination not only for refugees but also for economic migrants, who together comprise about 10% of the population (see City Report). Yet according to the City Report's conclusion (Rome City Report, 2014: 37), 'there is a strongly felt need of a more structured approach to multilingualism and multiculturality in the city'.

Overall, Rome has a number of unique attributes: as the capital city of Italy; as a major world tourist attraction thanks mainly to its monuments from antiquity and glorious Renaissance art heritage; and as the administrative centre of the Catholic Church and home to the Vatican. It embraces the concept of multiculturalism but, according to the report, there is no vision yet of how multiculturalism and multilingualism will drive change and transform society in the future.

Utrecht, situated in the centre of the Netherlands with a population of around a third of a million, is the fourth largest city in the country. The demographic profile of the city is youthful and multi-ethnic. A thriving university sector accounts for a student body making up about a fifth of the population, of whom half live in the city. Two key factors contribute to the linguistic landscape of the city: first, the university in Utrecht which opened its doors in 1636, ushering in a long tradition of mobility and plurilingualism among the better educated citizens. Secondly, there is the role of the Roman Catholic Church as a powerful driver of multilingualism; as the centre of the Archbishopric, Utrecht attracted dignitaries from the Catholic world all over Europe until Catholicism was forbidden after the Reformation. In 1853, the Dutch government allowed the bishopric of Utrecht to be reinstated by Rome, and Utrecht once more became the centre of Dutch Catholicism.

In more recent times, the 1960s marked a turning point in the social and linguistic history of Utrecht. The first Mediterranean 'guest workers' – Greeks, Spaniards and Italians – arrived in 1960, as did the Turks and then Moroccans, followed by the first Yugoslavs in 1969. Although only 3% of the population have a Surinamese/Antillean background, this community is an important legacy of the Dutch Empire; likewise a similar number of inhabitants, approximately 11,000, have their roots in the former colony of Indonesia. Today, just over a third of the city's residents have a migrant background according to the City Report. It suggests that 'the city of Utrecht seems to be rich in small initiatives that celebrate multi/plurilingualism. Their structural impact, however, is limited' (Utrecht City Report, 2014: 32).

Multilingualism accrues high status for instrumentally useful languages such as English, German and French ('prestigious multilingualism' in the report); it is valued and features prominently. Multilingualism in languages of the immigrant minority communities (Arabic, Berber, Turkish) is not valued in mainstream society ('plebeian multilingualism' in the report), and is sometimes even considered to be 'an obstacle to successful integration' in Dutch society (Utrecht City Report, 2014: 28).

Utrecht describes itself as a 'multilingual hotspot' and there is much goodwill and civic support for the vision of a truly multilingual city. Yet much remains to be done to valorise the languages of all its communities. Strong pressure is exerted on newcomers to learn the national language, as in all the cities, but, as the Utrecht research team comments, 'encouraging the acquisition of Dutch should not be linked to discouraging the home/mother/minority language' (Utrecht City Report, 2014: 29).

Varna, a major holiday resort situated on the Black Sea, is the third biggest city in Bulgaria with a population of approximately 350,000. Varna has a very ancient and complex history of multilingualism due to successive colonisations: Thracian, Miletian Greek, Roman and, eventually, Ottoman (1389–1878). It played a key role in several decisive conflicts. Notably, one of the last major battles of the Crusades was fought outside the city walls (in 1444) when the Turks routed an army of 20,000 crusaders led by the King of Poland. This defeat made the fall of Constantinople inevitable, leading to Ottoman domination of Bulgaria for over four centuries. Today's process of 'colonisation' is provoked by tourism and the sale of real estate to Russians and other foreigners seeking holiday homes. The Varna City Report (2014: 22) suggests that the essentially seasonal nature of tourism leads to:

> a shift from a multicultural city to one much smaller in numbers and poorer in cultures and actively used languages [...], and ultimately impedes the development of regular diverse city life and attitudes. This makes the perception of language use shift from social competence to employment skill.

26 The Multilingual City

Figure 1.3 Varna sign (LUCIDE network, 2014)

The report also suggests that neither tourist-led nor migrant-led multilingualism have yet been associated with any long-term policy initiatives. Moreover, there appears to be a growing gap in the perception of multilingualism between older generations and young people, with the latter seeing their own plurilingualism (mostly mother tongue + English) as the route to employment and advancement.

Cities built on immigration

Madrid has a population of 3.3 million, although the wider metropolitan area comprises 6.5 million inhabitants. It enjoys a rich and ancient tapestry of multicultural and multilingual influences, notably Sephardic and Arabic. In medieval times, however, Madrid was overshadowed by its more powerful neighbour, Toledo. A picture of a true 'Babel' emerges, with Latin, Sephardic, Hebrew, Berber, Arabic and Castilian merging with dialects and mingling with the languages of foreign visitors. From the Middle Ages to the 20th century, there was a steady flow of immigration from the Auvergne region of France. After the conquest of America beginning in 1492 and the establishment of the Spanish Empire, Madrid, as its capital, was transformed from a medieval European city into a global metropolis.

Today Madrid is home to inhabitants from almost 200 different countries comprising about 15% of the population and speaking a wide variety of languages. These include significant numbers of speakers of European languages such as Romanian, Quechua-speaking immigrants from South America, and speakers of languages and cultures from North Africa (Moroccan Arabic), sub-Saharan countries and Asia (Chinese). There is no overt hostility to multilingualism reported by respondents; rather, one senses an indifference to multilingualism unless it concerns valued languages associated with the notion of economic success, such as English. Importantly, the LUCIDE Madrid report draws attention to the way in which 'different nationalities share urban spaces but in monolingual or bilingual communities' (Madrid City Report, 2014: 27) and the corresponding lack of cross-over between communities. Demographic change has, as the report suggests:

> generated a double linguistic impact resulting in two different landscapes: on one hand, the 'official face' that accommodates primarily European languages with the strong presence of English; and on the other, the 'unofficial' space, resulting from immigration languages which have a greater impact in the urban area, with much more influence on the dimensions of urban space and life than the former. (Madrid City Report, 2014: 26)

Hamburg, the second largest city of Germany, has a population of about 1.8 million inhabitants with over a third being migrants from nearly 200 different countries. As elsewhere in Germany, Standard German is spoken but, as is typical for northern Germany, the original language of Hamburg is in fact Low German which has remained as a dialect today.

The city lies on the river Elbe on the southern point of the Jutland Peninsula between Continental Europe to the south and Scandinavia to the north, with the North Sea to the west and the Baltic Sea to the northeast. The geographical location has provided an excellent arena for intergroup exchange. As a thriving port, from the 13th to the 17th centuries it was a member of the Hanseatic League – a network of flourishing cities across Northern Europe which benefited from mutual privileges in trade and diplomacy. Sephardic Jews from Spain and Portugal came as religious refugees to build new communities in the 1620s; Dutch refugees sought refuge from the repressive measures of the Counter Reformation in the Netherlands. Later immigrants, however, were labour migrants – traders, craftsmen and mechanics such as the Italian flooring traders in the 19th century. In the same era of expansion, Chinese boiler-men and launderers were recruited in a period of increasing steamship traffic.

Another distinctive feature of Hamburg's history is its function as a transit area. Over 7 million people migrated via Hamburg to North America: from the foundation of the Hamburg Shipping Company in 1836, emigration

28 The Multilingual City

and transit migration were economically important for the city up to the early 1900s.

Germany suffered an acute shortage of labour in the extensive period of postwar reconstruction: the number of 'foreigners' living in the Federal Republic of Germany rose from roughly 1% in the late 1950s to more than 10% in the late 1960s. Today, according to the Hamburg City Report:

> Linguistic diversity is visible and audible throughout the urban space in the city of Hamburg. English can be found in public transport services and in street signage for places of interest. Whereas this points to the city's 'international flair', the heritage languages tend to be visible only in districts where many migrants live or where they trade. (Hamburg City Report, 2014: 21)

Hamburg is embracing multilingualism and has set up a variety of structures to support different communities and their languages. For instance, the large number of mosques attests to the presence of a substantial Islamic, largely Turkish, community, which constitutes the largest ethnolinguistic minority. Communities originating in Poland, Russia, Afghanistan, Kazakhstan, Iran, Serbia, Portugal, Vietnam and China also form significant parts of the cityscape. However, according to the City Report, the dominant

Figure 1.4 Hamburg jeweller (LUCIDE network, 2014)

position of Turkish, supported by a well-established community, tends to eclipse other mother tongues.

London, by far the largest of the LUCIDE cities with a population of over 8 million, faces two ways: east towards mainland Europe but also west across the Atlantic towards North America; moreover, 'as a city it is seen as a financial punctuation mark between New York and the Far East' (London City Report, 2014: 44). This gives the city a truly global position that makes it a magnet for people and institutions from all parts of the globe, including powerful international companies, oligarchs and entrepreneurs, highly educated individuals, economic migrants and asylum seekers. Its multilingualism is youthful, globally diverse and substantial according to the City Report. For instance, nearly 40% of Londoners have an immigrant background; over 200 languages are spoken by London's schoolchildren; 15 different ethnolinguistic communities have numbers greater than 50,000 with the three largest being Polish, Bangladeshi and Gujarati (according to the 2011 Census which for the first time included a question asking for the respondents' main language). Speakers of the official minority languages of the UK – Welsh, Irish, Ulster Scots, Scots, Scots Gaelic and Cornish (since 2002) – are, on the other hand, rare in the nation's capital.

London has a long history of immigration. Protestants fleeing religious persecution on the European continent, first from the Spanish Netherlands and later from France, constituted the most significant influx of immigrants in the early modern period; the number of Huguenots fleeing to Britain in the late 17th century has been estimated at between 50,000 and 80,000. The growth of the British Empire and the corresponding increase in international trade (in both goods and slaves) between 17th and 19th centuries led to the

Figure 1.5 London street signs (LUCIDE network, 2014)

establishment of African and Asian communities. Numerically, the most significant influx of migrants comprised Russian and East European Jews (120,000–140,000), who fled their homelands from economic hardship and persecution between 1880 and 1914.

In the aftermath of WWII, and the independence of most of Britain's colonies, the UK economy suffered from a shortage of labour. Within a few years more than 300,000 European nationals (mainly from Italy, Poland, Romania, Bulgaria and Yugoslavia) had been recruited to work in the UK, and from the 1950s and 1960s onwards they were joined by hundreds of thousands of immigrants, first from the Caribbean, then from partitioned India, Africa and Hong Kong. Britain withdrew the rights of most Commonwealth citizens to settle and live in the UK after 1962. The 1970s, however, brought the arrival of many Asians from Kenya and mainly Uganda, while the 1971 Bangladesh War of Independence led to a further increase in the Bengali community. From 1992, membership of the EU has led to considerable economic migration – most recently from Eastern Europe.

Despite its rich multi-ethnic fabric, London does not fully embrace its multilingual capital. Official integration policies for immigrants are aimed at acquiring English, while French, Spanish and German dominate schools' languages curricula, with Mandarin Chinese increasingly represented and some provision for Japanese and Italian. However, there are no restrictions on which modern languages can be taught within the national curriculum so, for example, Bengali, Urdu, Portuguese and Turkish among other heritage languages are offered in some schools, while in common with many other LUCIDE cities, the maintenance and learning of minority community (heritage) languages is widely taken on by communities themselves who set up 'complementary schools'. London is undeniably a vibrant global city in which hundreds of languages are used on a daily basis in a wide range of contexts. However, the authors of the London City Report conclude:

> our research paints a rich and dynamic picture of London as a hub of multilingual activities. [However behind] this richness and dynamism is a language hierarchy [...]. Speakers of languages which are perceived as high status – either because of their current economic value or historical circumstances – experience London in a fundamentally different way to those who speak less prestigious languages. (London City Report, 2014: 76)

Melbourne, with a population of nearly 4 million, is the capital of the state of Victoria. Before the arrival of European settlers in the early 19th century, it is estimated that the area was occupied for about 30,000–40,000 years by hunter-gatherers from five language groups (probably under 20,000 inhabitants). Today 18,025 Aboriginal and Torres Strait Islanders make up 0.5% of the population.

The LUCIDE City Report identifies four significant waves of immigration. The first wave of immigration, mainly from the UK, occurred in the 1830s. The second wave, which saw the arrival of a considerable number of Chinese, occurred in the 1850s during the Gold Rush. The third and biggest wave of immigration took place in the wake of WWII and consisted of refugees and displaced people but also assisted migrants from Europe. The fourth wave of immigration, mainly from Cambodia and Vietnam, occurred after 1970. Since 2006, the largest number of migrants has originated from India, China, Sri Lanka and the Philippines, with significant numbers also from Afghanistan, Pakistan, Sudan and Burma. According to the Melbourne City Report, 44% of today's inhabitants of Melbourne were born overseas.

Melbourne emerges from the LUCIDE project as another vibrant multilingual city in which plurilingualism is fostered through public and private structures, notably in the sphere of education. For instance, the City Report refers to community or heritage languages being supported with state and national funding, benefiting nearly 150 language communities (including teacher training programmes). Vibrant multicultural and multilingual cityscapes are present in Chinese, Vietnamese, Greek, Italian, Arabic, Jewish and Turkish districts. The City Report, however, leaves us with questions about the status of oral indigenous languages, which do not play a key role in economic prosperity and which in some cases are in danger of extinction.

Toronto, the capital of Ontario and the commercial centre of Canada, is situated towards the western end of Lake Ontario in an officially unilingual English province. It is the largest city in Canada, with just over 6 million inhabitants (or about 18% of Canada's total population) in the Greater Toronto Area. As in Australia, the multilingual and multicultural traditions of indigenous peoples were also suppressed by English and French colonisers in Canada. In the aftermath of the Seven Years War (1756–1763), France ceded most of its territory there to Britain, and 'during Canada's infancy, when it was still British North America, many attempts were made to assimilate Aboriginal and French people into the dominant English group' (Ottawa City Report, 2014: 4). It is this history of conflict and assimilation that underlies the sensitivities of language policy in the cities of Canada today. While indigenous peoples' languages have been nearly decimated, modern Canada is based on federal and official English–French bilingualism. Canadian cities also attract immigrants with their own linguistic histories from all parts of the world. It is noteworthy that indigenous communities form extremely small proportions of these cities today, and the City Reports do refer to some interesting efforts at the revitalisation of their languages. Whatever the outcome, official bilingualism means that language issues remain central to Canadian identity.

Toronto is growing fast as it is the most popular destination for new immigrants to Canada, and can claim to be one of the most diverse cities in the world with nearly 50% of its residents being born outside Canada and 47% of its inhabitants having a mother tongue other than English. Toronto used to have substantial Yiddish and Italian-speaking populations until late in the 20th century when new waves of immigration had the effect of shrinking the relative size of these communities, while younger generations spoke their parents' mother tongue to a lesser degree. Today Toronto's demographic profile is closer to that of Vancouver, with English dominating and Chinese and South Asian languages having significant vitality.

Toronto is perhaps the most global of all the Canadian cities according to the report. It has embraced diversity in various public and private spheres to a substantial degree and there are indications that multilingualism can thrive in such a positive civic environment. Today, the city has a motto that expresses great pride in and ownership of its multilingual profile: 'Diversity Our Strength'.

Vancouver is situated in the province of British Columbia on the Pacific Ocean, with English as the official language. The Greater Vancouver metropolitan area has 2.3 million residents, constituting the third largest metropolitan area in Canada. It is reportedly the third favourite destination in Canada for newcomers after Toronto and Montreal, and its strategic position as a port facing the Pacific-rim nations contributes to its vibrancy and multilingual character. As in the case of Melbourne, the 19th-century Gold Rushes acted as a stimulus to multilingualism. Before WWII, Chinese and Japanese communities were well established, comprising 5% of inhabitants. In the 1950s and 1960s significant numbers of northern European immigrants (Germans, Scandinavians and Ukrainians) together with Italians diversified the city further and, by 1961, 21% of the population in Vancouver reported a mother tongue other than English. Today this proportion has almost doubled to 41.5% claiming a mother tongue other than French or English. Chinese and South Asian languages are the largest minority languages according to the report, while Francophones and speakers of First Nations languages constitute very small proportions (some 1–2%) of the population. The city of Vancouver is prosperous and multilingual, facing across the Pacific to Asia. As a 'young' city relative to Montreal, Toronto and Ottawa, it is increasingly developing services in multiple languages, giving substance to its linguistic capital.

Cities new to multilingualism

Athens, with a population of about 3 million (metropolitan area), is the capital of Greece and spreads across the plain of the Attica basin with access to the eastern Mediterranean through the port of Piraeus. Notwithstanding its antiquity, Athens may be categorised as being relatively new to multilingualism due to a period of large-scale emigration of Greeks to other parts of the world post-WWII, and the relatively recent arrival of significant populations of immigrants from different parts of the world. The city of Athens itself is not in fact the focus of the Athens City Report: it concentrates rather on the multi-ethnic municipality of Aghii-Anargyroi Kamatero (AAK), which consists of 65,000 inhabitants of whom about 10% are of non-Greek origin: Albanians the largest, then Pakistanis, Bangladeshis, Roma and some other Eastern Europeans. However, reference is also made to the wider area of Athens.

Greece has had a turbulent history throughout the 20th century. Poverty and the harsh socio-economic conditions experienced by a large portion of its population, including the bitter civil war after WWII, resulted in waves of mass emigration over decades. The Greeks emigrated to various countries throughout the world, especially to the United States, Germany and Australia – hence the substantial Greek population in Melbourne. Immigration to Athens is actually a very recent phenomenon, dating back only to the 1970s and peaking in the 1990s, and may explain why 'the Greek state, along with Greek society, has appeared reluctant to accept the fact that immigrants are here to stay' (Athens City Report, 2014: 12). According to a respondent cited in the Athens City Report, 'Greek cities have not had a pre-existing infrastructure to enable them to receive and integrate immigrants in a balanced way' (Athens City Report, 2014: 17).

Recently Greece faced a severe economic crisis in the context of the world recession that was triggered in 2008. This disastrous economic context also provided a fertile breeding ground for the rise of xenophobia and the increasing appeal of extreme far-right anti-immigration rhetoric, adding fuel to the further devalorisation of other languages and resistance to multilingualism. Athens probably constitutes the city where the attitudinal gap is at its widest between valued bilingualism, in particular English, and the devalued multilingualism of minorities (Albanian, other Eastern European, Pakistani, Bangladeshi and Romani). There is a strong culture of and love for foreign language learning among the Greek population when it comes to European languages, especially English, but little interest in minority languages.

On the other hand, Athens is a truly multicultural and multilingual city and voluntary organisations that promote immigrants' rights and fight racism have proliferated in the last few years. These organisations place special emphasis on the promotion of multiculturalism and the provision of language courses for immigrants.

Sofia, the capital of Bulgaria, with a population of nearly 1.3 million according to the last national census in 2011, stands at a crossroads of the east/west and north/south axes in Europe. Sofia shares with both Athens and Limassol the experience of subjugation under the Ottoman Empire but over a greater time span (nearly five centuries). Nation formation was associated with the Bulgarian language as the expression of national consciousness and, after the liberation from the Ottomans in 1878, there began a process of internal migration from the countryside to the capital (in parallel with

Athens) which has continued to the present day. Today, according to the City Report, almost a fifth of Bulgaria's inhabitants reside in Sofia. At the end of WWII, Bulgaria was absorbed into the Soviet bloc, and at the end of 1989 the process of democratisation began with multi-party elections and the transition to a market economy.

In Bulgaria, four minority languages are recognised with official rights to mother-tongue education: Turkish, Roma, Armenian and Hebrew, although the last two have few speakers. Despite such a policy of official recognition of minority languages, the neglected position of the Roma people is highlighted as an issue by the Sofia City Report (2014: 20): 'Bulgaria needs serious efforts to improve its internal climate of tolerance and understanding of minorities (particularly Roma but also Turks).'

The accession of Bulgaria to the EU in 2007, which facilitated both emigration and immigration, has already had an impact on the demography of the city as Sofia has become a final destination for some immigrants rather than a transit point in their journey. However, it remains a predominantly monolingual, Bulgarian-speaking city with a Bulgarian ethnic population of 96.4%. Overall, multilingualism appears to be a hidden asset in Sofia that excites little overt interest. Linguistic capital is measured mainly as an economic tool, with English holding a primary role.

Oslo, a fjord port, is the capital of Norway, with a population of approximately 600,000; the greater metropolitan area, however, has a population of 1.5 million. It is the most northern of our LUCIDE cities in Europe. Norway is a member of the Schengen group, but it lies outside the EU unlike all the other European cities in our project.

After the Viking Age (8th–11th centuries), there was no further colonial expansion, and Norway instead endured a long nationalist struggle against Danish rule from the end of the 14th century until 1814 when it was ceded to Sweden, from which it achieved independence in 1905. Due to the nationalist struggle for autonomy Norway has wide experience of language planning and policy elaboration. As the City Report explains:

> Bokmål is today the preferred written standard for the majority of Norwegians, including in Oslo. The second written standard, Nynorsk ('new Norwegian'), was developed during the nineteenth century. As an alternative to the Danish-influenced language, it was based on the spoken language of rural Norwegians at that time. (Oslo City Report, 2014: 5)

Nynorsk is spoken mainly in the west of Norway. There are thus two official versions of Norwegian, a situation referred to in the LUCIDE report as 'parallelingualism – an accommodation of two standards' (Oslo City Report, 2014: 5). The autochthonous languages (Sami languages and Kven) together with Romani, were at first discouraged by the new Norwegian state with a ban on their use in schools only being lifted in 1959. These languages are now protected and have official minority status. Neighbouring languages, Swedish, Finnish and Danish, are widely spoken in Oslo. English is described in the City Report (2014: 22, 30) as very important: 'Professionally, however, English is used as the preferred language.'

According to the City Report, global diversity is a recent phenomenon for Oslo, a city characterised by decades of net emigration rather than immigration. Earlier immigrants, however, included Jewish migrants from Eastern Europe who arrived in the early years after independence. With the expansion of the oil and gas industries at the end of the 1960s, Norway experienced severe shortages of labour and welcomed migrants mainly from Turkey, Morocco and Pakistan to make up the shortfall.

As might be expected of the home of the Nobel Peace Centre, Norway has a tradition of welcoming refugees from around the world: Hungarians in the 1950s, Chileans and Vietnamese in the 1970s and more recently refugees from the Balkan countries, Iraq, Afghanistan and Somalia. There are sizeable populations of Swedes and Poles who live and work in Norway; Somalis and Eritrean migrants also constitute significant minorities in Oslo according to the City Report (2014: 26): 'As a relatively compact capital of a small European country, Oslo has experienced astonishing demolinguistic changes in the past decade.' These migrant populations can be very concentrated: in some Oslo suburbs one in two of the inhabitants is from a migrant background. In the wider area of the suburbs, immigrants comprise about 15% of the population, but this proportion rises to just over 30% within the city itself.

Dublin, the capital of the Republic of Ireland, is a port city on the east coast with Dublin city and suburbs having a population of 1.27 million – around 28% of the total population (LUCIDE Dublin Report, 2014: 6). By the end of the 18th century Dublin had become the 'second city' of the British Empire, as the city's wealthy Anglo-Protestant population thrived on trade and commerce. Around this time movements for the revival of the Irish language – a member of the Celtic branch of Indo-European – were mostly led by the educated, liberal and wealthy Anglo-Irish. Once the vernacular of the island of Ireland, Irish had decreased dramatically in usage. *Conradh na Gaeilge* (the Gaelic League), founded in Dublin in 1893, became the leading organisation in the revival and was founded on non-political and non-sectarian principles. However, this movement became increasingly politicised as the struggle for independence from Britain intensified. The City Report notes:

> the Irish language became embroiled in polarised politics. The equation of 'one language–one nation–one state', as used by nationalists across Europe at that time, linked Irish with politics and with a 'pure' past – despite the fact that actual Irish-language usage had dramatically decreased among the population, most obviously in Dublin. (Dublin City Report, 2014: 4)

Following Partition and the establishment of the Irish Free State (1922–1937) came the birth of Éire. The 1937 constitution declared that 'the Irish language as the national language is the first official language'; English was recognised as the second official language (Government of Ireland, 1937: Art. 8). Census data (CSO, 2012) suggest that almost half of Dublin households have at least one Irish speaker, although this is a somewhat misleading figure given that it is likely to include a significant number of children who study Irish at school and who are unlikely to use Irish at home. Language planning and policy efforts have been restricted to the role of Irish in the public or educational spheres.

The Irish experience of immigration remained modest for centuries: Protestant refugees fleeing wars of religion in continental Europe at the end of the 17th century; Jewish populations fleeing from pogroms in the Russian Empire (modern-day Lithuania) in the 1870s; a few hundred German families in the wake of WWII; some Hungarians in 1956; and modest numbers of Chileans, Vietnamese and Italians later.

Large-scale immigration to Ireland is a recent phenomenon, boosted by the enlargement of the EU in 2004 and again in 2007. At the time of the 2011 census (CSO, 2012), one in six Dublin city residents was a 'non-Irish national'. The booming construction sector, based on a property bubble, began to slow down in 2007 and, with the meltdown of the 'Celtic Tiger' economy in 2008, immigration slowed but did not entirely cease. A generous tax regime has attracted some high-profile multinationals to Dublin (and Ireland as a whole) including, among others, Amazon, eBay, Facebook, IBM, LinkedIn, Microsoft,

Figure 1.6 Dublin hairdresser (LUCIDE network, 2014)

PayPal and Twitter, all of whom recruit outside the European Economic Area for highly skilled, multilingual staff. The hospitality sector continues to be a major employer of economic migrants in Ireland. The most significant ethnolinguistic groups today include Polish, Romanian, Chinese, Brazilian, Lithuanian and Russian.

According to the Dublin City Report, 11% of Dubliners reported speaking languages other than Irish or English at home in 2011, with over 180 languages being mentioned in census returns. The report cites evidence of much awareness of Dublin's changing 'ethnoscape', with pragmatic responses to the challenges of multilingualism in the public sphere. However, the official status of Irish and English eclipses other languages in the school system.

Border and bilingual cities

Limassol is an eastern Mediterranean port situated on the southern coast of Cyprus, poised between the Middle East, Africa and Europe with a population approaching a quarter of a million. It is the second largest city in Cyprus but one of our smaller LUCIDE cities. Although the major influence is Greek, it has a rich multilingual history. For instance, French was used during medieval times (1192–1489), Italian under Venetian Rule (1489–1571) and Turkish since the Ottoman Era (1571–1878). Indeed, both Turkish and Greek are official languages of Cyprus, but the use of Turkish is now concentrated in the area established as a separate Turkish Cypriot political entity in the north after the Turkish invasion in 1974. In Limassol, formal interactions usually take place in Standard Modern Greek (SMG) rather than in the Greek Cypriot variety, according to the Limassol City Report (2014: 4). This distinctive diglossia has led to the characterisation of the city as 'de-facto bilingual' in the report. Last but not least, there is English which has a unique status not only as the international language of trade but also as the language of the former colonial power, as the British ruled Cyprus from 1878 to 1960. Close ties remain between the two countries – many British citizens reside in Cyprus and there are still British bases on the island.

Cyprus (like Greece) has a long history of emigration for economic reasons; more recently, between 1960 and 1975, especially following the Turkish invasion of the island in 1974, there was a renewed wave of emigration to countries such as the UK, the United States and Australia (Gregoriou et al., 2010). Conversely, the phenomenon of immigration is a relatively new experience for Cypriots. There is a culture of suspicion of newcomers in Limassol, tactfully reported by a respondent in the Limassol City Report (2014: 28) as 'linguistic diversity is not always welcome'. The Limassol research team also note that Cyprus ranks second last on the Migrant Integration Policy Index, an EU measure of the support afforded to new migrants.

Limassol today, according to the report, is a very diverse multilingual city with over a fifth of its inhabitants coming from a variety of countries including Russia, Poland, Romania, Slovakia, Bulgaria, Latvia, Ukraine, Belarus, Syria, Egypt, Lebanon, Jordan, Sri Lanka, the Philippines, India, Bangladesh and China. Limassol has also received a multilingual boost as a consequence of becoming an increasingly important tourist centre in the Republic of Cyprus since 1974. However, recent demographic changes have represented a shock to a traditional, strongly ethnocentric society in which only bilingualism with valued languages like English is understood and prized. At the same time, the increasing visibility of Russian and Chinese in Limassol shows the interconnection between language visibility and economic strength. Structures of support are emerging from the pressure of necessity, but also under the influence of good practice exemplified in other EU countries.

Osijek, founded by the Romans, is situated in eastern Croatia. Today it has a population of 108,000 and the official language is Croatian. It shares a common experience of Ottoman rule with Varna, Athens, Sofia and Limassol, but over a shorter time period as Ottoman rule lasted only until 1687 when Osijek became part of the Habsburg Empire. In the empire, dominated by Austria and Hungary, Latin was the official language (until 1848 in Croatia), but German also enjoyed high status. As the Osijek City Report points out, by the end of the 19th century German speakers made up more than half the population of Osijek and the significance of German in Osijek lasted until the establishment of the new Slav state – The Kingdom of Serbs, Croats and Slovenes – in 1918, which aimed at a unifying policy, making Croatian and Serbian one language. The linguistic landscape was thus dramatically changed by the outcome of WWI. Subsequently, WWII ushered in the communist era with the establishment of the Socialist Federated Republic of Yugoslavia in 1943, which maintained the single language policy. The City Report explains further:

> During the course of the 40 year-long communist system many issues were ignored [...] Those who spoke German as their mother tongue, and were not prosecuted or did not flee, either hid this fact and spoke it only at home or abandoned German altogether [...]. (Osijek City Report, 2014: 8–9)

Thus German became a 'secret' language and the distinctive pidgin known as *Essekerisch* (a German base incorporating elements of Croatian, Serbian, Hungarian and Yiddish) died out.

The more recent conflict known as the 'Homeland War', 1991–1997, caused further seismic shifts in population, including a reduction in Osijek's population by at least 20,000 inhabitants. Croatia entered the EU in July 2013, and greater demographic mobility is predicted – both emigration and immigration (minorities are very rare at the moment according to the City Report).

In Osijek the balance of languages is still dictated by history, giving Hungarian and German a particular position as heritage languages (see Chapter 5). However, the new element is the prestige of English, especially among the youth for whom employment abroad is a very attractive prospect.

Strasbourg in the French region of Alsace is one of LUCIDE's smaller cities, with a population of under 300,000 inhabitants. However, its modest size belies its status and role at the heart of Europe. The key to Strasbourg's past and present lies not only in its location in France close to the German border but also in its role as a 'European' city and host to a large number of transnational European institutions.

The regions of Alsace and Lorraine have a unique history of dual identity which began in 1681 when Louis XIV invaded and Strasbourg became part of France. Later, over a period of only 75 years, Germany and France were to exchange control of these regions four times. The defeat of the French by Germany in the Franco-Prussian War of 1870 restored Strasbourg to German control. Following WWI, Alsace became French again, but was to be annexed by Germany in 1940 until a return to France in 1944, at the end of WWII. The city became a symbol of reconciliation between France and Germany and accordingly in 1949 was chosen as the seat of the Council of Europe; in 1992 it became, with Brussels, the joint host of the European Parliament. Today more than 20 different European institutions are based in Strasbourg.

The Alsatian language, a Low Alemannic variety of German, is still sometimes used in everyday life in the city. As the Strasbourg City Report (2014: 6) comments concisely: 'Strasbourg is an interesting case study as a multilingual city because of its endogenous linguistic diversity and the exogenous linguistic variety due to immigration.'

A further contribution to the multilingual character of the city is made by the *travailleurs frontaliers* who daily cross the border from Germany as they commute to Strasbourg for work. In schools German is the first foreign language taught, unlike in other French regions where English predominates. Likewise the presence of over 1000 international companies boosts the linguistic capital. Strasbourg today has the largest university in France with over 43,000 students enrolled, according to the City Report. Strasbourg's unique history, border position and also the various European institutions provide it with a key political and economic role in Europe. It operates as a global city with a strong commitment to valued ('elite') bilingualism or multilingualism, with German on a par with English.

Today Strasbourg's diversity has intensified with small but significant multi-ethnic minority populations (probably under 10%, although statistics are unreliable) originating from a more varied set of regions and countries, including Turkey, North Africa (Algeria and Morocco), West Africa (Senegal and Cameroon), Southeast Asia (Cambodia, Laos and Vietnam), as well as Eastern Europe (Institut National de la Statistique et des Etudes Economiques,

2012). However, the Strasbourg City Report, echoing the mood in Athens, noted some strong negative associations with multilingualism in Strasbourg:

> for them it is a term that they think is inclined towards the tolerance and acceptance of the practices and language of those adherents of Islam. There is a fear that too much inclination to multilingualism would mean a loss of national and regional identity. This feeling of anxiety is consistent with right-wing press surveys. (Strasbourg City Report, 2014: 33)

Ottawa, the capital of Canada, is a city of about 1.25 million, situated in Ontario (officially English at the provincial level) on the border with Quebec (officially French at the provincial level), and housing many public federal institutions. The Ottawa City Report points out that under the Languages Act of 1969, which granted French and English equal status in the governance of Canada, the federal courts, parliament and all federal institutions are governed by an official policy of federal bilingualism. Accordingly, nearly half of the region's inhabitants are bilingual in the two official languages (French and English), although according to the City Report, the City of Ottawa has experienced a decline in the percentage of Francophone inhabitants from 40% in 1941 to just under one-third today.

The City Report also reports that Ottawa fell from its position as fourth favourite Canadian destination for immigrants in 2006 to seventh position in 2011. It argues that a key factor in dissuading immigrants from settling in Ottawa is the issue of employment – the federal public service is the city's main employer and it hires only Canadian citizens for full-time employment. However, it is a more favoured choice of Canadian city among refugees, retaining fourth position. Overall, and because of the dominance of public sector employment, Ottawa appears less attractive as a final destination to economic migrants than other Canadian cities.

Montreal, the largest city in the province of Quebec, sits at the head of the St Lawrence Seaway, a series of locks and channels that link the Atlantic Ocean to the Great Lakes. The total population of the Montreal metropolitan area was just under 4 million in 2011. The linguistic profile of Montreal reveals that its population is effectively French–English bilingual. Interestingly, after Paris, Montreal is the biggest French-speaking city in the world (Roussopoulos & Benello, 2005). While Canada is an officially bilingual country at the federal level, most provinces and cities are officially unilingual (the exception being New Brunswick). Montreal stands in a distinctive position because its official language is French rather than English.

Following the early history of French and English immigration and colonial conflict, Ashkenazy Jews fleeing pogroms in Russia and Eastern Europe in the late 19th and early 20th centuries constituted the next substantial wave of immigrants; they were, in the majority, speakers of Yiddish. According to the City Report, by 1939 their population in Montreal numbered 60,000 out of a total population of 900,000. From the 1940s onwards Italians formed the second major wave of immigration.

According to the City Report, in 2011 the majority (64.5%) of Montreal's inhabitants stated that their mother tongue was French, followed by English (12.5%) and a number of other languages (23.0%). The report indicates the changing diversity of Montreal in recounting how different ethnolinguistic groups have become a significant part of the scene over time. For instance, although in 2006 Italian remained the third largest language group in Montreal (after French and English), its position fell to fifth, with Arabic occupying fourth place after Spanish in 2011. As the reports from Canada point out, the linguistic profile of Montreal is quite different from that of Vancouver and Toronto, where South Asian languages are the most commonly spoken languages after English and French.

Despite the overwhelmingly francophone majority in Montreal, and despite being part of a city where over half of the population in the greater metropolitan area is bilingual in both official languages of Canada, a significant proportion of respondents in the LUCIDE Montreal City Report thought that 'fear of English' was reconfigured in Montreal into 'fear of multilingualism'. Nonetheless, the reality, according to the City Report is that 'today's Montreal, even though it is an officially unilingual city in an officially unilingual province in an officially bilingual country, is highly multilingual' (Montreal City Report, 2014: 4).

The Vitality of Urban Multilingualism across LUCIDE

These brief introductions to the LUCIDE cities have focused on their distinctiveness, in size, geography, history and ethnolinguistic composition as gleaned from the City Reports. This section provides an overview analysis of the vitality of their urban multilingualism in terms of demographic, institutional support (and control) and status factors. The focus here is first on more settled populations and then on temporary migrants such as tourists, international students and others. Tourists are undoubtedly an increasingly important aspect of the ecology of many LUCIDE cities (e.g. Varna, Rome), while international students are significant in several others (e.g. Utrecht, London). Their contribution to the degree and form of the vitality of urban multilingualism is important, and is indicated by the presence of many languages, especially English, in the sights, sounds and services in cities (see Chapter 2).

Demographic factors

Demographic factors relate to actual numbers and their distribution throughout urban areas, including immigration, emigration and exogamy (Giles *et al.*,

1977; Sachdev *et al.*, 2012). Ethnolinguistic diversity in LUCIDE cities varies not only in terms of sheer numbers and size of communities, but also in terms of their relative proportions and distributions (see Chapter 3 for an articulation of city size and identity).

Patterns of recent migration, within the EU and across the world, have led to increased diversity in most cities. Freedom of mobility and exchange across EU countries, coupled with the globalisation of markets, money and migration, and enhanced by an increasing ease of travel and communication, are primary contributors. Larger cities like London, Toronto, Montreal, Melbourne, Madrid and Dublin report languages and groups from all continents of the world, fuelled by freer movement within the EU and by recent immigration, including refugees, from Africa, Asia and the Middle East. The spread of languages and groups is perhaps narrower and more regional in smaller cities such as Sofia, Varna and Osijek, which are more influenced by the legacies of older empires such as the Roman, Austro-Hungarian and Ottoman, as well as by significant populations of Roma.

Hundreds of different languages and groups are reported across the cities (e.g. 190 in Hamburg, 183 in Madrid, 233 in London), including those in a diglossic relationship to more standard, official varieties such as Greek in Limassol. It is important to note that there is probably an under-reporting of non-valorised dialects and varieties, which undermines overall estimates of the vitality of multilingualism in the cities. In most LUCIDE cities, ethnolinguistic minority populations make up 10–25% of the populations, with Toronto (47% having a mother tongue other than English) and Osijek (less than 5% with mother tongue other than Croatian) representing the extremes. Most cities report large numbers of languages being spoken in their school-aged populations, auguring well for the vitality of multilingualism, albeit in a strong climate of 'monolingual conservatism' (see also Chapter 5). Colonial ties account for some of the representation of this diversity, resulting in patterns such as the significant South Asian presence in London and the impact of Latin American residents in Madrid. Being at the crossroads for trade and commerce provides for different profiles that include Turkish and Polish in Hamburg and Russian and Arabic in Limassol. Although LUCIDE reports provide little quantitative data about the distribution of plurilingual speakers across cities, some qualitative data are provided concerning the multilingual landscapes of minority neighbourhoods (see Chapter 2).

Border cities are exemplary in displaying high levels of local and regional multilingualism. For example in Strasbourg, in addition to the official national language, French, and Standard German which are learned at school, families may speak Alsatian at home. Ottawa, with its relatively high levels of bilingualism, may also be considered a border city at the provincial level between two officially unilingual provinces (English Ontario and French Quebec), although its special status as the official bilingual federal capital makes the issue more complex. Proximity to the Asia-Pacific region (away from francophone Canada) influences the multilingual fabric of Vancouver (over 40% neither English nor French mother tongue) with Chinese (mainly Cantonese, 15%) and Punjabi (6%) being the largest minority languages. The Asia-Pacific region also has a significant impact on Melbourne (30% speak a language other than English at home), with significant Mandarin-, Cantonese-, Vietnamese-, Punjabi- and Hindi-speaking communities alongside various European minorities (e.g. Greeks, Italians).

Based on the LUCIDE City Reports, an overall loose classification may suggest that the cities in Canada, Melbourne and London display perhaps the highest levels of demographic VUM, with Utrecht, Hamburg, Dublin, Strasbourg and Madrid being close behind, followed by Rome, Limassol, Athens, Sofia, Varna and Osijek.

Status factors

Status factors pertain to sociohistorical prestige as well as social and economic status in local, regional and global contexts (Giles *et al.*, 1977; Sachdev *et al.*, 2012). Although demographic factors (including size and geolinguistic spread) are important in contributing to the vitality of urban multilingualism, sociohistorical legacies stretching back to antiquity through millennia of different empires, colonisation and regional integration also contribute to systematic variation in the multilingual fabric of cities. The most enduring legacy – 'one language-one nation' – has left most cities officially monolingual, with the exception of Dublin (Irish and English official), and cities in Canada (English–French bilingualism official at federal, but not provincial level). The status of languages in eastern and central European cities that were late entrants to the EU bear vestiges of a succession of empires from antiquity (Greek, Roman) to the end of the Austro-Hungarian and Ottoman empires in the early 20th century. Languages of the Roma accrue perhaps the most consistently low status in this region. The status of languages in western Europe appear to be influenced strongly by recent colonial histories and the emergence of the EU in the aftermath of WWII. In a related way, the ethnolinguistic fabric of modern Canadian and Australian cities (built primarily on recent immigration) is also rooted in their colonial histories, at the expense of indigenous languages and cultures.

Regardless of the demographic variation across cities, LUCIDE reports suggest that a fairly clear hierarchy of status accrues to different languages. In addition to the official and/or national languages, English receives the highest prestige on cultural, educational, commercial and other (international) dimensions in all cities. The special high status of English as a globally facilitating lingua franca may facilitate biliguality among non-Anglophones yet be an inhibitor for the development of their plurilingualism, or even of bilingualism for Anglophones (e.g. in UK, Ireland, Canada and Australia). Some European languages such as French, German and

Spanish are on an almost equivalent level, and are often valued highly in education curricula (see Chapter 5) and also in a variety of transnational official contexts (e.g. in Strasbourg's various European institutions).

The tourism industry also involves high-status languages, primarily for instrumental reasons and economic benefits. For instance, Varna's seasonal Russian tourist industry promotes Russian, whereas the more international attractions of Rome, London, Athens and Madrid favour English. Across all LUCIDE cities, the languages of ethnolinguistic minorities from Asia, Africa and the Middle East appear on the bottom tier.

Government decision makers at the city as well as the national level are key in formulating public policies regarding the management of diversity. In some countries, first- and second-generation immigrants are not recognised as full citizens, and government support for their languages and cultures may be tenuous or non-existent (e.g. minorities in Athens and Limassol). By creating second-class citizenship categories such as temporary resident, 'guest worker' (Hamburg, Utrecht) and 'landed immigrant' (Canada), state integration and language policies legitimise the non-recognition of the languages of first- and second-generation immigrants who, nevertheless, pay the same income and consumer taxes as dominant majority members.

The sum total of these processes results in high- and low-status forms of urban multilingualism (e.g. 'prestigious' versus 'plebeian' multilingualism in the Utrecht City Report) that are apparent in all cities, and perhaps most clearly discussed in the reports from Utrecht and Strasbourg, to which we will return in subsequent chapters. This distinction encompasses not only value and opportunities, but also institutional support, control and representation in society.

Institutional support and control factors

Institutional support factors refer to representation in, and control of, formal and informal institutions in the spheres of education, politics, religion, economy, culture and media (Giles *et al.*, 1977; Sachdev *et al.*, 2012). In democratic states, members of majorities usually command greater institutional support and control relative to those of minorities. A few states offer minority languages some recognition; most ignore, and some actively oppress the languages and cultures in their midst – as was the case for many indigenous minorities (Edwards, 1994; Sachdev *et al.*, 2006; see the City Reports from LUCIDE's Canadian partners and from Melbourne).

Legacies of 'monolingual conservatism', where attitudes are usually shaped by one nation–one language ideologies, exist in the institutions of all the national states of LUCIDE cities: institutional support and control are associated with dominant groups and their ideologies. Thus public educational, social, cultural and media institutions in cities are generally in the official languages – monolingual in most cases in Europe (except Ireland) and Australia. Interestingly, whereas Canada's official bilingualism applies to public federal institutions, many provincial public and private anglophone and francophone institutions in cities are effectively monolingual, including many major universities, reinforcing the image of Canada as a nation of 'two solitudes' (MacLennan, 1945). LUCIDE City Reports also suggest that non-official multilingual education in Canadian cities faces challenges akin to several cities in Europe in terms of institutional support and control (see Chapter 4).

LUCIDE cities represent varied sociopolitical settings within which multilingual communication takes place. In Europe, the loosening of EU boundaries has led to an increase in the institutions (formal and informal) of and for migrant populations. For instance, Polish-language minorities have significant social, cultural, educational and religious institutional representation in Dublin, Hamburg and London. Indeed Polish is now the second language in the UK in terms of numbers of speakers. Turkish minority institutions (religious, social and cultural), not always with equivalent recognition status, are found in Limassol, Hamburg, London, Utrecht, Sofia and Varna.

In all LUCIDE cities, language institutions in the mainstream educational sphere continue to promote the learning of high-status and valued ('elite/prestige/international') languages like English, French, German, Spanish and most recently Mandarin Chinese (e.g. in London), and language policies are implemented to foster the 'successful' integration of linguistic minorities within the dominant majority mainstream (see Chapter 5). In the not-so-distant past for most LUCIDE cities, this generally meant assimilation – expecting linguistic minorities to abandon their language and culture for the sake of adopting that of the dominant majority. Although this still appears to be the case today as an implication of many government policies implicitly, and perhaps most explicitly in Athens and Limassol, a shift away from assimilation may be happening in some places. For instance, Melbourne, London, Dublin, Utrecht and Hamburg and cities in Canada, although still expecting minorities to adopt dominant languages and cultures, have set up institutions to accommodate the linguistic needs of minorities (in social, health, municipal and other services; see Chapter 4), although they are generally intended to avoid 'emergencies'.

Respect for, and sometimes even promotion of the cultures and languages of linguistic minorities is also beginning to appear on city and national agendas (e.g. London, Toronto, Hamburg, Utrecht), but does not always extend to providing sufficient public funding needed to develop sustainable multilingualism and plurilingualism (e.g. via education and the setting up of public institutions), although Melbourne provides an interesting model in many respects. Several City Reports note that the global economic crisis beginning in 2008 has further dented available public funding, and in many cases even led to hostility against immigrants (especially in the media in Athens, Dublin and London). The absence of official and institutional recognition and financial support for ethnolinguistic minorities allows free market forces to reinforce the attraction of dominant and high-status languages to the detriment of minority languages.

Whereas valued multilingualism attracts public institutional attention and resources across societies, LUCIDE City Reports also provide evidence suggesting that many ethnolinguistic minority populations have managed to set up their own private institutions catering to their cultural, religious and linguistic needs. Multilingual landscapes of minority neighbourhoods are found in many LUCIDE cities (as explored in the next chapter) and ethnolinguistic minority institutions include a diverse array of places of spiritual and social welfare, commerce, media (print, radio, TV, new media), as well as language classes (see Chapters 3 and 4).

Based on the above and other details in the LUCIDE City Reports, it is clear that, whereas most cities display the highest levels of institutional support for linguistic vitality in valued languages (usually European including English), there is greater variability in support for the less valued languages of indigenous and immigrant minorities. City Reports often document non-official and private institutional support, as well as citing some good practice at official levels for less-valued languages in cities such as Melbourne and, to a lesser degree, in Utrecht, Hamburg, Dublin, Toronto, Vancouver and London. Overall, the vitality of urban multilingualism involving less valued languages, especially in official, educational, social and economic domains, remains to be fully nurtured and celebrated across the vast majority of LUCIDE cities.

The Increasing Vitality of Urban Multilingualism

This chapter charted multilingualism and plurilingualism from antiquity to the modern day, and attempted to provide an overview of VUM compiled from LUCIDE City Reports. The brief overview of the LUCIDE cities focused on their distinctiveness, especially in size, geography, history and ethnolinguistic composition, and focused largely on overall data concerning individual languages and groups, understating the rich, textured, dynamic, and changing multilingual LUCIDE cityscapes (covered in the following chapters). Considerably more data are required about societal multilingualism and individual plurilingualism as a composite to develop a comprehensive assessment of VUM. Degrees of vitality here are inferred but can be somewhat imprecise, underlying the importance of collecting reliable and accurate statistics for mapping diversity and enhancing VUM (Extra & Yağmur, 2012).

This overview suggests, however, that in spite of a legacy of monolingual conservatism associated with the formation of modern nation states, recent urbanisation and super-/hyper-diversity (Tasan-Kok et al., 2013; Vertovec,

2007) and the vitality associated with it are here to stay and increase further. The vitality of multilingualism varies systematically as a function of mobility, history, geography, politics, economy and technological advance. How this is reflected in observed cityscapes is considered in the next chapter. In the LUCIDE City Reports, official authorities are often cited as expressing positive attitudes and pride in the multilingual profiles of inhabitants, perhaps best exemplified by Toronto's motto, 'Diversity Our Strength'. An exploration of attitudes, perceptions, identities and beliefs of city inhabitants – in other words, the 'subjective' aspects of vitality – is also important to our understanding (see Chapter 3).

Multilingual communication is a consequence of the interaction between macro-level factors (such as ideologies, state policies) and micro-level factors associated with sociolinguistic norms and rules, and as mediated by social psychological factors which include plurilingual and pluricultural competencies, perceptions, identities and attitudes (Sachdev et al., 2012). It is important to adopt an intergroup approach to multilingual communication involving group identifications, intergroup perceptions, stereotypes, beliefs and attitudes. This is illustrated most ironically in the Dublin City Report, where a white, female, Irish-speaking respondent recalled:

> [...] recently I was racially abused on a bus when I was speaking on the phone to my father [in Irish]. A [Irish] woman started blasting that she was sick of us, and we were taking jobs, and her daughters were home with no work and it was because of the likes of us. (Dublin City Report, 2014: 37)

As has been observed, the abuser would probably have spent at least 12 years 'learning' Irish at school! How individuals and institutions experience and express the vitality of urban multilingualism is the focus of the next chapter.

This chapter is about the visual evidence of multilingualism and the languages we hear in Europe's cities, indeed the new varieties that seem to be emerging as a result of close language contact. In what follows, we will explore the languages we see in the streets of Europe's cities as well as the soundscapes created and experienced by their citizens. The written language we see all around us in a city – official and permanent signs guiding traffic or providing public information, signs generated by the marketplace, unofficial or temporary notices, even graffiti – are all indicators of the various languages that may be spoken by the city's residents and visitors. Most city dwellers do not necessarily pay much attention to the languages they see and hear around them – sometimes ignoring them, sometimes taking them for granted, often failing to distinguish between them. Sociolinguistics and researchers in the field of study described as linguistic landscaping argue that the languages we see (or do not see) reflect the power and social relations in a city, inclusion or exclusion, solidarity and belonging. This is an important area of city life to scrutinise, as we know very little about how the multilingual repertoires of citizens are operationalised in their daily lives. How do multilingual (and monolingual) citizens use the various languages at their disposal in their interactions with others? Do the various spheres of city life reflect the type of daily language usage that occurs, and the speech communities who are present? In the LUCIDE City Reports, the research teams examined what local residents and tourists notice about the cityscape. Through interviews with respondents and photographic evidence, the City Reports provide a snapshot of contemporary multilingualism in its manifestations in city streets. The last part of the chapter turns from the visual landscape to consider two aspects of the audioscape: multilingualism in the airwaves and the phenomenon of multiethnolects.

2 The Sights and Sounds of the Multilingual City

Lorna Carson

> *Cities have the capability of providing something for everybody, only because, and only when, they are created by everybody.*
> Jane Jacobs, *The Death and Life of Great American Cities*

Within a short distance from my home beside Dublin Bay, I regularly walk past two park benches on the footpath which seem to be pointing the wrong way. They face away from the road (unlike benches located near bus stops), and instead they are angled towards a stone wall. The beach ends about 100m before the benches. When I stop to investigate, I see the top of the wall, some trees, bushes and a grassy area on the other side of the wall and, on the horizon, an industrial area with a power station, water treatment plant and so forth. What a peculiar site for park benches! Why are they there, and what are people supposed to look at when they sit down?

To answer these questions, a passer-by needs to know some of the history of Dublin Bay and its reclaimed land. Previously, the wall that these park benches face was the sea wall, and on the other side was the beach. The beach that now ends several hundred metres away continued on, and passers-by would have once enjoyed a sea view before the land was reclaimed. What caught my attention when I first saw these benches was the notion of indexing – we assume that park benches are deliberately placed in locations which point us towards a view, and indeed in many parts of national parks and other areas of beauty, we often find a welcome bench for a picnic or just a rest which also orients visitors towards features in the landscape. In the study of linguistic landscapes, the idea of indexicality (or pointing us towards something) helps us understand something about the presence and vitality of languages in a city and in turn their speech communities.

Taking another example, the Dutch city of Utrecht is often described as a multilingual hotspot. However, despite the many visible languages in the city, there are not very many instances of East Asian languages. One sign stands out because of its use of Japanese. The information sign about a museum, the *dick bruna huis*, uses Dutch, English and Japanese to inform

Figure 2.1 Bench beside Dublin Bay (LUCIDE network, 2014)

readers about ticket purchases. The uses of Dutch and English are not surprising. But why Japanese here, and not elsewhere in Utrecht? Why not French or Spanish, for instance, like the tourist menus in the city? The Japanese language is almost invisible in the rest of the city.

To understand why Japanese is used here, we must understand something about the museum itself. This permanent exhibition celebrates the work of Dick Bruna, creator of the *Miffy* series of children's books, and the choice of including Japanese language in the sign provides a clue as to the popularity of the central character, a cartoon rabbit, in Japan. *Miffy* is such an important part of Japanese popular culture that many people assume she is a Japanese creation, like Hello Kitty. Indeed, the museum describes how some Japanese couples choose to organise their honeymoon around a visit to the *dick bruna huis* (Figure 2.2), and Utrecht is mentioned as 'the city of Miffy' in all Japanese tour guides. In other words, we learn that the choice of Japanese in this part of the city is a deliberate choice. Yet it stands out as there are very few other instances of Japanese elsewhere. Knowledge of Japanese popular culture explains the popularity of Miffy and the reasons for *this* sign. Building on this knowledge and the fact that many Japanese tourists are present suggests that more signs could usefully display information in Japanese to help such tourists and perhaps attract more.

It is also important to note early in this chapter that some examples of multilingualism can be incidental rather than indexical, meaning that some instances of the multilingualism we see and hear around us may be less salient than others. In Osijek, trams imported from Germany still display German language signage. In Varna, the instructions on vending machines often remain

The Sights and Sounds of the Multilingual City 51

Figure 2.2 dick bruna huis in Utrecht (LUCIDE network, 2014)

in the original language of their country of origin. Sometimes a translation in Bulgarian is provided, but not always. A medical technician interviewed by the authors of the Strasbourg City Report explained that most instruction manuals for medical devices are in English. The same respondent described a similar situation when using computer software. These appearances of German, Bulgarian and English say something about trade and globalisation, and how employees or even customers must sometimes cope with other language varieties in their sphere, but they are not necessarily indexical of the key issues experienced in Osijek, Varna or Strasbourg. The approach employed by the LUCIDE research sets out to capture some of the most relevant features of a city's linguistic landscape, the instances that help us understand how multilingual citizen communities most typically live and work and which point to the vitality of the languages in a city environment.

Investigating Multilingual Cityscapes

Cities are sites of intensive language contact. Our daily activities are surrounded by visual messages in a variety of scripts and registers. Sometimes

52 The Multilingual City

Figure 2.3 Dublin shop front (LUCIDE network, 2014)

a place can be famous for the signs that appear in the cityscape – think of Times Square in New York, the tourist trade in reproductions of Parisian street and café signs, Chinatown in London. But it is not simply about the signs or the languages used. Our cities are 'the interweaving of *human* patterns' (Raskin, in Jacobs, 1961: 229): 'They are full of people doing different things, with different reasons and different ends in view, and the architecture reflects and expresses this difference – which is one of content rather than form alone.' The city's streets provide its main visual focus for citizens and visitors. Jacobs describes the 'detail and activity' therein:

> [Streets] make a visual announcement (very useful to us for understanding the order of cities) that this is an intense life and that into its composition go many different things. They make this announcement to us not only because we may see considerable activities itself, but because we see, in different types of buildings, signs, store fronts or other enterprises or institutions, and so on, the inanimate evidences of activity and diversity. (Jacobs, 1961: 378)

The streets of the LUCIDE cities were the focus of the network's primary and secondary data collection. As outlined in the Introduction, the theme of urban spaces, or the 'cityscape', was one of five key spheres of city life identified by the research team. By 'urban spaces' we mean all publicly visible and audible aspects of a city, or what Scollon and Scollon (2003) describe as discourses in place. This includes the analysis of language in public signage, advertising, official and unofficial street art, instructions and announcements. These visual and audible aspects of multilingualism are the external markers of a city's many speech communities. Very often, however, citizens may be blind to the languages which appear in the cityscape, and unaware of the decision-making behind them. This is not just a case of monolingual bias, but also a case of efficiency, and only selecting or decoding that which is necessary within a language environment.

For instance, while a walk around the central business district or most residential neighbourhoods of any European city would allow us to hear a wide variety of languages (especially if we are able to distinguish between them), we may not see any written examples of these languages in what is described as the linguistic landscape of a city. In fact, some of the languages present in a city may be entirely invisible, or appear only in unofficial signs. And what about the predominance of some languages, especially English, in the marketplace or in tourism? What is going on when we see multiple languages in a city street? How do these connect with daily life? Are they meaningful at the level of society or politics? Are they indexing different types of relationships between communities? Who decides to place such signs? What language choices do these decision makers face? As Bogatto and Hélot explain,

> the production and display of such messages are in no way trivial or insignificant. On the contrary, they are used to mark a given space even if only symbolically, to mark oneself out as different from others or to express one's identity in various ways and through different processes. (Bogatto & Hélot, 2010: 17)

While interest in how languages and scripts (and which languages and scripts) feature in city life has existed arguably since the Rosetta Stone, the academic study of manifestations of language use in the cityscape has gathered considerable momentum in recent years, especially in areas where language choice is politically and socially contested. Rosenbaum *et al.* (1977) examined signage in Jerusalem; Tulp (1978) looked at the distribution of commercial billboards in French and Dutch in Brussels; Monnier (1989) explored compliance with the law in French language use in shop fronts in Montreal. The term 'linguistic landscape' was coined by Landry and Bourhis:

> The language of public road signs, advertising billboards, street names, place names, commercial shop signs, and public signs on government buildings combines to form the linguistic landscape of a given territory, region, or urban agglomeration. (Landry & Bourhis, 1997: 25)

This field of study employs photography and mapping techniques to capture and analyse the languages that surround us. It draws on disciplines such as geography and urbanism, sociology and political science, to understand what is going on within and behind the written discourse in the public (and sometimes private) spaces of contemporary society. The 'mushrooming' of multilingualism in cities is not something incidental or adjacent to everyday life, like a decorative Chinese arch when entering Chinatown, but is meaningful, in the way that the languages we see in signs and hear around us in fact point to the presence of vitality in speech communities. The visible evidence of multilingualism in cities – on noticeboards, billboards, electronic screens, instruction leaflets, in graffiti and in public announcements – form part of a dialogue between those who place such signs and those who read the signs. Below, we explore how such visual and audible evidence points to varying degrees of vitality in the languages represented.

A Snapshot of LUCIDE Cityscapes

In the cityscapes described in the LUCIDE City Reports, the private and economic spheres of city life tend to be sites of multilingual language use, whereas signs that appear in the public sphere tend towards either monolingualism or bilingualism as set out by law. For example, the authors of the Montreal City Report (2014: 4) describe it as 'an officially unilingual city in an officially unilingual province in an officially bilingual country', but go on to point out that it is in fact a highly multilingual city. Commercial properties in the city are subject to the Charter of the French Language, explored in more detail below, but increasingly languages such as Spanish and Arabic are also visible in the city. The Saint-Michel area is home to a Maghreb community, with many stores, coffee shops and restaurants, and Spanish is visible in the streets of the Rosemont-Petite-Patrie area.

All of the LUCIDE City Reports refer to the vitality of multilingualism in central districts as well as in specific neighbourhoods, some of which are designated as a 'Chinatown', 'Little Italy' or 'Little Greece', as explored in the next chapter. The visual character of these named areas grows from waves of immigration in neighbourhoods where immigrants first settled. It is interesting to compare cities with established patterns of immigration and cities with more recent experiences of immigration. The City Reports from Melbourne and Dublin point to old and new versions of specifically named ethnolinguistic areas. In Australia, gold was discovered in the Victorian goldfield in the 1850s. Thousands of Chinese immigrants emigrated to Melbourne, and the impact of the Chinese remains evident throughout Melbourne. This is especially the case around the area that is described as Melbourne's 'Chinatown', Little Bourke Street, where shoppers pass under a traditional Chinese arch. The author of the Melbourne City Report describes it as a 'a lively and colourful precinct filled with shops and restaurants', which is an established part of Melbourne's cityscape (Melbourne City Report, 2014: 3).

On the other hand, while the city of Dublin has resisted creating a designated district, the arrival of many Chinese entrepreneurs in the north inner city has created a de facto Chinatown. Mottiar and Walsh (2012) provide an insight into one street in this part of the city, Parnell Street East. This deprived inner-city district of historical significance was known briefly as 'Little Africa' before transforming over the last 10 years into an area with many Asian entrepreneurs. The authors describe the aspirations of local business owners to erect an arch marking this status, as in other international cities with a 'Chinatown'. Their paper points to 'the tension that exists between whether areas should be encouraged and supported to develop as specific monocultural areas such as a Chinatown, or in a more multicultural form encompassing other immigrant and local groups who operate and use such urban space' (Mottiar & Walsh, 2012: 29). A group of restaurants in this district have created a website which promotes Dublin's Chinatown (including Japanese and Korean restaurants), despite the city's reluctance to endorse the name.

Melbourne's Italian immigrants arrived between the 1920s and 1950s, and many settled in the neighbourhood of Carlton. While the percentage of Italian residents has declined over the years, Lygon Street, where the city's famous café culture was born, remains at the heart of Melbourne's 'Little Italy'. In Dublin, it is evident that the City Council has sanctioned the naming of the city's new 'Italian Quarter' through mentions in official documentation such as its Public Realm Strategy (although 'Chinatown' is conspicuous by its absence). This newly designed district was the result of urban planning in coffee shops and restaurants rather than representing the site of Ireland's original Italian population. One Dublin interviewee touched on the peculiarities of newly 'branded' areas when asked about language visibility. She noted 'a lack of signage and knowledge of the Italian quarter' among locals, despite its being described as such in tourist guides to Dublin (Dublin City Report, 2014: 28). Italian migrants came to Ireland between the late 18th and early 20th centuries, finding work in the stucco, mosaic and terrazzo industry of Dublin's grand building projects (Reynolds, 1993; Dietz, 2011). Later, other Italian immigrants found work in catering and hospitality; many Irish-Italian families are descended from a single chain migration, which commenced in 1912 in the region of Lucca, and they still continue the fish and chip trade in Dublin (De Tona, 2006; King & Reynolds, 1994). However, these well-established fish and chip shops (named, for instance, after the Borza, Macari, Cafolla and Aprilies families) are not located in the city's 'Italian Quarter'.

We will return to the discussion of specifically designated areas and fears of ghettoisation in Chapter 3, but it is worth drawing attention to the question of branding, authenticity and the gradual shift of newly arrived immigrants from inner-city neighbourhoods to the suburbs. The authors of the Toronto City Report trace the relocation of the main 'ethnic' linguistic neighbourhoods from the downtown to the suburbs. Hence, while the city's

Chinese community was originally concentrated near Elizabeth and Hagerman Streets, it is now concentrated in the suburbs of Scarborough, Markham and Mississauga. In Toronto, less than 10% of all areas in which Chinese immigrants are concentrated are downtown; they are for the most part located in the suburbs. An article in the *Toronto Star* newspaper makes the point that Chinatown, Greektown and Little Italy now resemble tourist landmarks, whereas new immigrant neighbourhoods grow in the suburbs. Another common feature is that these types of distinct urban areas are not exclusively sites for one speech community or ethnicity. According to Agrawal, an expert in ethnic enclaves and urban planning, 'The Greektown is not Greek; Chinatown is not Chinese. They are just ethnic business enclaves where you go, eat, play, have fun and go home' (Keung, 2013).

There are sometimes inconsistencies and contradictions in the language services and language choices provided in city spaces, as we will address in terms of policy in Chapter 4. For instance, the authors of the Athens City Report describe a dearth of street signs in languages other than Greek in most parts of the city, and point out the difficulties that this can cause for visitors. Official street art, sculptures and some attractions are only described in Greek. Aghii Anargyroi, the district investigated during the LUCIDE project, includes the site of Peisistratus's Olive Tree, a natural monument which dates back 2500 years and represents the ruler's edict to farmers to grow olive trees. The significance of this ancient olive tree is only described in Greek; the Athens City Report describes this situation as a missed opportunity. When another language does appear alongside Greek in this district of Athens, it is invariably English (Athens City Report, 2014: 36).

In Rome, despite significant tourist spending from South and East Asia and Eastern Europe, only European languages feature in the city's self-service rail ticket machines (English, French, German and Spanish). The main tourism website for the city only features the same languages. The website of the *Roma Migranda* initiative, which provides bespoke walking tours of the city by guides from immigrant backgrounds, is available only in Italian.

Multilingual manifestations in urban spaces can emanate from the activities of private citizens as well as the actions of the municipality or public bodies. The London City Report demonstrates some of the pragmatic efforts made by local authorities to communicate in the languages most relevant to local communities, such as the bilingual information sign in Tower Hamlets on the disposal of rubbish in English and Bengali (see Figure 2.4). Somali also appears in some local authority signs and newspapers in this district of London.

In central London, and in the centres of other cities that are major tourist destinations, most visible multilingual manifestations tend to be aimed at visitors rather than locals. The Transport for London website provides content in 15 languages other than English. Detailed information is provided about transport options, the city's Oyster cards and contactless payment methods,

The Sights and Sounds of the Multilingual City 57

Figure 2.4 Bilingual London recycling sign (LUCIDE network, 2014)

but these are hidden at the very bottom of the homepage under a link to 'Other Languages'. The link is in English, in a small font, and near the terms and conditions section of the website. The London LUCIDE team describes the limited effectiveness of some measures. For instance, one respondent describes how, 'In a mainline London station, a notice read: "If you need an interpreter, go to platform 8"' (London City Report, 2014: 64). All the LUCIDE City Reports point to serious lacunae in public transport. In London, despite multilingual welcome signs, the really useful information tends to be provided in English only, both in notices and in announcements.

In Utrecht (Utrecht City Report, 2014: 26), tourists and non-Dutch speaking residents of Utrecht may find it difficult to navigate around the city using public transport, as information is often provided only in Dutch. At Utrecht Central Station, for instance, all signs are in Dutch apart from information about international trains or trains to Schiphol Airport. Few public signs in the city give information in any other language but Dutch (apart from the Japanese example cited above). They provide the example of the Dom Church, with its famous Dom Tower. A public sign pointing to it and to other local museums and tourist sites is provided only in Dutch, with the exception of the sign pointing to the Aboriginal Art Museum, which does not have a Dutch name. Residents interviewed by the report's authors pointed to the need for more 'internationalisation' of the city. One respondent mentioned that this could be done through 'providing more English subtitles throughout the city, for instance on street signs or boards or in restaurants'. Several respondents from Utrecht noted that their municipality's interest in language issues was 'noticeable and refreshing', but drew attention to the fact that much of a fascinating blog on multilingualism in the city is provided only in Dutch! To consider these issues in greater depth in the following section, we will now explore three cities surveyed by the LUCIDE network, drawing on the primary and secondary data collected on visible manifestations of multilingualism in Hamburg, Strasbourg and Dublin.

Views from Three LUCIDE Cityscapes

Hamburg

The authors of the Hamburg City Report describe the multilingual landscape of the city and contrast the use of English in street signage and public transport with the use of heritage languages, which tend to be only visible in districts where migrants live or shop. Located near the main railway station, the St Georg district in Hamburg is a district that would be recognisable for many Europeans, a 'hot spot for social, ethnic and linguistic diversity' (Scarvaglieri *et al.*, 2013: 49). Scarvaglieri and other researchers from the universities of Neuchâtel, Hamburg and Greifswald studied the languages seen and heard in this part of the city. Overall, the district is characterised by its density, a young population and a high percentage of recent migrants, especially from Turkey and Central and Eastern Europe. There are fewer families living in St Georg than elsewhere in the city. The St Georg district divides into two clearly distinct zones: *Steindamm* and the *Lange Reihe*. *Steindamm* is composed of grocery stores, cafés and snack bars mostly selling products from Turkey, Iran, the Middle East and East Asia, as well as being known for prostitution and gambling. Just a few metres away, *Lange Reihe* is often described as a 'gentrified' part of the district, home to higher end shops and more expensive restaurants offering Italian and Portuguese food. *Lange Reihe* is visited both by tourists and locals, and is home to a sizeable gay community. Here, languages such as English, Italian and Spanish are clearly visible.

While German-language signage seems to be a predominant feature in St Georg overall, a closer look confirms that about a quarter of the 1034 documented signs in the district do not in fact include any German at all (Scarvaglieri *et al.*, 2013). And although about two-thirds of the signs are monolingual German signs, in line with some 'dominant domestic discourse' (Scarvaglieri *et al.*, 2013: 56) that considers Hamburg to be monolingual,

Figure 2.5 Hamburg food packaging (LUCIDE network, 2014)

the remaining third of the signs are either bilingual or multilingual. The less prosperous *Steindamm* is more linguistically diverse than *Lange Reihe*, with twice as many bilingual or multilingual signs. Grocers advertise their produce in Arabic, Turkish or Farsi, and the travel agents, hairdressers and snack stands cater to a clientele who speak a range of languages.

The research team describe a typical Turkish grocery store, *Sönmez Markt*. *Markt* is the German word for market, while *Sönmez* means 'never dies' in Turkish. A slogan below the name of the shop is provided uniquely in Turkish, which is translated by the researchers into English as 'Our strength comes from quality' (Scarvaglieri et al., 2013). The shop front also includes Turkish and English bilingual signage. The crates of fruit and vegetables are described in small individual signs; these are only written in German, as well as the units for prices (*Stück*, or per item). The research team propose that the different languages used in the signs perform different communication functions. They suggest that 'non-domestic languages are typically used to set up an interaction system' – affiliation, attracting passers-by and advertising (just Turkish or Turkish and English). The German language is only used once customers have been attracted into the shop and are browsing the goods, to find out the prices or to see what is at a reduced price – 'for performing linguistic actions which are at the *core* of an already *established* action system' (Scarvaglieri et al., 2013: 61, original italics).

The multilingual cityscape of *Steindamm* is shaped by labour migration to Hamburg, and by the plurilingual repertoires of individuals who use a variety of home languages as well as German to carry out everyday transactions. On the other hand, the multilingualism of *Lange Reihe*, with displays of international languages such as English, Spanish and Italian, reflects the gentrification of the street and high symbolic value of these languages, which perform a decorative function, indexing fashion and luxury products. In a similar vein, one respondent interviewed by the authors of the London City Report described 'pseudo-Italian restaurants' which use Italian simply as a branding technique to entice customers:

> You go to a so-called 'Italian' restaurant and the menu is in Italian (more or less) but actually no one there is Italian! So you get the impression you can speak Italian but if you do, it doesn't work! (London City Report, 2014: 61)

In the case of the St Georg district in Hamburg, it is clear that the Turkish language continues to play an important role as a marker of belonging; otherwise in the commercial world the shopkeepers simply wouldn't bother. The German language proficiency of shoppers is such that all the names of the fruit, vegetables, sales items and pricing are provided in German, pointing to code-switching between German and Turkish. It is also likely that monolingual German speakers use these shops. The use of German signs provide evidence of Turkish–German bilingualism, and suggest that most shoppers who may self-identify as Turkish speakers and choose to buy their groceries in stores which index the Turkish language are fully proficient in German. The Turkish speech community may be considered as having assimilated linguistically, pointing towards a low vitality for the Turkish language, yet seems to maintain a distinctive collective identity, which is generally an indicator of high language vitality.

Strasbourg

Strasbourg is a site of intense language contact, given its geographical position, its status as a border city where workers cross daily from France to Germany and vice versa, and the presence of many European institutions. In 2010, Bogatto and Hélot conducted the first empirical study of Strasbourg's linguistic landscape. This study focused on the commercial signs on the shop fronts in the district described as the *Quartier Gare,* around the railway station:

> As a micro context of cultural, social and linguistic mixing the Quartier Gare lends itself particularly well to an analysis of linguistic diversity and of the possible spatial delimitations, appropriation and construction linked to the production and display of urban written signs. (Bogatto & Hélot, 2010: 6–7)

The features of this part of the city are common to many other European cities: it is quite an old district, with a multi-ethnic population of varied socio-economic status, and there are many small shops as well as the infrastructure serving the train station. Choosing such a district for analysis provides rich data in the study itself, but also allows for future comparisons with similar districts in other cities. The study focuses on shop fronts as 'instances of individual discourses' (Bogatto & Hélot, 2010: 7), which point the reader or sign viewer towards expressions of the shop owner's local or global identity. As in other studies of this type, the researchers organise the photographs of the shop fronts according to units of analysis, which may contain several photos of different aspects of the same shop front. In the *Quartier Gare* in Strasbourg, Bogatto and Hélot collected and analysed 170 'signs' or units of analysis.

Their findings clearly indicate the dominance of the French language in this district, with 87% of the signs featuring French. The use of French indexes features of the local area (for instance, *Délice de la laiterie* refers to the site of a former creamery) as well as choices by shop owners to refer to their global identity through the medium of French (*Restaurant Le gourmet d'Afrique, Délices d'Asie, La boutique antillaise, Restaurant Le Cappadoce*). These signs point to Africa, Asia, the French Antilles and Turkey.

The Strasbourg City Report describes the use of Alsatian in the city. While Alsatian is highly visible in Strasbourg's street signs, it is not so apparent in the city's commercial signs. For instance, only five of the 170 signs described by Bogatto and Hélot (2010) contained instances of Alsatian on

Figure 2.6 Strasbourg restaurant (LUCIDE network, 2014)

display; four of these referred to restaurants serving Alsatian dishes. The remaining sign on a shop front read: 'We speak Alsatian' (*Mir rede Elsassisch*). Turning to the visibility of the neighbouring language of German, again a small subset of four signs featured German text. As in the case of Alsatian, three of the four referred to restaurants and were destined for tourists. An analysis of the city's linguistic landscape suggests that not all of the languages of residents are visible in the streetscape. For instance, only Arabic, Thai and Mandarin Chinese were recorded as visible around the *Quartier Gare*, and Bogatto and Hélot (2010) only recorded six instances overall of their use, on restaurant signs, on an Asian supermarket sign, on grocery stores and on a mobile phone shop. They describe how the appearance of these signs, alongside French, provide a decorative function for readers who cannot decode their meaning:

> Therefore it is not the content of the message which is important but rather its presence which brings to mind distant lands and a certain exoticism, all the more since it is always made explicit by meta discursive language, for example: *Traiteur chinois, Spécialités thaïlandaises, Téléboutique, Boucherie Traiteur Alimentation*, etc. (Bogatto & Hélot, 2010: 15)

A noteworthy aspect of this study of the neighbourhood around the railway station is how the use of Turkish family names is featured in signage. Eleven signs contained the Turkish language, and these featured family names rather than messages in Turkish:

> [I]t could be one of the specificities of the Quartier Gare since this expression of identity through the display of Turkish names seems to be clearly assumed, whereas in other areas of Strasbourg, it is not rare for Turkish shop owners to hide under less stigmatised identities such as a Greek one for example. (Bogatto & Hélot, 2010: 16)

Dublin

Dublin's linguistic landscape reflects the significant population changes in Ireland in recent years. Kallen (2010: 43) describes how the linguistic landscape in Dublin was 'very much a two-language affair' until recently. English was the dominant language in private signage and many public signs, with bilingual signs in Irish and English in 'state-related functions such as street and place-name labelling, traffic regulation and the identification of public buildings of various kinds' (Kallen, 2010: 44). Irish is visible in some private signs on shop fronts, although there are fewer of these in Dublin than in other towns and cities in Ireland. In his study of Dublin's changing landscape, Kallen (2010) refers to three key phenomena which have resulted in changes in the cityscape: changes in tourism flows, especially in the countries of origin of tourists which are more diverse than previously; growth of international retail and commerce, to which we also add the growth of multinational companies who have set up their headquarters in Dublin; and immigration. His study explores the role that inward migration has played in the development of the city's linguistic landscape.

Irish/English bilingualism is initially the most salient feature of the Dublin cityscape. As Carson and Extra (2010: 8) remark, 'Travellers who arrive at Dublin airport from abroad easily receive the impression that they have arrived in a bilingual country'. However, outside the public (or civic) and educational spheres, Irish is not as visible as public signage suggests. One of the interviewees in the Dublin City Report notes: 'Having lived in Dublin for several years I am surprised by the lack of people that speak Irish. Only on occasion over the past 10 years have I heard Irish language conversations.' One interviewee describes displays of Irish as haphazard, and suggests a different model: 'In Canada, French and English appear on all domestic goods, although perhaps it doesn't help with the usage of language, it helps with the visibility of it' (Dublin City Report, 2014: 31).

The Irish language has a protected status in the public sphere (including education) due to its constitutional recognition as 'first official language' of the Republic of Ireland (Government of Ireland, 1937, Art. 8). The Constitution recognises English as the second official language. Although Ireland's public sphere has operated bilingually in many respects, the Official Languages Act of 2003 seeks to strengthen the provision of Irish in public services. For instance, according to the Act,

> oral announcements (whether live or recorded) made by a public body, the headings of stationery used by a public body and the contents and the lay-out of any signage or advertisements placed by it shall, to such extent as may be specified, be in the Irish language or in the English and Irish languages.

Figure 2.7 Dublin street sign (LUCIDE network, 2014)

Ireland's official language policy is immediately visible on traffic signs: 'The use of Irish on the country's traffic signs is the most visible illustration of the state's policy regarding our official languages, Irish and English. The road authorities are obliged to adhere to the obligations imposed on them with regard to the use of those languages on traffic signs under the Traffic Signs Manual' (An Coimisinéir Teanga, n.d.). A Statutory Instrument in 2008 provided clarity on the presentation of bilingual signage placed by public bodies, which must either be provided in the Irish language, or in the Irish and English languages. The following provisions apply to bilingual Irish and English signage (Government of Ireland, 1937, Art. 7.2):

(a) the text in the Irish language shall appear first;
(b) the text in the Irish language shall not be less prominent, visible, or legible than the text in the English language;
(c) the lettering of the text in the Irish language shall not be smaller in size than the lettering of the text in the English language;
(d) the text in the Irish language shall communicate the same information as is communicated by the text in the English language; and
(e) a word in the text in the Irish language shall not be abbreviated unless the word in the text in the English language, of which it is the translation, is also abbreviated.

Ireland's legislation explains the visual – although not always grammatically accurate – prominence of the Irish language in Dublin in the civic sphere. As Kallen (2010: 47) notes, '[b]ilingualism here is not dependent on linguistic vitality in the sense of everyday language use'. While Irish is not as visible in the city's economic sphere, what Kallen and Ní Dhonnacha (2010: 22) describe as 'Celticised English' is ubiquitous in Dublin city centre, its symbolism pointing towards Irish authenticity. This often includes the use of English names in a Celtic script rather than lexical items. One well-known online restaurant guide lists 600 restaurants in Dublin city centre, of which only eight have Irish names. While Dublin is geographically distant from the *Gaeltacht* areas of Ireland (mostly located in the west of Ireland and where Irish is recognised as the community language), the Irish language is audible in the city. Nevertheless, just how often (and how much, and how well) Irish is spoken in everyday public life is a subject of controversy. Take, for instance, an extract from a tourist information website (www.dublin.info):

The language spoken in Dublin is English. Street signs and official buildings are signposted in both English and Gaelic, the indigenous Irish language. Despite this, you are highly unlikely to hear any Gaelic spoken on your travels across town. You are, however, likely to come across a lot of cursing in casual conversations. Relax, it does not carry the same connotations it might in other languages.

The intersection between the languages most likely to be heard in Dublin is beautifully illustrated in a short film by Daniel O'Hara (2003), entitled *Yu Ming is Ainm Dom* (My name is Yu Ming). A young Chinese man decides to come to Ireland, having picked his adventure at random by spinning a globe. Before coming, his next step is to learn Irish. However, on arrival in Dublin, he is perplexed to discover that no-one understands him. He meets an elderly man, Paddy, in a pub who explains, *Ní labhraítear Gaeilge anseo, labhraítear Béarla anseo, ó Shasana!* (Irish isn't spoken here, English is spoken here, from England!). The eavesdropping barman is amazed at the conversation between the two, and exclaims, 'Did you know that ol' Paddy could speak Chinese?' The young Chinese man happily finds a job in the Connemara *Gaeltacht* (Irish-speaking area), where he can use his language skills to welcome American tourists. While this Irish language learner is featured as moving to the west of Ireland, significant concentrations of Irish speakers have emerged in Dublin as a result of revitalisation activities. These speakers are in addition to those from the Meath *Gaeltacht* which was established in the 1930s, just outside Dublin. The recent Gaeltacht Act (Government of Ireland, 2012) allows for recognition to be given which is based on linguistic criteria rather than geographical location. This has led to much speculation that areas with concentrations of Irish speakers (such as the suburbs of Clondalkin or Ballymun in Dublin) may attain some sort of Irish-speaking status (O'Carroll, 2012), and the notion of *Urban Gaeilge* is now raised in the discussion of Irish language policy making (McMonagle, 2012).

Together, the visual evidence from the public spaces of Hamburg, Strasbourg and Dublin points to the different circumstances that have brought together each city's inhabitants – both permanent and temporary, as the next chapter will explore – and illustrates the dynamic of multilingual communication within and between the various speech communities present. In the next section, we address some salient common features which emerged from our comparison of different linguistic landscapes in the LUCIDE cities: the role of English, monolingual signs in multilingual cities, and languages on the edges of city life, in graffiti and informal notices.

Some Visible Features of Multilingual Cityscapes

English language usage

When it comes to understanding the significance of multilingual signs, unpicking what is informational and what is symbolic can be helpful. Hult

(2009), in his research on multilingual signs of two areas in the Swedish city of Malmö, distinguished between symbolic and instrumental language use. For instance, in a shop sign in both English and Swedish, the use of English gives no information about what a shop sells, only serving to index globalisation. The Swedish language sign fulfils the communicative function of telling visitors that it is a food store. English in such instances indexes globalisation, pointing towards modernity, prosperity, youthfulness and so forth in order to sell goods. The English language is visible in all the cities in the LUCIDE network, and its use in commercial signs and advertising, on storefronts and in other aspects of a city's linguistic landscape is ubiquitous. The nature and extent of English language use in Europe's cities have been the subject of several empirical studies. Data from these studies suggest that English plays a variety of roles according to sphere. For instance, Ball (1989) suggests that in France, English-language tokens tend to feature in luxury or entertainment establishments such as travel agents and florists, cafés and night clubs, rather than in shops which provide the everyday necessities (bakers, butchers, hardware stores). A study by Schlick (2003) explored the use of English in clothes stores in Austria, Italy and Slovenia. In an investigation of English shop signs in Macedonia, Dimova (2007) notes that the 'extent of English present in shop signs varies among cities depending on their size and their roles in commerce, diplomacy, foreign trade, and tourism'.

Part of a city's linguistic landscape is of course derived from the brand names and slogans of multinational companies. In addition to these, many of the English or 'English-ised' names have been created locally, for regional or national changes, or for individual establishments. It can be argued that these signs are not simply deployed to attract customers who can read them in English, but that they are also on display for the whole population, indexing prosperity, luxury, prestige, and so forth. In the St Georg district in Hamburg mentioned earlier in this chapter, English is the most frequently deployed language in signage apart from German: 30.6% of the signs recorded in *Steindamm* contained English (Scarvaglieri *et al.*, 2013). The English language features in 15% of the signs analysed by Bogatto and Hélot in the *Quarter Gare* in Strasbourg; three of these were monolingual signs, uniquely in English. Their study explores the connotative aspects of English-language use in these signs in Strasbourg, indexing modernity, cosmopolitanism and fun, in clothes shops, restaurants and bars and mobile phone and photocopying shops. The findings here confirm Ball's (1989) suggestion that in France, English-language tokens tend to feature in luxury or entertainment establishments such as travel agents and florists, cafés and nightclubs, rather than in shops which provide the everyday necessities (bakers, butchers, hardware stores).

The authors of the Osijek City Report (2014: 45) pinpoint two parallel trends in the city's linguistic landscape: the appearance of English in the

Figure 2.8 Hamburg coffee shop (LUCIDE network, 2014)

names of pubs and shops and in graffiti, and the trend of 'keeping history' through using the names of famous figures from the past, particularly German and Hungarian names. The ubiquity of English is particularly evident in the hospitality industry in Osijek. The City Report provide examples of how English is used in the names of cafés and bars. The researchers surveyed a directory of establishments; those which offer wifi to customers are listed below:

- Brooklyn
- Caffeteria Exclusive
- Cat
- Goldfinger
- Golden Sun Casino
- Lounge Bar Nox
- Matrix Caffe
- New York
- News
- Old Bridge Pub
- Saloon
- San Francisco Caffe Bar
- Sporting Caffe Bar
- St Patrick's Pub.

All of these names are based on place names from the English-speaking world or use English-language markers. Many of the signs are unilingual. Croatian is not deployed as a marker. As in Dimova's analysis (2007) of shop signs in Macedonia, these names demonstrate a distinct orthographical feature. Although most English words in these names maintain their original and correct English spelling, the word *café* is written as *caffe* (or *caffeteria*) in almost all signs. While the English language is used in the names of cafes and bars, the city also demonstrates an *essekersich* tradition where establishments display German names in memory of famous citizens, for instance the *Waldinger* hotel (a famous painter from the city), the *Guesthouse Maksimilian* (a café named after a renowned 19th century *Bürger*), and the *Beckers* café (marking the commander of the Osijek fort, General von Beckers). Streets are also named after famous German or Hungarian residents. One of the residents interviewed for the Osijek City Report describes how Hungarian is only audible in the marketplace, and went on to point out, 'globally, it is all about English [...] the names of the shops, bars'.

Some cities in the LUCIDE network are subject to legislation which impacts on the languages used in advertising and storefronts. In Montreal, commercial signs are subject to the Charter of the French Language, or Bill 101. In its original form, this legislation required signs to be in French only. Following amendments to the Charter, some resulting from litigation, it now requires in the case of bilingual signs that the French part of the sign must be predominant. Bouchard (2008) reported that French was clearly predominant in 85.2% of the businesses surveyed, not predominant in 7.4% and absent in 7.4%. Only a small percentage (6%) advertise in a language other than French or English. In Strasbourg, the city's public services and commercial operators are subject to the Toubon Law of 1994:

> The use of French shall be mandatory for the designation, offer, presentation, instructions for use, and description of the scope and conditions of a warranty of goods, products and services, as well as bills and receipts. The same provisions apply to any written, spoken, radio and television advertisement.[1]

In the streets of Strasbourg, as elsewhere in France, this has resulted in continued use of English and other languages in advertising, which are marked with an asterisk. The French translation appears in a miniscule font at the bottom of the billboard or sign. In Varna, municipal regulations on advertising, published in 2009, stipulate that all texts in public outdoor advertising, on noticeboards and in public notices should be written in Bulgarian, and should only use foreign trademarks or brands if they are associated with companies which trade internationally. Shop signs demonstrate heterogeneity, with a combination of unilingual Bulgarian signs, combinations of English and Bulgarian, and the use of foreign words transliterated

The Sights and Sounds of the Multilingual City 69

into Bulgarian. While establishments aimed at younger customers tend to use unilingual English signage, many small businesses in the city continue to use the Bulgarian language in an exclusive manner, although sometimes two separate shop signs are provided, one in Bulgarian and another in English or another language.

Monolingual signs

Sometimes monolingual signs target a specific language community for specific purposes, indexing specific social situations, or are used where a bilingual or multilingual sign would have been more useful – perhaps pointing to a lack of funds, lack of will or lack of knowledge on the part of the provider. In Dublin, a temporary sign, written in Russian, appeared beside the sauna at a public swimming pool in the city centre. The information contained in the sign was not provided in English or in any other language, and by implication it was specifically targeting the behaviour of Russian-speaking users of the sauna. In English, the translation reads, 'Attention! It is strictly forbidden to bring or consume alcoholic beverages and also to be under the influence of drink. Offenders will be punished' (personal communication with Sarah Smyth). We can make several inferences from this sign: first, that there have been sufficient 'offenders' bringing alcoholic drinks with them to merit this sign, that these individuals have been Russian speakers, and that the management of the pool do not deem other groups to be in need of a similar warning (e.g. Polish speakers or Mandarin speakers). The full import of the sign requires deeper cultural knowledge: for visitors from a Russian background, the Russian style of using a sauna or *banya* (áàíÿ) will almost inevitably involve drinking vodka or cold beer (or tea) during cooling periods before re-entering the sauna. However, in Ireland, alcohol is banned throughout the country in all swimming pools and spas, steam rooms and saunas.

In 2012, many residential buildings in the neighbourhood of Kanaleniland in Utrecht were evacuated due to large-scale exposure to asbestos caused by renovations by housing corporations. More than three-quarters of residents in the district are not ethnically Dutch, and there are large communities of Moroccans and Turks in particular. The evacuations occurred rapidly and streets surrounding the apartment buildings were barricaded by the police while investigations were carried out by inspectors. Warnings and announcements about this emergency situation were provided only in Dutch, including street signs about extensive road closures (Figure 2.9).

Languages on the edges

Liminal spaces – the 'in-between spaces' of cities – are often sites of particular interest in the study of a linguistic landscape. Scollon and Scollon (2003) identify 'transgressive discourses' in urban space as one of types of dialogue which occur between those who place signs and those who view

Figure 2.9 Utrecht information sign (LUCIDE network, 2014)

them. Transgressive discourses refer to signs that are not presented in a conventional manner, or 'meaning out of place' (Scollon & Scollon, 2003: 161). The most typical example of transgressive discourse is graffiti. Another interesting aspect of the liminal landscape is that which only exists temporarily: posters, private notices and so forth. Kallen draws our attention to the detritus zone, the accumulation of waste with languages printed on them, such as a cigarette packet, a discarded ticket or an abandoned leaflet. According to Kallen (2009, 2010), those random and scattered wastes are indexical of population movements and the trace of their presence in Ireland. In his work, Kallen suggests that the detritus zone deserves due attention, playing its own particular role in the cityscape.

In the LUCIDE cities, the Athens research team report a predominance of English in graffiti and street art in the city, sometimes alongside Greek but often only in English. The city of Varna also provides examples of graffiti in English. The Latin alphabet, rather than the Cyrillic alphabet, and the English language dominate graffiti in this Bulgarian seaside resort. Varna regularly hosts graffiti and street art events, and the Varna City Report tells us that local artists have recently been promoting the use of Cyrillic alongside English. In Croatia, Osijek has also been host to graffiti competitions, and in this small city much of the graffiti is, as in Athens and Varna, in English. In Oslo, there is predominance of graffiti in English (Figure 2.10). Much of the graffiti in the city demonstrates influences from the United States and the UK, including music (heavy metal groups, hip hop) and political statements.

Public noticeboards are also located in a city's liminal space, representing an ever-shifting dialogue between the private sphere and the civic or urban sphere. These types of bulletin boards include advertisements for services

The Sights and Sounds of the Multilingual City 71

Figure 2.10 Oslo graffiti (LUCIDE network, 2014)

and events posted by individuals or associations, and reflect the languages spoken in a district. The noticeboard in Figure 2.11 is particularly interesting, with three adjacent yet distinct signs. From the left side, the first sign is bilingual, in Norwegian and in Arabic. Posted in Oslo during Ramadan, it explains opportunities to donate according to the practices of *fidya* and

Figure 2.11 Oslo billboard (LUCIDE network, 2014)

kaffara. At the bottom of the sign, a slogan in English identifies the 'Helping the Needy' charity. The next sign is a notice of a forthcoming protest at the Pakistani Embassy in Oslo, following the violence of the 'Model Town massacre' in the Punjab. The sign is predominantly monolingual, although the slogan 'state terrorism' appears in English. The third sign, a notice from the Ghousia Muslim Society, is almost exclusively in Arabic. At the bottom of the noticeboard, a poster for the Oslo Extra Large publicity campaign (OXLO) is visible. Another noticeboard from the Oslo Public Library (see Figure 2.12) advertises language courses in Italian and Japanese in Norwegian with some display aspects of Italian and Japanese. English is used alongside Norwegian to advertise theatre and concerts (Still in Silence, Desert Blues, The Crimson ProjeCKt, Mad Fingers Ball, The Golden Voice of Mali).

Figure 2.12 Oslo library noticeboard (LUCIDE network, 2014)

The Sounds of the Cityscape

> You go out in the streets and you hear so many languages, on an everyday basis so it's more and more accepted, and the world is getting smaller because of movies and the internet and everything, so it's more and more accepted. And for our generation, but still, our generation thinks this but those who decide now are actually our parent's generation. So I hope it will be better but I don't think because of the political programme, but because this is how the world is going. The world is getting smaller and we talk to each other on more spaces than we did before, social websites and everything so it's more natural to hear – in the music, in the movies, and everything. (Oslo City Report, 2014: 58)

While the study of written discourse in the linguistic landscape can be illuminating, the voices of speakers are an important aspect of understanding the vitality of a multilingual cityscape. In this last part of the chapter, we turn to some of the sounds and voices that we hear in European cities, in the public and private spheres of television and radio broadcasting, and in the new varieties and practices that seem to be emerging as a result of close language contact.

We can apply the same questions to the concept of audibility as to the concept of visibility: why are certain languages audible, what is their impact on listeners, who chooses the languages which feature in announcements or in broadcasting, and why? Scarvaglieri *et al.* (2013: 63) build on such questions, and assert that 'the linguistic soundscape offers insights into language use trends within a given society'. They report on their 'soundwalks' in the St Georg district, which involved ethnographic observations and recordings of public utterances and conversations in bars, shops and restaurants where interlocutors gave their permission to be recorded. While the majority of conversations in both *Steindamm* and *Lange Reihe* were in German, the proportion was much higher in the gentrified *Lange Reihe* area (83% German) than in *Steindamm* (39% German). Apart from German, in *Steindamm* the two largest language groups were Turkic languages (17%) and Arabic languages (8%). In *Lange Reihe*, 3% of conversations featured Turkic languages and 2% featured Arabic languages.

Cronin (2004: 9) cites a Romanian journalist's experiences of Dublin's transforming soundscape in 2001. Anna Lebedeva writes: 'Walking around Dublin these days is like travelling the world. The streets echo the languages of the city's newly found diversity and one cannot stroll the span of the Ha'penny Bridge without bumping into a foreigner.' But the Dublin City Report illustrates how linguistic misunderstanding can lead to tense situations. One interviewee describes a communication breakdown witnessed on public transport in Dublin due to a passenger's lack of proficiency in English:

> Every country in the world is represented [on my bus] and you see a lot of racial clashes. The last time was last week [...] the card wasn't working and there was quite a tense exchange between her and the bus driver. She didn't quite have the English to – she just kept saying, 'It not work, it not work,' and he was going, 'Show it to me, it's out of date' and there was a whole issue. (Dublin City Report, 2014: 33)

The same interviewee, a native speaker of Irish, describes how the Irish language itself may not be recognised by hearers in Dublin, despite the fact that Irish is a compulsory component of formal schooling throughout the primary and secondary cycles. In the primary cycle, four hours in the curriculum each week are dedicated to Irish as a Second Language. Yet, as this interviewee describes, many Irish people are unable to identify the Irish language when spoken by native speakers:

> I think we're not terribly attuned to language generally, and on a personal basis I'm probably asked three times a week what language I'm speaking when I'm speaking Irish by Irish people. [...] People occasionally get a bit shy around me [when I'm speaking Irish] or a bit defensive. When people ask me what language I'm speaking, the response is 'Well I always hated [Irish] in school, I can't stand it'. It always initiates a strong emotional response, whether it's positive or negative. (Dublin City Report, 2014: 34)

Television and radio broadcasting

Public service and independent broadcasting are an important part of the multilingual landscape in the city, despite the growth in news and entertainment accessed via the internet. The LUCIDE City Reports demonstrate some of the diversity of broadcasting, the extent of support for local language needs and visibility of language varieties.

Some of the LUCIDE City Reports mention the provision of signed language programmes. Television broadcasting can offer a vital source of information and entertainment for Deaf viewers. The use of signed languages in the television sector varies across the cities surveyed in the project. In Athens, the Greek national television broadcasts a summary of the daily news each evening in Greek Sign Language. In Sofia, the Bulgarian national television service provides a daily news broadcast in Bulgarian Sign Language. The status of Bulgarian Sign Language was bolstered by the establishment by the Union of the Deaf in Bulgaria of a National Centre for Sign Language in 2004. While Irish Sign Language lacks legal recognition in Ireland, the national public service broadcaster RTE (*Raidió Teilifís Éireann*) has been engaging recently with the Irish Deaf community to extend programming in Irish Sign Language (ISL), including during primetime slots. Currently, three and half hours of programmes are broadcast each week in ISL in addition to the daily news and weather.

Radio has long been a lifeline for migrant communities and community radio plays a particularly important and cost-effective role in the visibility and maintenance of languages. Community radio stations are generally independent, not-for-profit initiatives. *Raidió na Life* is an independent radio station based in Dublin (the name of the city's river Liffey is derived from its name in Irish, *An Life*) which provides a platform for Irish language organisations, Irish speakers, people with an interest in the language and music lovers of all kinds – including those who would not necessarily have regular contact with the Irish language. The station takes care to include a wide range of interests in its programmes, with a focus on Dublin city and county as well as the commuter belt. It is a multicultural and diverse community vis-à-vis the range of interests, age profile, level of fluency in Irish and active participation in the Irish language community.

London's Resonance FM 104 provides some output in Farsi, Serbian and Albanian; the Voice of Africa Community Radio broadcasts in English and African languages with some French and Portuguese output. In Melbourne, 64 community groups work with the city's community radio station (3ZZZ), and some 400 volunteers broadcast in 57 languages each week. Rome has a similarly vibrant community radio sector. For instance, many of the community stations feature programmes for the city's Filipino population. The Filipino population in Rome tends to work in the healthcare and domestic service sector as carers, housekeepers and nannies, gardeners and drivers. As well as featuring news and music from the Philippines, the programmes address aspects of living as an immigrant in Rome, including visa issues and migrant rights.

- *Buhay Pinoy* ('Pinoy Life', on Radio Spazio Aperto);
- *Kaibigang Pinoy Radio* ('Pinoy Friends Radio') and *Radio Pinoy Balitang Bayan* ('Pinoy News Round Town', both on Radio Roma, 103.95 FM);
- Radio Sentro Pilipino Ng Vaticano ('Vatican Radio Association', on Radio Vaticana, 1611 AM)
- *Ugnayan sa Himpapawid* ('Contact the Air', on Radio Città Aperta, 88.9 FM), celebrated its 15th anniversary in 2014;
- *Bato-bato sa Langit* (Radio Onda Rossa, 87.9 FM), established in 2004.

There are over 2000 community radio stations across Europe and they can be heard in most of Europe's cities (Buckley, 2010). A European Parliament Resolution in 2008[2] noted that community media are 'an effective means of strengthening cultural and linguistic diversity, social inclusion and local identity'. The Resolution describes how community media 'promote intercultural dialogue by educating the general public, combating negative stereotypes and correcting the ideas put forward by the mass media regarding communities within society threatened with exclusion, such as refugees, migrants, Roma and other ethnic and religious minorities', and stresses that 'community media are one of the existing means of facilitating the integration of immigrants and also enabling disadvantaged members of society to become active participants by engaging in debates that are important to them'.

Multiethnolects

A fascinating and relatively recent phenomenon resulting from the interplay of languages and culture in contexts of migration, language contact and second language learning has been the emergence of new kinds of urban communication – the multiethnolect. There are examples of this in increasing numbers of cities, including in the LUCIDE cities, most notably Utrecht and London. This, too, is becoming part of the multilingual city's soundscape. The convergence of people inevitably involves regular language contact which impacts on linguistic practices. For instance, in their study of Hamburg's soundscape, Scarvaglieri *et al.* describe how a variety of languages are deployed on the streets and inside the grocery stores of the *Steindamm* area in St Georg:

> [...] the employees behind the counter chatted amongst themselves in Arabic, with their customers waiting in line and conversing in small groups. One group of customers was speaking in Ewe, another group in English, a third group in Kurdish. Still, when issuing an order and thereby communicatively transcending the borders of their own language group, each of the groups regularly switched to German. The German used in these cases at times had a non-native soundscape, in other cases it could be recognized as native German; no matter how the German sounds, however, ethnographic observation allows us to identify German as the intergroup-language, facilitating communication amongst people from different and diverse language groups. (Scarvaglieri *et al.*, 2013: 68)

One of the respondents interviewed by the Hamburg team refers to the emergence of German-Turkish, a variety of Turkish that is influenced by German syntactical and lexical features, particularly the use of the definite article. This example and other data suggest that language practices in Europe's cities are audibly changing and that new urban varieties or styles of speech are emerging, especially among young people and in sites of high-density housing with an elevated percentage of second language learners from diverse origins.

In the Netherlands, Dorleijn and Nortier (2012: 480) have explored the 'very specific slang-like linguistic varieties [that] pop up among urban, multi-ethnic adolescent groups', variously described as youth slang or youth language, or the language of the street. In Germany, it has been described as *Kiezdeutsch* (Wiese, 2009), and in Sweden as *rinkebysvenska* (Kotsinas, 1988).

Cheshire *et al.* (2011) coined the term Multicultural London English for the variety that is apparent in London. Dorleijn and Nortier point out that, despite different locations (in Utrecht, Hamburg or London, for example), these emerging varieties share similar features and characteristics. They provide the following definition of a multiethnolect, a term coined by Clyne in 2000, as:

> a linguistic style and/or variety that is part of linguistic practices of speakers of more than two different ethnic and (by consequence) linguistic backgrounds, and contains features from more than one language, but has one clear base-language, generally the dominant language of the society where the multi-ethnolect is in use. (Dorleijn & Nortier, 2012: 481)

While Nortier and Dorleijn stress this is not a new linguistic phenomenon, citing work on African urban youth languages, on African American Vernacular English and among Puerto Rican-American groups, it is clear that European multiethnolects are found in cities among adolescents with a migrant background 'involved in the process of constructing and presenting a social identity, [...] an unavoidable consequence of living in the highly dynamic circumstances [of] multiethnic neighbourhoods in large urban areas' (Nortier & Dorleijn, 2013: 233). Cheshire *et al.* (2011: 190) trace the beginnings of Multicultural London English from the 1980s onwards, and describe the social conditions as: 'the presence of an exceptionally high proportion of speakers of language varieties other than the local variety, here, London English – 50 percent or higher in parts of some boroughs, sustained over a considerable time by continued immigration.'

Cheshire *et al.* explore how the addition of the host language to children's repertoires influences the development of a multiethnolect:

> People of different language backgrounds have settled in already quite underprivileged neighbourhoods, and economic deprivation has led to the maintenance of close kin and neighbourhood ties. [...] In these communities, there is often a rapid shift to the majority language by the children of the migrants, possibly accelerated by the fact that there are a large number of languages spoken in areas without strong residential segregation. Because majority-language speakers may be in a minority in parts of these districts, the availability of local, native models of the majority language is weaker than elsewhere. This means that the majority language may be acquired from other second-language speakers. (Cheshire *et al.*, 2011: 153)

The presence of speakers of other varieties creates covert prestige features. Nortier and Dorleijn (2008) refer to occurrences of Dutch pronounced with a Moroccan accent in Utrecht, even by speakers who are not of Moroccan origin. Such vernacular speech styles, deployed for intra-group communication, tend to include regular code-mixing as well as distinctive phonological, morphosyntactic and lexical features. These include 'exaggerated and consciously stereotyped features characteristic of second language learners (grammatical structures, pronunciation, prosodic features)' and 'insertions of (non-dominant-language-) formulaic expressions, greetings, discourse particles, all kinds of interjections, (taboo) content words and even occasionally function words of diverse linguistic sources', as well as word revision in some multiethnolects. The following example, taken from Nortier and Dorleijn (2008: 132), sheds light on a lexical feature as well as the speaker's awareness of the choices made according to interlocutor and context:

R: Dat is het slechte Nederlands
I: En heeft dat ook een naam?
R: Ja, niet echt, maar 't is in principe dan eh lidwoorden die gebruik je dan expres verkeerd.
I: Ja, ja, die gebruik je dan exprès verkeerd, net als–
R: Ja dus
I: Die meisje
R: Die huis zeg ik dan. Terwijl ik weet ik bedoel ik weet heus wel dat het dat huis is, maar 't staat zo dom als ik dat op straat zeg, als ik zeg
I: Ja
R: Als ik zeg dat huis
I: Jaja
R: 't Is gewoon die huis. Maar als ik met jullie spreek dan wordt 't gewoon dat huis.

R: That is the bad kind of Dutch
I: Does it have a name?
R: No, not really, but in principle you uhmm ... just use the articles deliberately in the wrong way.
I: Right! So you use them in the wrong way deliberately? Just like–
R: –Yes, like
I: **Die meisje** ('that girl' – **dat meisje** in standard Dutch).
R: I would say: **Die huis** ('that house' – **dat huis** in standard Dutch). At the same time I know, I mean, I am very well aware of the fact that it should actually be **het huis**, but it would make a stupid impression if I would say ...
I: Yes
R: If I would say **dat huis** out on the street
I: Yes, yes
R: It is just **die huis**. But when I speak with you (the authors – both Dutch and middle-aged) it is just **dat huis**.

Interviewees in the Utrecht City Report refer to this multiethnolect as *Straattaal*, (street language) 'this strange Dutch/Moroccan street language' or 'a nice mix of Dutch, Moroccan, Antillean and Surinamese words and expressions'. One respondent describes how his teenage children help him to understand it.

Cheshire et al. (2011) describe the emergence of Multicultural London English in terms of its phonological and morphosyntactic features as well as the use of a new expression introducing quoted speech, *this + speaker*. Other quotatives such as *here's me + speaker* and *I was like + speaker* are also deployed, as well as use of *was* in the second person past tense (*you was*), non-standard negatives (*I weren't*). Unlike Cockney English, there is no h-dropping. The quotative *this is + speaker* is illustrated by Cheshire et al. (2011: 172) in the following examples:

(1) *this is them* 'what area are you from. what part?'
(2) this is me 'I'm from Hackney'
(3) *this is her* 'that was my sister'
(4) *this is him* 'don't lie. if I search you and if I find one I'll kick your arse'
(5) *this is my mum* 'what are you doing? I was in the queue before you'
(6) *this is my mum's boyfriend* 'put that in your pocket now'

The intensity of the social and linguistic contact in many parts of our cities does not always create an easy context for hearers. In the Netherlands, the type of multiethnolect used by young people is described by themselves as 'the bad kind of Dutch'. Multicultural London English has been described – and rebutted – in the media as threatening, connecting speakers to gang culture and terrorism (Hill, 2013). The audible mix of languages may not be seen as a benefit to the city but rather as a threat. As one interviewee in Oslo described succinctly, the attitude of many citizens to the city's new linguistic diversity is 'By all means, talk Somali, just not so I can hear it'. In Limassol, one of the respondents interviewed by the authors of the City Report describes how some citizens complain about 'foreigners who are "destroying" the city's civilisation [...] and contribute to the loss of the city's identity; everywhere you go, people speak another language'.

On the other hand, many respondents in the LUCIDE cities saw multilingualism as a badge of honour, a sign of the creativity and spirit of their city. In some cities, a functional bilingualism is part of daily life for many cities. In Oslo, for example, English occupies a particular place in most citizens' repertoires. The regular and extensive use of English was described by one of the Oslo respondents as being 'bilingual in the way that all Norwegians are bilingual in Norwegian and English'. In Montreal, one of the respondents distinguishes between the roles that English and French play in the repertoires of its citizens:

Montréal est une métropole importante. Nous travaillons très fort à la positionner sur l'échelle mondiale. S'ouvrir sur le monde, c'est un acte de partage. Parler anglais, c'est se donner une chance de pouvoir s'ouvrir au monde. Parler le français c'est respecter nos valeurs et nos différences. (Montreal City Report, 2014: 15)

Montreal is a major metropolis. We work very hard to place it on the world stage. Opening up to the world is an act of sharing. Speaking

English gives us the opportunity to open up to the world. Speaking French is a way of respecting our values and our differences.

A respondent from Hamburg, who speaks German, Turkish and English, sees the advantages in a multilingual citizen community:

I realize that when people are multilingual they are more open, this is very pleasant. Also they are more able to see things from a different perspective and don't stay in their cultural networks [...] Especially concerning the resolution of conflicts, multilingual people are better able to compromise and bring the opposing parties together, they find arguments for both sides. (Stakeholder interviewed by the Hamburg research team)

Ordinary Multilingualism

Of course, theory and praxis always clash. I notice that people talk very slow to me because of my Turkish accent. When I am talking Turkish on the phone, people in the subways tell me to lower my voice. When I talk in German nobody says anything. (Stakeholder interviewed by the Hamburg research team)

The park bench I describe at the beginning of this chapter points to a changed situation in the city of Dublin. A landscape that was previously coastal is now a semi-industrial zone; the original view has been irrevocably changed. In many ways, most European cityscapes have undergone the same transformation of their linguistic landscapes. New views include frequent English-language signage in public transport or road signs, in shops and restaurants, as well as other non-indigenous languages used to sell products and demonstrate affiliations. New varieties of languages are emerging through language contact. In the same way that the park bench is an example of indexicality, pointing us towards an interesting state of affairs, the visibility and audibility of the many languages present in any particular city direct us towards inherent and specific power relations, symbolism and choices.

In the cities described in this chapter, where speakers of many languages live and work in close proximity, the everyday contact and interchange between language speakers must be at the heart of how a city manages its resources, maintains its neighbourhoods and sells itself to the rest of the world. There are large population flows of tourists, international students and temporary workers. For many of these people, English is a lingua franca and a language through which some services may be delivered. As well as citizens who speak the officially recognised language(s) of the city, there are citizens whose languages exclude them from full access to services. As Lamoureux and Clément (2012: 2) ask, should a city reflect the languages spoken by its citizens and residents, or should these citizens and residents adapt to how their city structures and manages language resources? One of the interviews from Strasbourg neatly sums up the challenge:

> I think the co-existence of multiple languages in a city is a real challenge for the local government in the sense that they need to take into account the people in their day-to-day life. You cannot ignore these people. (Strasbourg City Report, 2014: 69)

A respondent from Montreal considers who should take responsibility for the provision of multilingual services, a theme we address in Chapter 4:

> *[...] je ne crois pas que l'administration publique doive assumer tout le fardeau de cette situation. A mon avis, un minimum d'information peut être offert au public, dans différentes langues, mais il faut responsabiliser les citoyens pour qu'ils trouvent eux mêmes un interlocuteur qui puisse faire le lien avec l'administration, en français ou si requis, en anglais.* (Montreal City Report, 2014: 15)

> I don't think that the public administration should have to bear all the burden of this situation. In my opinion, some minimal information should be provided for the general public, in different languages, but citizens should also take responsibility themselves in order to find someone who could help them connect with the administration, in French, or if necessary, in English.

The data from the study of a city's landscape often say less about the demolinguistic composition of its inhabitants than about the prestige of some languages or the influence of language policies. This is particularly the case when we consider the prominence of the English language in all of the LUCIDE cities. The English language has a particular status in Europe and internationally due to its role as a lingua franca and world language or, as Coluzzi describes it (2012: 239), as a language *super partes*. Sometimes English is bounded by legislation (as in Dublin, Strasbourg and, to a lesser extent, Varna); elsewhere it is a neutral resource upon which attributes of globalisation or internationalisation can be hung without threat to local or national identity (as in Osijek, Utrecht and Madrid). In many cases, it is used for display and decorative purposes, perhaps not even partially intelligible to all local residents but sending out messages about prosperity and creativity. In Dublin, the role of Irish – the first official language yet used rarely for daily communication by most residents in the city – is protected by the Irish Language Act in the public sphere, yet it is almost invisible in the economic sphere, including in Dublin's busy hospitality industry. In Strasbourg, Alsatian is visible in official street signs, yet it is rarely used in the city's restaurants and shops. In Osijek, the Hungarian language is identified by interviewees as the one language in particular need of a 'visibility boost' in the city, despite a language education policy which provides for schooling through Hungarian (see Chapter 5). Hungarian and Serbian are rarely heard in the city outside the marketplace and the Reflata district, and the authors of the Osijek report describe minority language use as 'a hidden practice'. Similarly, while many Sámi live in Oslo, the language is almost invisible in the city's linguistic landscape and national legislation means that administrative services cannot be conducted through Sámi in the city. In sum, even within contexts where regional and minority languages are supported by legislation, these varieties occupy a rather marginal place in the visual landscape of cities.

While the languages of immigrants in cities are very distinctive in some spheres of city life and in neighbourhoods with high percentages of citizens from non-indigenous backgrounds, not all of the languages spoken in a city appear in the city's visual landscape in the public sphere. Romani, for instance, remains an invisible language in most of the LUCIDE cities despite its vitality in Roma speech communities. A parent in Hamburg described how,

> If you speak Turkish in a bus or train people look at you strangely. It's not a curious look but rather a downgrading look, a different look than when you speak English or French. My daughter was asked why she spoke Turkish. (Stakeholder interviewed by the Hamburg research team)

The words of another respondent from Hamburg, again a German/Turkish bilingual, are poignant, pointing to the hidden languages of some citizens:

> My parents are from Bosnia. It was sad for me that they never spoke Bosnian to us. When I ask them now they say everyone in our environment spoke Turkish and we wanted to make sure that you speak a flawless Turkish as well. They thought that learning two languages simultaneously would deteriorate the mother tongue. Bosnian was a secret language for them. My mother also didn't speak to my children in Bosnian even though we urged her to do so but she said that they don't react on it, she didn't have the patience. Later she saw many Kurdish families speaking Kurdish in our neighbourhood, this was the first time she realised that she should have spoken Bosnian to us. (Stakeholder interviewed by the Hamburg research team)

It is important to ask whether the symbolic use of migrant languages observed in many cities (for instance in welcome signs or in an information leaflet) would have helped in these particular cases. Would it have reassured the mother that Bosnian was a language worth maintaining? The LUCIDE City Reports suggest that these types of signals – while perhaps tokenistic in some cases (e.g. greetings in multiple languages at entrances to buildings) – are a step in the right direction towards the more visible and sustained use of many languages in multiple spheres of city life. Research by Cenoz and Gorter (2006) confirms that the appearance of minority languages in the linguistic landscape does raise language status and bolster maintenance. In other words, even small and symbolic instances contribute to enhanced language vitality and send out positive signals to local residents that their languages are worthy to be used, to be maintained and to be learned. The authors of the London City Report suggest that once the language of a speech community attains a critical mass, it starts to be reflected in the physical surroundings of the neighbourhood. Other varieties, with smaller numbers of speakers, remain less visible. When the languages of local communities are embedded in the fabric of an area, this can both create a sense of ownership and belonging as well as reflect a degree of valorisation on the part of the whole community (London City Report).

In her ethnography of a multi-ethnic street in London, Hall (2012: 108) writes of 'ordinary cosmopolitanism, a living among and recognition of difference without a convergence to sameness'. The streets of our cities have changed irrevocably over the previous century, with the blurring of physical boundaries and distance, unprecedented global mobility of goods and people, and the development of unimaginable technological and communication tools. As we close this chapter and turn to questions of place and belonging, perhaps we can ask whether Hall's definition could equally apply to *ordinary multilingualism* – an accepted intermingling of different language varieties (regional, minority, indigenous, non-indigenous, prestigious, non-prestigious) in both private and public settings, where we do not fear languages we do not understand, but instead seek to distinguish between them. In the words of a respondent from Hamburg, 'The invisible borders are easier to overcome, to accept the new, the different because in some way it's part of oneself' (stakeholder interviewed by the Hamburg research team). The next chapter will explore the images and representations of cities, and what connects citizens – or otherwise – to their multilingual city.

Notes

(1) LOI n° 94-665 du 4 août 1994 relative à l'emploi de la langue française, Article 2, http://legifrance.gouv.fr.
(2) European Parliament Resolution of 25 September 2008 on Community Media in Europe (2008/2011 (INI)).

The concept of the city is central to our understanding of modern life. The rich complexity of the multilingual city is observed not only in its sights and sounds, but in the image that it presents to its inhabitants and to the world beyond. How do people position themselves vis-à-vis the urban multilingual environment? What can help us to analyse multilingualism as a social fact and to understand the diverse attitudes towards the ways in which the city transforms reality? Mobility has abolished the city walls – the external limits of cities – making them instead an exemplary kind of mobile space. However, this raises anew the problem of internal delimitations within cities and of the city as a site of affiliations (bonds) and new identities. How can we explain the links between the phenomena of multilingualism and identity formation in urban settings? How do we interpret people's different attitudes in relation to the multilingual profiles of the city? How are people's expressions of identity recomposed in the changing multilingual city environment? Does city multilingualism redefine the contours of normality and the extent to which difference can be embraced? This chapter offers thoughts on how we can read city multilingualism in relation to the shifting identities of the people who live there – the 'city-zens', and the vitality of their languages.

3 Urban Multilingualism: Bond or Barrier?

Maria Stoicheva

> *Remember, Parviz, we're all foreigners in this city!*
> Amara Lakhous, *Clash of Civilisations over an Elevator in Piazza Vittorio*

Chapter 1 identified common features that allow us to classify cities as multilingual, but also introduced us to variations in their multilingual character. Chapter 2 explored the sights and sounds of the city as seen through the prism of multilingualism and shaped by the presence of a variety of different languages (sometimes rather distinct from one another). The image of the city in this sense is a description of language practices, a memory of past language presences and their urban reminders, a recurrent use of different languages that can be heard or read in urban spaces and an image of its multilingual entity. The scale of city multilingualism is another way of representing the city as a site of multiple differences.

This chapter further analyses this multilingual reality of constructing and sustaining the image of the city in a process of continual revitalisation. It considers how people position themselves vis-à-vis the urban multilingual environment. First, we consider the concept of the image of the city (what it is and what it wants to be). This in itself is a powerful symbol of a complex society that influences individual identity formation and representation. Next, we look at the city as an arena of language contacts in which groups, communities and individuals negotiate and embed their identities. These agents of linguistic diversity shape the reality and the multilingual profiles of the city. The permutation of the city narrative in cultural and linguistic terms is identified as a major factor for identity formation. Valued and less-valued forms of multilingualism and their visibility are indicators of polarised urban landscapes and of the perception of city boundaries with specific cultural and economic markers. The third part of this chapter considers the symbolic attachment to language and the intertwining of language with group identity. It problematises the particular relation between place and language in the city environment. Cities demonstrate different micro publics through the everyday sharing of space. This part of the

Figure 3.1 Sofia city centre (LUCIDE network, 2014)

chapter also draws on some literary narratives of city life, in which the link between language and identity is explored and questions are asked about communication and understanding in the multilingual setting of the condensed space of the city.

The Image and Identity of the City and Why It Matters

The concept of the city is central to our understanding of modern life and it is beyond doubt that cities shape the lives of people. We are still accustomed to the representation of the city as a collection of buildings surrounded by walls, although now walls are either demolished or are considered of tourist and archaeological significance. Cities are no longer built to keep people out or for defensive purposes, but it does not mean that the concept of boundary as a barrier is not applicable to the concept of the city. The idea of the city is filled with the tangible and intangible, of history and concepts of structure and organisation. It is a mixture of old and new, big and small, core and periphery, uniform and diverse, which combine to give the impression of the city as a whole. What does city multilingualism add to the perception of the cityscape and is it a source for developing bonds with the place and points of reference for self-categorisation?

A fundamental characteristic of the current age – and therefore of the modern city – is that of mobility (Castells, 2000; Castles & Miller, 2009; Cresswell, 2011; Pinder, 2011; Urry, 2007). Not only were walls and gates to the city demolished, but the space of the city has become the exemplary kind of modern mobile space. In many aspects our focus shifts from fixed things to process and circulation; social life is often perceived as held together by travel and communication technologies. However, it is still the case that we often assume a stable point of view, a world of places, boundaries and territories rooted in time and bounded in space. From this perspective, the city is a 'concentration of different, changing cultures which somehow manage to create a new identity' (King *et al.*, 2011: 39).

As we have already argued in some detail in the Introduction, most studies of cities and urbanism have underestimated the language issue – either ignoring it completely or regarding it only as a marker of ethnic or national identity. The LUCIDE City Reports, therefore, are a starting point and resource for considering the intersection of multilingualism, identity and city space. The reports attempt to elaborate on what can influence the mindsets of city inhabitants and on the role of the ordinary encounter of multiple languages in contemporary urbanism as a way of life. 'City' is a core concept and there seems to be a consensus on which cities can be considered emblematic multilingual cities, for example, London, New York or Sydney (Hall, 1984, 1996; Sassen, 2001, 2005). City identity refers to people's connections (bonds) with cities and reflects their socialisation in the city.

However, when applied to the city, the concept of identity may carry two different meanings. In its first meaning it has a clear reference to the 'place' and describes its unique character and how it was sustained and continued through time. We will use the notion of 'image of the city' in order to differentiate this meaning from the second understanding of city identity, which is a specific component of each individual's self-identity. City identity in this sense is defined as a dimension of the self in relation to the physical city environment. The notion of 'attachment' is relevant here because it refers to connections that people develop with cities, with the place where they live, work or enjoy themselves. The evolution of people's perceptions is monitored in various public opinion polls (see Eurobarometer, 2004–2014, 2013). There is a distinct degree of self-categorisation in attachment to the city, in feeling first and foremost a resident of a city or of a part of a city.

City identity in both its meanings includes a tangibility of place, embedded in what we call a bond, different from the identification with the nation as an imagined community. There is a cognitive aspect to this 'city bond', shown in the awareness of the history of the place, in knowing its stories and songs, and demonstrated in vivid collective memories of the distant and near past. Behavioural components are not easy to measure, although sociology provides an interpretation of urban movements and their engagement with the city and its transformation. Human action is closely linked to a vision of the future of the city and a dream of the best city in which to live. Can we then consider a city's many languages as adding to the sense of self of city dwellers and citizens and to their overlapping multiple identities? The next section deals with the language aspect of the increasing complexity of the urban context.

City Linguistic Diversity as a Social Fact

Size of the city and multilingualism

Recent data based on the revised urban–rural Eurostat typology show that 68% of the EU population live in urban areas (Eurostat, 2011). Population size is definitely one of the categories that suggest a typology of cities as multilingual entities. Ever since Aristotle it has been recognised that increasing the number of inhabitants in a settlement beyond a certain limit affects the relationship between them and the character of the city (Aristotle, 1946, vii 4.4–14). London is the most populous city among LUCIDE cities (and in the EU as well), with a population of 8 million. The rest of the LUCIDE cities fall into three approximate categories according to their population size: large cities with populations of between 1–5 million inhabitants (cities such as Rome and Madrid); medium-sized cities with populations of between 100,000 and 600,000 inhabitants (cities such as Utrecht and Limassol); and smaller urban centres such as Osijek (a city with around 100,000 inhabitants).

It seems intuitive that the multilingual character of the cities can be considered partially as a function of size. The higher the numbers of inhabitants, the more potential speakers of different languages – mother tongues, heritage languages, migrant languages or local dialects. However, among the LUCIDE cities there are cities of a comparable size but with rather different multilingual situations (e.g. Hamburg and Montreal, Sofia and Dublin). It seems that size is not the only factor. Three other important factors, all related to mobility in today's world, also shape the linguistically diverse landscape of the city – migration flows, the mobility created by the freedom of movement of people within the EU and educational mobility.

Migration flows are referred to as the major factor for linguistic diversity in the City Reports. Intrastate mobility does not appear to significantly affect the multilingualism of the city, even when it is related to the mobility of minority groups. Internal EU mobility (inter-state mobility), however, has proved to be as significant as migration from non-EU countries, especially after the Eastern European enlargement in its two consecutive waves in 2004 and 2007. When there are more immigrants to the city, there are more encounters with languages that people might not understand, creating situations in which language barriers are to be overcome. When asked about the ways language barriers can be handled in the city context, a respondent from Strasbourg makes the following remark:

> Yes, I think the co-existence of multiple languages in a city is a real challenge for the local government in the sense that they need to take into account the people in their day-to-day life. You cannot ignore these people. You need to ... if it is one per cent of the population, there is no issue, but if it ten per cent in terms of ... yes, maybe, you need to bring them all support. (Strasbourg City Report, 2014: 80)

We do not focus here on the challenges that this situation poses to local policy and governments as these are dealt with in the next chapter. Instead, it seems important to elaborate on what this Strasbourg interviewee mentions at the end of his comment. He refers to the relative size of the population

Figure 3.2 London street food sign (LUCIDE network, 2014)

(migrant population in this case) as a very significant factor not only for local government, but for the encounters with various languages and for the multilingual image of the city. Three cities that belong to different tiers according to population size show similar proportions of populations with an immigrant background: London (with an estimated 37%), Hamburg (estimated 30%) and Utrecht (estimated 32% non-native Dutch inhabitants). Madrid, Dublin and Strasbourg form another group with around 15% of the city population composed of migrants. It is not clear whether there are similar trends among the rest of the cities (9% is the estimate for Rome; Limassol has 20.6 % non-national inhabitants). The reports on multilingualism from the four Canadian cities tell us that 'close to 250,000 immigrants arrive each year, settling mostly in Toronto, Montreal and Vancouver, but increasingly in Calgary, Edmonton and Winnipeg'. In terms of figures this means that as of 2007 nearly 'one in five Canadians was foreign-born' (Toronto City Report, 2014: 5).

The difference in this variable has a direct effect on the multilingual image of the city. There is a considerable difference in the way the city is perceived if every third or fourth resident can potentially use and speak a different language in some of the spheres of city life compared to the perception of diversity where this applies to only one in 10 of the population. However, the relativity of the perception of multilingualism is conditioned by whether these speakers of other languages are inhabitants or visitors and by the situation in other parts of the country. For example, the Utrecht report makes the observation that the number of non-native Dutch inhabitants is relatively low, but only compared to Rotterdam, The Hague and Amsterdam where the proportion of migrants is closer to 50%.

Which people? Which languages?

The composition of the city's minority inhabitants or migrant groups has an effect on shaping the multilingual image of the city. For example, around 3 million Londoners were born outside the UK. Of these, 1 million were born in Europe, 970,000 were born in Asia and the Middle East, 620,000 in Africa, 325,000 in the Americas and the Caribbean, and 84,000 in Australasia and Oceania (London City Report, 2014: 6). Whether this results in a similar scale of multilingualism in London is another matter. The answer can be found in the demolinguistic profile of the city. In the case of London the report tells us that 'more than 1.7 million Londoners over the age of three speak a language other than English as their main language' (London City Report, 2014: 14). There are 15 large community languages (also defined as language groups ranging from 50,000 to 100,000 resident speakers). In size, the speakers of one London community language are equal to the whole population of the smallest LUCIDE city of Osijek. Again we observe significant variations among the cities. For example, the Madrid report presents data for two main migrant groups – those of EU origin (Romania) and those from Latin America (Ecuador, Bolivia, Peru, Colombia). In the area of Athens under scrutiny by LUCIDE researchers, two large migrant communities are described: Albanian and Pakistani. Sixteen ethnic groups are listed by the municipality of Rome; 43% of the migrant composition of Rome is reported to come from Romania, Morocco, China and Ukraine. The Hamburg City Report describes two large migrant groups from Turkey and Poland. Utrecht and Strasbourg present a similar model with two large migrant groups with labour migrant history from Morocco and Turkey. A much more diverse picture is observed in Melbourne and the four Canadian cities, which can generally be identified as cities based on immigration. As noted in Chapter 1, the colonial past influences the specific linguistic landscape of some of the cities. For example, the multilingual profiles of Utrecht, London and Madrid include groups from former colonies.

The languages of the large migrant communities have a significant degree of visibility in the city environment so they are, or become, associated with the city environment and image. A predictable model of possible language encounters can gradually emerge, which contributes to the legibility of the multilingual environment and to the perception of the city as multilingual. However, the ways in which different people read their linguistic environment is a completely different matter. It seems that the number of languages that citizens can encounter in the cities is much higher than just those represented by the major migrant groups. Some of the reports tell us that close to 200 languages are present in their city environments, some of them spoken by very few or even by single city inhabitants. The Hamburg City Report tells us that the number of languages that could theoretically co-exist exceeds 1000. The Madrid City Report mentions 183 countries of origin, with Dublin mentioning 182. Osijek, the smallest of the LUCIDE cities, tells us of 151

Figure 3.3 Rome Termini station (LUCIDE network, 2014)

recorded other languages. Although recorded, most of these languages remain invisible and their influence on the city identity as a multilingual city is very low. In such a diverse demographic situation, with few people representing a particular national or ethnic group, the role of their language as a marker of group identity could significantly diminish.

Variations in perception of the city's multilingual reality

The images of the multilingual cities that emerge from the City Reports are diverse. They reveal a linguistic particularity rooted in cities' distant and recent history, making links with historical transformations and attempting to embed the current image of the city into a historical narrative. They are combinations of what the city is and what it wants to be. Cities like Melbourne, London and Hamburg sustain the image of cities of extraordinary linguistic diversity and multicultural histories. Others like Utrecht strive to be a European hotspot and laboratory for multilingualism. Cities such as Sofia and Varna are still perceived as monolingual but with a large number of people capable of holding a conversation in another language and of welcoming tourists and visitors. The multilingual image of Madrid emphasises the presence of languages and dialects affected by global migration processes. The image of Osijek is formed through a mixture of ethnic minority languages and neighbouring languages with a high percentage of bilingual citizens.

To what extent are these city images publicly shared views of what the city is like and how it should be perceived? The shared image of the city is a matter of interaction. It is the result of a two-way process between the citizen as the observer and his or her environment. Lynch talks about cities as pieces of architecture, as physical entities to be enjoyed:

> The city is a construction in space, but one of vast scale, a thing perceived only in the course of long spans of time. City design is therefore a temporal art, but it can rarely use the controlled and limited sequences of other temporal arts like music. On different occasions and for different people, the sequences are reversed, interrupted, abandoned, cut across. It is seen in all lights and all weathers. (Lynch, 1960: 1)

Even in this sense the city is not just a physical entity. The city landscape suggests distinctions and relations, and the observer selects, organises and endows with meaning what he/she sees. Different people can see the city in a different way and have a different image of it in their minds. In addition, people care deeply about where they live; time and familiarity breed particular attachments to the parts of the city that they inhabit. Images of the city are imbued with memories and meaning – personal or shared. They can therefore be partial, fragmentary, often mixed with other concerns. And there is 'more than the eye can see, more than the ear can hear, a setting and a view waiting to be explored' (Lynch, 1960: 1). As the city is a product of many builders who are constantly modifying the city structure, so is the city an object that is perceived by millions of people of very diverse cultures and character. The image of a city reality may vary significantly for different observers. It is an object, which can be enjoyed and exploited, or it can provoke uneasy attitudes or a neutrality of attachment. Diversity has a powerful role to play in this image formation. To a large extent individual perception is influenced by the personal constructs of the limit of diversity, beyond which there can be unease and uncertainty.

The image of the city as multilingual is not a widely shared concept among the stakeholders interviewed by LUCIDE's research teams. The City Reports suggest at least three explanations for this. The first is a normative explanation related to the language policy of the nation state. The argument is that, if there is only one official national language, then the city is or rather is supposed to be monolingual. The second explanation represents the ambiguity of the term. For example, an interviewee from Strasbourg (Strasbourg City Report, 2014: 66) does not consider her city multilingual although there are multiple languages, because individual people do not speak many languages. In her view, a city should be called multilingual if 'everybody speaks multiple languages'. This is a further complicating factor in understanding the image of the multilingual city. Is it a city of many monolingualisms or a city of plurilingual inhabitants? There is a third explanation for the way people might understand multilingualism and multilingual reality. They consider their city as multilingual only if it comes close to established models of multilingual cities such as London, Sydney and New York. For example, an interviewee from Sofia (Sofia City Report, 2014: 11) says that 'Sofia is not a multilingual city like London or New York'. The interviewee from Strasbourg cited above talks about her city, a multilingual city in many aspects, and talks about Strasbourg as 'almost' or close to multilingual, clearly comparing it with cities that can be considered paradigmatic cases of multilingualism, thinking of that ideal multilingual city where 'everyone speaks multiple languages'.

The Linguistic Legibility of the Cityscape

In his study of the image of the city, Lynch considers legibility crucial in the city setting and defines it as a 'visual quality: apparent clarity of the cityscape' (Lynch, 1960: 2). With this he means the 'ease with which its parts can be recognised and can be organised into a coherent whole' (Lynch, 1960: 2). An underlying inspiration of most of the City Reports is to transcend individual opinions and to make an attempt to explore the public image of the city as multilingual. On the one hand, this is related to visibility, to objects that are not only able to be seen, but which are presented sharply and intensely to the senses as discussed in the previous chapter. On the other hand, it is linked to the readability and predictability of the city environment and to the clarity and legibility of city multilingualism. People can get 'lost' in a city in a sense which is not only related to space and place uncertainty but also to cultural points of reference. These perceptions can arouse uncertainty and a desire for withdrawal. This is possible in an environment of close physical contact and distant social relations, of segmentation and anonymity of human contacts, which are all assumed to be characteristics of urban life.

In the same way that we use route-finding devices to help us navigate the complexity of the modern city, linguistic legibility or clarity serves as a frame of reference for understanding urban multilingualism and attaching meaning and sense to it. It stimulates informal connections, communication and mixing among people who know each other and those who meet for the first time. Like the streets, parks and city landmarks, languages, although less tangible, are also the marks that make a city legible and clear, while accommodating people not only from different cultures but from different walks of life. This enables the formation of the city as a community in which, through engagement and identification, bonds are created. To adopt Anderson's (1983) terminology, these bonds can be defined as 'imagined communities' of strangers in the city.

Reading the logic of the languages of the city lends form to the city image. The dynamic of the association of place and language makes a city 'ours' or 'mine' when I know it and when I feel comfortable in it. People create their maps of legibility that contain language markers incorporated in the image of the city. It seems that identification with the city is mediated by such maps and markers. They constitute an important component of what we mean by the identity of the citizen as *city-zen*, e.g. Londoner or a citizen of Madrid, Hamburg, Sofia, Athens, Rome, Utrecht, Osijek.

Figure 3.4 Strasbourg parking sign (LUCIDE network, 2014)

The point of reference for identification is the city as a place and as a way of life. It is defined in specific urban terms rather than in terms of ethnicity, origin or culture. This does not mean that the latter are no longer identity markers. However, they seem to combine more easily, openly and chaotically in the individual identities of the *city-zen*.

The legibility of the linguistic surroundings can evoke positive values of cultural curiosity and openness, of emotional satisfaction and a sense of emotional security. They can affirm the positive vitality of certain forms of perceived diversity, even disorder and transformation (Sampson, 2009; Sennett, 2009). Diversity is very often associated with the emotional sense of enrichment of everyday experience and can carry a great force of attraction. It can add to the vividness and depth of the emotional experience if it is not taken by surprise. City language profiles can be considered as points of orientation and reference for understanding the multilingual environment of the city.

Agents of urban linguistic diversity

Let us now examine how the speakers of different languages affect what we have called the language profile of the city and by implication the city identity. The language profile is the outcome of the way in which languages combine in the city environment. It represents the languages people speak in the city, the languages they bring to the city, the languages they learn in the city. These are the languages they feel comfortable with. We can talk of specific language constellations associated with the cities as well as of specific associations of languages and places in the city environment. Taken together, they refer to the distinctiveness and exclusivity of the particular city.

The breadth and vitality of today's city multilingualism emerges from some of the LUCIDE City Reports. It can be considered a result of a dynamic relationship between people and the physical environment in which the people *create* an environment that reveals the nature of the self and the environment in turn gives back information to the person. It is a process both of reinforcing self-identity as well as of changing the person in some way. Therefore we can talk about speakers of different languages in the city as agents of the city's linguistic diversity.

The weight of monolingualism or 'when in Rome, do as the Romans do'

So far we have discussed the multilingualism of the LUCIDE cities as a social fact that finds its reflection in the images of the city held in the minds of inhabitants and visitors alike. In other words, we have argued that, to differing degrees, city inhabitants accept or welcome the multilingual reality and see the need to find appropriate ways to respond to this reality. As we have also mentioned, there is no consensus on the nature of the cities' multilingualism among the City Report interviewees, but there are some shared

96 The Multilingual City

Figure 3.5 London Korean Anglican church (LUCIDE network, 2014)

views about this reality as a social fact. Most of the City Reports tell us that multilingualism is not a new phenomenon and there is an underlying argument that many languages have been historically associated with the city environment. Moreover, as discussed in the previous chapter, this social fact has become or is becoming a visible feature of the city landscape.

Most of the LUCIDE cities, however, are located in states with one official language, which has direct implications for how urban life is organised, how public communication is carried out and for the expected standard language repertoires. Although various languages are associated with the city, each city has a predominant language. This means that when we talk about city multilingualism we talk about a contextualised multilingualism. Many of the interviewees attempt to deal adequately with 'new linguistic realities', as the Hamburg report tells us, yet a monolingual mindset continues to prevail. To a large extent, this 'monolingual habitus', to use Gogolin's (1994) term that captures the essence of the understanding of linguistic normality that is widely encountered in a city context, is 'likely to be shared by representatives of the multilingual groups themselves' (Hamburg City Report, 2014: 6). For example, this is often expressed in the uncertainty of some parents concerning their children's language education or the benefits of intergenerational language transmission. The established language regime has its normative aspects as well. Thus it presupposes an equation between the official state language(s) with the city language community and anticipates that communicative success in the urban setting entails a set of normative rules about which languages one ought to learn and speak in specific domains. The language configurations in the city are therefore reflective of the national community and in many cases this is reinforced by the implementation of policies in the areas of education, administration and social services and culture. The perception of what is normal linguistic communication in the city environment has a further effect on people's judgements on what is accepted regarding normal linguistic behaviour. This inevitably limits the range of languages used in communication. However, multilingual city realities require a way to deal with the specificities and difficulties that can arise in everyday life. We will see some examples of political and practical responses at the level of the city in the next chapter.

What is relevant here is the effect of the established language regime on identity formation in the city environment. For example, the objective of 'integration' is frequently based on this limited understanding of linguistic normality that favours monolingualism. Often it is understood as a one-way process, facilitated by lessons in the language of the host country. An argument from 'common sense' also seems relevant in this case. This is best expressed in the proverb, 'When in Rome, do as the Romans do'. Asked what 'to integrate in the French way of living' means, an interviewee from Strasbourg (Strasbourg City Report, 2014: 43) says: 'Yes, learn French. That is a requisite, I think. No, even to adapt. They can keep their own culture, but they are living in France and so they have to adapt to the ways in France.'

The City Reports also give voice to a different view expressed in the concern that cities are not only sites for language vitality and multilingualism, but also sites where language loss is observed. For example, this is the concern of the 'fairly fragile status of migrant languages' (Hamburg City Report, 2014: 16) or the observation that 'a pattern of subtractive bilingualism seems to be the only likely outcome' with the consequence that the present linguistic richness provided by immigrant pupils is not likely to be sustained (Broeder & Mijares, 2004, cited in Madrid City Report, 2014).

Linguistic minorities

Linguistic minorities enjoy a special status in the general scenario of multilingualism, especially in Europe. In particular, some historical regional and minority languages in Europe are protected and promoted under the Council of Europe's Framework Convention for the Protection of National Minorities and the European Charter for Regional and Minority Languages. Osijek, Sofia and Varna present a picture of multilingualism shaped by local ethnic minorities sustaining their minority languages in their local communities. Historically, as the reports explain, language contacts took place under conditions of social and political inequality – wars and consequent reshaping of political maps, conquest, forced migration, political domination. These conditions have eventually resulted in a linguistic situation of relative stability and acceptance instead of language loss and assimilation. It is often within the narrative of language maintenance that stories of language loss are intertwined. The Osijek City Report tells us about the loss of the local mixed language *Essekerisch* (*das Osijeker Deutsch*), urban reminders of which are still kept in city landmarks – restaurants, cafes, hotels. The Utrecht City Report mentions the local variety of Dutch, associated with the lower social classes and in contrast to the higher status Amsterdam variety. There is the story of Alsatian in Strasbourg which, although extensively studied by academics and linguists in the region, seems to provoke emotions and fears of extinction and loss. The outcomes of the language contacts, therefore, cannot be clearly predicted as they reflect complex social, economic and power forces and relations.

The Canadian City Reports, situating the issue of multilingualism in the broader context of federal and provincial institutions, also talk about legal instruments providing support for minority communities, although concerning mainly French and English as the official languages of Canada and as languages of the 'original European settlers'. These reports note the absence of similar policies promoting Aboriginal peoples and preventing the loss of their languages. It was late in the 20th century that legislation was put in place to protect Aboriginal languages and their autonomous education system. A citizen of Toronto notes:

> I think the most underserviced and least visible languages are Aboriginal languages. Given that City of Toronto has the largest urban Aboriginal population in Canada (approximately 70,000 according to community estimates), it is a community that ought to be recognised and their diverse language needs addressed. (Toronto City Report, 2014: 32)

Migration

The City Reports link the cities' multilingualism to stories of migration. They present migration processes as closely interconnected with each city's history and as something which has always been the case. For example, Hamburg experienced various types of migration with its function as a transit area and a gateway to the Hanseatic League, a flourishing network of port cities and harbours in Northern Germany, England, Flanders, France, Sweden and Norway that benefited from privileges in trade and diplomacy. An important part of Madrid's story of multilingualism goes back to history before the nation state – 'a time when immigration through conquest was common' (Madrid City Report, 2014: 4).

For cities built on migration, like Melbourne and the Canadian cities, waves of newcomers gradually shaped and transformed the multilingual and multicultural images of the cities. Toronto is one of the most diverse major cities in the Western world (Toronto City Report, 2014: 4), and has turned its multicultural nature into a selling point and source of pride. This is still the case today as the high rate of immigration to Canada continues to transform the linguistic landscape of the country and its cities. In Europe, too, the story is told of successive waves of economic migrants and refugees. London is a striking example of this, with Huguenots from France, then Jews from central Europe and Russia and more recently Bengalis and others from the Indian subcontinent arriving and settling near the docks in the East End. Economic migration from beyond Europe, as mentioned in some City Reports, was a result of special campaigns to attract much needed labour in post-war Europe ('guest workers' from Turkey and Morocco, for example, or post-war Afro-Caribbean immigrants in London). This was a major influence on city multilingualism (in Utrecht, Hamburg and London, for example) until very recently.

Mobility within the European continent also had a historical impact on introducing new languages to the big European cities (for example, the Italian flooring traders who settled in Hamburg in the 19th century or the Italian stucco workers who helped create Dublin's Georgian buildings). This has taken on added importance within the context of the EU and its founding principle of the free movement of labour, now identified as equally important as migration from outside the EU. Indeed most 21st-century migration flows are an immediate consequence of the EU enlargement processes when 11 Eastern and Central European countries joined the EU in two consecutive waves in 2004 and 2007. Romanians are the largest migrant group in Rome according to the Rome City Report, and Polish and Lithuanian nationals are among groups with the highest net migration to Norway. Romanians are one of the two largest groups (Moroccans are the other) of non-Spanish speaking populations in Madrid. The largest migrant groups in Hamburg come from Turkey and Poland. The Athens-AAK City Report tells us that there are two large communities (Romanians and Bulgarians) of EU citizens living in AAK but also makes the important point that reliable data on EU citizens in the city are not available since they do not need a residence permit.

As with some migration flows in the past, employment is the most important reason for immigration for European 'migrants'. However, it is difficult to measure the scale and dynamics of mobility within the EU and therefore the extent to which this influences city inhabitants' attitudes.

There are, however, indications in the current debates about freedom of movement – for example in France and the UK – that a rather intolerant view is being promoted by some politicians and in the media which is having an impact on public views. What enables this large-scale mobility within the EU is the right to freedom of movement, which underpins the common European market and constitutes a core component of European citizenship and, to a large extent, of the project of European identity formation. Interestingly, even in the City Reports, this aspect of the identity of mobile European citizens exercising their rights to mobility in a union is often ignored or understated. In most cases the large groups of people coming from new EU member states are presented as groups of migrants among other migrant groups without specific reference to common citizenship or other markers of common identity.

Transient city inhabitants

In 1938 Wirth considered the city as a relatively large, dense and permanent settlement of heterogeneous individuals. Nowadays this aspect of permanency is largely contested as a result of the unprecedented scale of contemporary mobility. Cresswell (2011) argues that we 'need to pay attention to process and circulation'. Pinder (2011), in the title of his volume, describes cities as 'moving, plugging in, floating, dissolving'. The implications of mobility find another expression in Sennett's definition of the city as 'a human settlement in which strangers are likely to meet' (Sennett, 1970: 39).

This aspect of city multilingualism finds its place in the City Reports through descriptions of the role played by visitors to the city (albeit occasional and of brief duration) in bringing languages to the city. According to the Strasbourg City Report, we should consider a separate category of people – transient city inhabitants (tourists and foreign students) who play a significant role in shaping the multilingual profiles of the city. This category can be extended to include some migrants and refugees, particularly those who stay in a city but who have a destination different from the country or city they have first entered. A prototype of the modern type of mobile individual can be found in history. The Hamburg City Report tells the story of substantial waves of transit migration to North America, estimated at more than 7 million from Hamburg alone, as one of the European gateways to the New World.

A specific case of this category is the group of the *travailleurs frontaliers*, as described in the Strasbourg City Report. These are workers whose residence is in Strasbourg but who leave home every day to work across the border in Germany or Switzerland. Similar situations are found elsewhere in Europe and the language factor is quoted as an important prerequisite for their success. This phenomenon is rather different from the commuting practices explored by sociology and urban studies. It is different in scale and nature and concerns people whose work and life is essentially cross-border.

Foreign students are also becoming a factor in the linguistic diversity of cities. Universities are a necessary and important component of every big city and they traditionally attract a large number of international students. Strasbourg, which hosts the largest university in France, has more than 8000 international and exchange students. Madrid, London, Rome, Hamburg and Dublin, as well as Melbourne and Montreal, are also examples of concentrations of international students. Student exchange programmes have become not just popular but are gaining the status of an indispensable part of good higher education. The city where the university is situated is also a major factor in the choices made by students. For example, it can be expected that the choice of university for an exchange programme is preconditioned by the attractiveness of the city and preformed attitudes (sometimes in a romantic way) of the city, its ethos and its potential for new connections. Additionally, foreign language teaching, apart from providing the necessary linguistic competences, develops understanding and emotional attachment to the national or city culture of the host country.

These are some of the emerging categories in the group of mobile citizens. There are other sectors of contemporary life in which mobility has become a norm rather than an exception. For example, this is the case with academics, researchers and in particular young researchers (doctorate and post-doctorate programmes) and people working in the financial and economic consultancy sectors. Years ago the *au pair* programme was a popular way for young people to spend time in another country and culture. Today, however, the numbers of people from other European countries working in childcare and also adult care is without precedent.

A particularly interesting group among the so-called transients are tourists. Baumann notes that 'the tourist used once to inhabit the margins of "properly social" action', while now tourism is among the activities practised by the majority 'in the prime time of their lives and in places central to their life-worlds' (Baumann, 1998: 26). All City Reports acknowledge the significance of tourism for the city's multilingualism. Some of them argue that this is the major factor which makes the city multilingual. There is good reason to consider tourists as legitimate agents of the city's multilingual image since they constitute a large group of people who 'conquer' the city's space and who may seem to be constantly present in the city environment. Their composition varies, but they represent a group of 'inhabitants' with a constant presence. In one sense, tourists can be considered legitimate 'owners' and recognised users of the city space.

Multilingual realities: Between vitality and status

The demand for recognition is one of the driving forces of nationalist, as well as social and political, movements (Honneth, 1992; Taylor, 1992). According to Taylor (1992: 25), identity, designating 'something like a person's understanding of who they are', is partly shaped by recognition or by absence of recognition. Language as a marker of cultural identity and, in a broad sense, as a mode of expression is closely linked to the formation and verification of identity in and through social relations of recognition. The multilingual reality of today's cities represents in this sense a set of institutionalised social relations of subordination that mirror the economic, political or cultural subordination in the social structures of the city. Thus some of the languages in the pictures of the City Reports enjoy a higher status and recognition, while others tend to be hidden or invisible.

In this context, the Madrid City Report (2014: 16) reminds us of the role of ideologies and hegemony of vision in the establishment of hierarchies of languages. It tells us that 'the languages issue' is still being addressed 'more as a linguistic challenge rather than an opportunity for growth and diversity'. There are also traces of a linguistic ideology that perceives diversity as a threat to the nation's political and economic objectives, which can be seen in the recent promotion of bilingualism in schools, oriented primarily towards the learning of English rather than any of the languages of the city. The imbalance in the efforts and investment put into this task and the neglect of other languages that inhabit the shared space of the city is another manifestation of status.

Perceptions of status and prestige

The City Reports use the notion of the 'face of the city' to interpret the dichotomy between multilingual reality and an established hierarchy in public opinion of the prestige and usefulness of particular languages. There are multilingual manifestations of the 'official face' of the city, essentially linked to tourism in capital cities like Madrid, Athens and Rome, which accommodate primarily European languages with the strong presence of English, as explored in Chapter 2. There is also the 'unofficial' face of the city into which some languages creep but do not receive any public recognition. However, it is felt that the languages in the 'hidden face' are gaining visibility and are becoming a factor that impacts on urban areas. In this sense, the lack of recognition is more acutely felt and can have implications for the identity formation in urban settings.

Multilingual repertoires are normal for large groups of the city population. However, most of the City Reports explicitly refer to the different status in public opinion of existing individual multilingualism/plurilingualism. This is reflected in different attitudes towards languages in terms of perception of status, prestige, usefulness and eventually of preference and recognition. In one respondent's opinion from Dublin some languages are 'devalued and marginalised' and 'some children in primary schools are embarrassed when their parents speak to them in front of their peers in their first language'. However, the respondent recognises how important it is that 'native speaking teens preserve their language skills and not be ashamed of their heritage' (Dublin City Report, 2014: 43). The emotional reaction of people confronted with a language they do not understand or are not acquainted with is described by another interviewee (Dublin City Report, 2014: 58): 'People occasionally get a bit shy around me [when I'm speaking Irish] or a bit defensive.'

The Utrecht report distinguishes between forms of valued and less-valued multilingualism (Jaspers & Verschueren, 2011) to explain people's attitudes towards languages in the city environment. Prestigious multilingualism is a form of multilingualism among highly educated people. It is perceived as a practical necessity for better employment prospects and eventually for better social status. In this sense, it is highly desired, worth the effort and investment and surrounded by positive attitudes. Non-prestigious individual multilingualism, as noted by the authors in Utrecht, is 'mainly found among urban migrant communities' (Utrecht City Report, 2014: 6). It includes languages other than Dutch whose place is often confined to the home and hence excluded from the educational system and largely from the public sphere and they are perceived as economically deprived of value.

Language as a proxy for ethnicity

Language status is closely related to national and regional identity. The memories of war and inter-ethnic conflict, for instance, give a negative charge to attitudes to some languages because they are perceived as markers of difference and a proxy for ethnicity and religious identity. The Osijek City Report (2014: 37) tells us that multilingualism is generally considered a sensitive issue. One interviewee (a doctoral student) believes multilingualism in the city to be sensitive 'mostly because of its recent history'. He goes on to say: 'There are different language statuses regarding the nationalities that speak them. They vary from negative to neutral, I don't think there are generally 'desirable' languages in Osijek social life' (Osijek City Report, 2014: 60). Another interviewee from Osijek (a librarian) makes the following observation:

> The Serbian language is a sensitive issue. Imagine someone came into a shop and asked for *hleb*, that would be a difference marker, and someone might react in a special way to this, different than if someone said the neutral word *kruh*. (Osijek City Report, 2014: 37)

An interviewee from Varna (a housewife), a long-term resident originally from Russia, shares a similar view about the ways in which attitudes to nations and states are transferred into attitudes to languages. Asked about difficulties in language communication, she replied: 'I had problems not because of a lack of proficiency in Bulgarian, but because in Bulgaria there are Russophiles and Russophobes' (Varna City Report, 2014: 40).

What these observations tell us is that there are situations where speaking a specific language can produce a negative judgement of the speaker related to his or her national, ethnic or religious identity. Speaking a particular language is interpreted as a means of expressing a different identity and can be used as an instrument of exclusion. Because of the proximity and density of contact, urban settings can be considered as an arena where these tensions and attitudes are expressed. However, because of the regularity of contact and engagement in the routines of daily life, some of these tensions can be reconciled and new attitudes developed and constructed.

The language used in social contacts (public or private) is not always a means of identity expression. The City Reports talk about situations where the intergenerational transmission of language is low, without the effect of assimilation into the dominant culture. Language can be a marker of identity (ethnic, national or social) but only one marker among others. Although some authors claim that language is the most 'potent' component of cultural identity (Arel, 2002: 92), the concept of the cultural nation or ethnicity cannot be reduced to a single linguistic marker of identity (Anderson, 1983; Gellner, 1983; Smith, 1991). Two examples from the City Reports are worth mentioning in this respect. First there is the status of Irish as the first official language of Ireland. Despite the fact that a very small percentage of the population claims to speak it on a daily basis and census returns demonstrate small increases in its knowledge and use, the Irish language sustains its power as a symbolic marker of national identity in and outside the country. At the beginning of 2007, Irish was granted the status of an official language of the EU.

Secondly we read of cases in the City Reports where ethnic dimensions of identity are separate from the language dimension. The Utrecht report, for example, talks about the different language situation of six immigrant communities in the city. Among them, the Turkish language enjoys a high status in the Turkish community and is used alongside Dutch, whereas this is not the case with the Moroccan community where identity (ethnic pride and self-esteem) is not 'expressed through language in the first place but through other identifying beliefs and activities, such as a common religion (Islam)' (Utrecht City Report, 2014: 8). This can also be seen in the fact that language use in multilingual settings is a matter of choice often driven by employment opportunities, by social relations, by the medium of study and work, and so on. How to communicate and who to contact is a matter of personal choice and circumstances. In this sense, using a language and developing a multilingual repertoire may have some influence on features related to identity, but it cannot be considered as a marker of a radical change in identity.

Language as a proxy for social identity

The distinction between prestigious and non-prestigious, valued and less-valued multilingualism can be viewed as representing the social stratification of urban life. Attitudes towards individual types of multilingualism and towards languages as a whole are closely linked to the social identities of groups within a city population. In contrast to the desirability and value attached to multilingual repertoires, including widely spoken languages or languages that are taught at school, there is an opposing attitude towards languages that are not considered as resources for their speakers and for others. Because of the social structure of society and the issues of poverty and deprivation, which are often the main reasons for migration and mobility to the city, some languages, dialects and accents can be considered as a mark of lower class origin or lack of education. Social identity thus marks the attitudes towards some languages and may trigger a negative judgement of the speaker. Respect for all languages present and belonging to the city, and recognition and support for them, are ways to sustain a city environment of inclusion rather than of social exclusion and partitioning, of creating bonds rather than barriers.

Languages and City Places

Languages as means of communication and as markers of identity find their expression in the physical urban environment. The notion of a monolingual national space is readily transformed into an attitude of standard monolingualism in the public sphere and often the lack of communicative competence in the main host country language provokes a negative and even reproachful attitude. It could therefore be argued that it is in the private sphere, above all, that multiple languages are accommodated. However, in today's society, people belong to many different kinds of communities: work, families, leisure and other social networks. Some of these communities cover an intermediate area between the private and the public and due to the density of population, they cross what can be considered a borderline between private and public. This means that some activities belonging to the private sphere find overt public expression and are manifested before much wider audiences than in the private sphere alone.

It is of course true that modern technologies offer unprecedented communication opportunities that radically change some assumptions about identity formation. Aspirational communities are built and sustained through the internet and social media. These communities do not necessarily bear any relationship to a city's physical environment. Yet, the city as a place, with the range of attitudes it triggers, remains a powerful factor for attaching meaning and sense to community formation, in understanding who we are and in forging strong connections between people.

A particular focus of the City Reports is multilingualism in the private sphere, encompassing activities related to family, friends and social networks, local or citywide activities. Community groups, migrant support organisations and community centres are an established part of the social fabric of all cities. For instance, some of the reports outline the role churches play in supporting linguistic diversity. The Strasbourg City Report identifies freedom of religious expression as a factor that allows cultural and linguistic diversity. The Limassol and Dublin City Reports include examples of religious ceremonies conducted in a range of languages. This creates some visibility of languages in the public arena.

The Montreal report talks about the first- and second-generation immigrants' choice of home languages. Use of the new national language in this context is often considered as a measure of successful integration, even though it can lead to the loss of migrants' first languages. The language distance between the new and host languages of the country and the language or country of origin are identified as important factors that can facilitate this process or slow it down. For example, coming from a Romance language country facilitates the transfer to French at home, while for other languages the transfer to French at home happens in approximately 13% of the cases (Béland, 2008, cited in the Montreal City Report, 2014: 6). It is noticeable that the City Reports as well as the individuals who participated in the city surveys do not share a common view on the relationship between language and integration. Often, integration at the cost of language loss is supported as the right path by interviewees. There are a number of factors that influence people's attitudes towards integration and cohesion, such as the extent to which multilingualism is reflected in local policy debates, national policy priorities (considered in the next chapter), and whether the collective city vision fosters an atmosphere of openness and accommodation of linguistic diversity.

City festivals

An important aspect of city life, crossing the border between the public and the private sphere, is the variety of festivities and celebrations. The LUCIDE City Reports share examples of publicly funded festivals and celebrations as well as those organised by local and voluntary associations. Although essentially cultural in nature, these festivities (e.g. Chinese New Year, *La Fête des Peuples* in Strasbourg, *Altonale* in Hamburg) provide space for the promotion of linguistic awareness of a range of languages and showcase languages and cultures that are present in the city. City and neighbourhood festivals and celebrations go hand in hand with an attitude of embracing multilingualism and the languages in the city environment. An interviewee from Dublin makes the following comment:

> I think it would be really interesting to try and use that new multilingualism that we have on our doorstep, to lock ourselves out of notions of monolingualism and bilingualism and embrace languages, because I'm

not sure we're very good at embracing languages. So I think there's an opportunity there – I think we could have a language festival. (Dublin City Report, 2014: 59)

Even as one-off events, the authors of the Hamburg report argue, festivals and similar events can contribute to the public acceptance of diversity in the city. However, as exceptions to the rule, they may not 'lead to sustainable change in the negative perceptions of linguistic and cultural diversity' (Hamburg City Report, 2014: 36). Citywide activities and festivals organised by local community groups have gained a ubiquitous presence in Canadian

Figure 3.6 Osijek poster for International Mother Tongue Day (LUCIDE network, 2014)

cities such as Ottawa, Toronto, Montreal and Vancouver, adding a significant dimension to their multicultural and multilingual character.

Music and dance are usually at the centre of neighbourhood and city festivals, thus making them a city stage for migrant cultures. For example, as the Athens Report tells us, the 2013 Antiracist Festival, held for the past 17 years, included dance and music from Madagascar, the Philippines, Albania, Bangladesh, a choir from the Greek-Bulgarian Cultural Association, performances by the Association of African Women, by the Georgian Community, traditional Kurdish music, Afghan music, etc. (Athens City Report, 2014: 24). City festivals also convey important messages concerning city life and social relations. For example, the Athens festival is known as the Antiracist Festival. All the continents are represented through songs, dances and different forms of entertainment at *La Fête des Peuples* in Strasbourg, which held its 21st celebration in 2013 (Strasbourg City Report, 2014: 28).

Organised by migrant and community associations and welcome by city residents, these events can be considered as manifestations of the demand for recognition and a contribution to the vitality of the city. Thus they are not just celebrations of culturally important events for the diverse city population. They become associated with places in the city and with particular times of the year and can be considered as drawing on and promoting urban values and a new changing identity of the whole city.

City festivals and public celebrations can also be interpreted as representing a form of public consent to reconstruct the city space and the image of the city as embracing difference and diversity. This can be achieved through scheduling them as annual events or linking them to the city's public calendar. These locally initiated activities provide a concentrated version of cultural encounters which open and enlarge the city's own identity.

Spatial language clustering

The previous chapter described how in every city there are emblematic sites of cultural and linguistic diversity. Some cities extend over large territories and have a highly polycentric metropolitan system with a complex pattern of living and working. Relatively large areas of the city are often distinguished by their specific identity or character, which might be experienced as a social boundary (Marcuse & van Kempen, 2000, 2002). It is sometimes the case that the edges or cores of the city spaces are linguistically marked with specific vital, visible and reiterated linguistic repertoires. Is spatial clustering an inevitable accompaniment to urban life? Are these city places to be interpreted as clues to the expression of polarised urban landscapes?

The LUCIDE City Reports present various patterns of clustering in the city space. For example, immigrants in Toronto tend to live in areas where 50% of residents are immigrants, whereas this is not the case for other

Figure 3.7 Ottawa Chinatown (LUCIDE network, 2014)

cities in Canada (Montreal and Vancouver) where the pattern of clustering does not exceed the averages of 31% and 42.5%, respectively. There are many examples of neighbourhoods, streets, squares and quarters related to different languages and language groups as part of their identity. This is also reflected in their names (Chinatown, Little Italy, Greek precinct, etc.). The dynamic of city life inevitably leads to transformations of parts of the city when the name stays but the reality changes. As a result of this, the Greek precinct may not necessarily be Greek anymore; Chinatown and Little Italy may become places where you go to eat. Districts with clearly associated historical roles in the city's history acquire new features and are revitalised with new languages as part of community life. This is, for example, the case with Piazza Vittorio in Rome, Usera or Lavapiés in Madrid, and Brick Lane in London, where linguistic, ethnic and cultural diversity are identified as markers of the space. These districts, streets and neighbourhoods are experienced as places that readily accommodate languages less visible in other parts of the city. It is where some of the hidden faces of the city come to the surface and are mirrored in people's perceptions. Each of these places tells its own little story of alterations that reinforce a new dynamic of identification with the place. These places can also be referred to as 'my' or 'our' street, place, neighbourhood or 'block', but also as 'theirs' and therefore alien.

Mobile citizens also cluster in close association with specific city places. Tourists, for example, represent in some sense a permanent group of people inhabiting the city although never in the same configuration. In ways similar to the residents of neighbourhoods and city quarters, tourists occupy clearly identified city spaces. They have 'their' streets along which they walk, 'their' quarters where they are accommodated, 'their' restaurants where they eat and their places of entertainment. In some sense these are recognised places that city inhabitants might not consider suitable for their status or taste – a perception embedded in the phrase 'too touristic'. Guided by a similar understanding, some tourists go in search of more 'authenticity' in the city environment and try to avoid crowded tourist places.

City multilingualism: Communication hindered or facilitated?

Cities demonstrate different micro publics through the everyday sharing of space. They are also spaces of encounters, contact and participation in identity building and commonality, in finding what people can easily share and how and to what extent they can support each other. Life in the city, with its dense concentration of diversity, reframes our schemes of communication and understanding beyond dominant cultural and linguistic expression by offering an immense diversity of options. What then makes the city a unified common picture, rather than a set of fragmented smaller narratives of city spaces? This is perhaps a question of central importance.

We argued above that people experience the reality of multilingualism in the city in different ways. However, there is also a perception of the linguistic balance in the city which is very much determined by the (imagined) capacity of people to communicate with other inhabitants. In this sense, the limit of linguistic diversity is reached when the city is perceived by its inhabitants as fragmented, partitioned and divided in terms of communication. Therefore, when talking about linguistic diversity it is useful to focus on the degree to which people can effectively communicate within the city. The capacity of communication is a path towards experiencing the city as a community. Historically, the emergence of a language community had a significant role in nation building (Anderson, 1983; Deutsch, 1942; Smith, 1991). The languages that become languages of the city now can be different, very distant from each other and new to the city setting. But whatever the language distance is, this cannot be considered as constituting a barrier to communication. The language repertoires of citizens become particularly important in enabling effective communication with city inhabitants. They are significant and necessary for a range of purposes: for communication with fellow citizens in view of the multilingual reality of today's cities; for travelling; for economic exchanges and mobility in a globalised world; for social mobility prospects; for cultural purposes; and for leisure activities. In some sense they represent the nature of communication in all aspects of contemporary life and consequently of urban life.

Even when linguistic skills are partial, distance between languages can be considerably shortened by a higher motivation and willingness to communicate. Because of the density of cities, people and languages rub along with one another. This is perceived to be normal by many people. The current picture of city multilingualism influences the redefinition of the contours of normality and the extent to which difference can be embraced. This is expressed very vividly by one of the interviewees from Varna:

> The more and various languages I hear every day, the happier I will be. That is why I would like to hear a new language every day. I would really like to hear more different languages coming from more distant places around the world. This will mean that every time I go out in the city, I will be undertaking a trip around the world. (Varna City Report, 2014: 44)

City language configurations are not automatically reflective of the language configurations of the state as markers of national and ethnic identity. There is a level at which engagement and attachment to the city is developed so that a city inhabitant might adopt first, or at least to a high degree, a multiplicity of identities: a Londoner, a citizen of Hamburg or Utrecht, of Madrid or Rome, of Limassol or Oslo, of Athens or Sofia, rather than a member of a national community. This may be reflected in the way cities are often advertised to tourists (for instance the 'I love this city' t-shirts), distinct from the pride of national identity.

Literary narratives about city multilingualism

The image of the city is a rich source for literature of many kinds, where language, attitudes and place mix in an expressive way. Before this chapter closes, we consider just two examples of many. Piazza Vittorio and Brick Lane are reference points in the Rome and London City Reports but also in two bestselling novels: *Clash of Civilisations over an Elevator in Piazza Vittorio* by Amara Lakhous (2008) and *Brick Lane* by Monica Ali (2004). Written by authors of migrant background, these novels add a narrative to the image of the city as a culturally mixed community and an eclectic mix of authenticity. They present micro-stories, but the places they depict are microcosms of the city's shifting cultural and linguistic patterns of diversity. They record people's interactions through the mixture of languages and emotions. In the *Clash of Civilisations over an Elevator in Piazza Vittorio,* place shrinks to the image of the elevator as a symbol of shared city space. People attach different meaning to this shared place and this causes disagreement and misunderstanding. *Brick Lane* is a glance behind the curtains of private life where fears and desires are articulated. It maps out a new, invisible London focusing almost exclusively on the lives of Bangladeshi women. It goes deep in order to ensure that the scale of the transformation is understood:

> 'It's a success story,' said Chanu, exercising his shoulders. 'But behind every story of immigration success there lies a deeper tragedy. ... I'm

talking about the clash between Western values and our own. I'm talking about the struggle to assimilate and the need to preserve one's identity and heritage. I'm talking about children who don't know what their identity is. I'm talking about the feelings of alienation engendered by a society where racism is prevalent. I'm talking about the terrific struggle to preserve one's own sanity while striving to achieve the best for one's family.' (Ali, 2004: 88)

The city places – Piazza Vittorio and Brick Lane – are the real protagonists of the novels as the scenes of diverse attitudes, uncertainties and questions asked privately and publicly. In *Clash of Civilisations over an Elevator in Piazza Vittorio*, these include questions about languages spoken and used:

Often people will say to me: 'You don't know Italian', or 'First, you have to learn the language better', or 'Sorry, but your Italian is very poor'. Usually I hear these poisonous phrases when I am looking for work as a restaurant cook and in the end they shunt me into the kitchen to wash dishes. [...] But I am sorry to inform you that I'm not the only one who does not know Italian in this country. I've worked in restaurants in Rome with a lot of young Neapolitans, Calabrians, and Sicilians, and I've discovered that our language level is about the same. (Lakhous, 2008: 15–16)

They also include questions about who lives in the city and the bonds to the place where they live: 'Mario, the cook at the restaurant at the Termini station, wasn't wrong when he said: "Remember, Parviz, we're all foreigners in this city!"' (Lakhous, 2008: 16). And questions about the nature of this bond if where 'we' are is 'seven seas and thirteen rivers' away (as *Brick Lane* was originally called): 'They were both lost in cities that would not even pause even to shrug' (Ali, 2004: 42).

Perhaps most apposite for this exploration of the identity of the multilingual city and its inhabitants and the new contexts in which it is expressed is this moving passage from *Clash of Civilisations over an Elevator in Piazza Vittorio*, with which we will conclude the chapter:

It's pointless to persist with this question: is Amedeo Italian? Whatever the answer is, it won't solve the problem. But then who is Italian? Only someone who is born in Italy, has an Italian passport and identity card, has an Italian name, and lives in Italy? As you see, the question is very complicated [...] you need a lifetime to understand its meaning, and only then will your heart open to the world and tears warm your cold cheeks. (Lakhous, 2008: 14–15)

Multilingual reality is a pervasive entity embedded in the continual revitalisation of society and cities. The images of the city, the changes of the city reality and the language components of citizens' identity create an image of the future and of the increasing complexity of the society we live in. When coloured with emotions and grief and when interpreted through the spectre of identity, the need for engagement, the richness of emotional attachment and the desire to set up one's own life, the co-existence of multiple languages in a city are real challenges for local government and local agencies. The next chapter will explore the policies and politics of urban multilingualism or what it means to take people's everyday lives into account when managing the multilingual city.

There are two central questions related to language policies and the politics of multilingualism. How do civic institutions respond to the challenges of governing increasingly multilingual urban communities and how do the inhabitants of these cities experience, view and influence these language policies? For all citizens and residents, access to vital material and symbolic resources depends on their ability to use their language(s) and linguistic repertoires successfully in numerous, everyday encounters with public service providers, co-workers, family members, friends and fellow citizens. As urban communities are becoming increasingly linguistically and ethnically diverse, more and more of these interactions involve the use of more than one language. In all the LUCIDE cities, the reality of urban multilingualism is shaped by a variety of developing national and local political frameworks and institutional arrangements, by political activism and initiative from below and by public debates and discourses about linguistic and cultural diversity and integration. The central language policy issues presented in the chapter concern the public use and status of languages, policies designed to facilitate language learning, and initiatives devoted to maintaining languages as well as the use of public service translation and interpreting. The analysis shows that public policies and discourses are framed by contradictory interests and ideologies. On the one hand, linguistic diversity is seen as an economic asset and also as a positive cultural good, while on the other hand, multilingualism is still seen as a possible threat to social and national cohesion.

4 Language Policies and the Politics of Urban Multilingualism

Peter Skrandies

> *The right to the city is far more than the individual liberty to access urban resources: it is a right to change ourselves by changing the city. It is, moreover, a common rather than an individual right since this transformation inevitably depends upon the exercise of a collective power to reshape the processes of urbanization. The freedom to make and remake our cities and ourselves is [...] one of the most precious yet most neglected of our human rights.*
> David Harvey, *The Right to the City*

The previous chapter has considered how the languages of citizens interrelate in dense urban settings, and how inhabitants perceive their multilingual cities. This chapter moves from individual experiences and perceptions to the larger policy context. Both descriptive and analytic in its focus, it explores language policies in urban settings as well as the politics of urban multilingualism. The main parts are concerned with the description, analysis and classification of public social policies and practices which have evolved in different cities as a response to multilingualism and the demands and needs of linguistic communities. Another focus is the description of everyday urban multilingualism as sustained by the activities of local citizens' organisations and NGOs central to organising the social lives of linguistic and ethnic communities and devoted to supporting their cultural and political rights. The final part of the chapter is devoted to a discussion of the politics and debates surrounding urban multilingualism. Multilingual policies and practices are simultaneously shaped from above, as politicians and policymakers try to manage and reconcile contradictory interests and ideologies, and from below, as communities struggle for the recognition of their needs and interests.

Public Policy and Urban Linguistic Diversity

Many areas of public policy are relevant in a discussion of urban linguistic diversity and its vitality, since most of 'the programs and policies by which officers of the state attempt to rule [and] exercise control' (Goodin et al., 2008: 1) will affect the socio-economic positioning, political status or general well-being of members of linguistic communities and will thereby have an impact on the cohesion of ethnolinguistic communities and networks, and on the vitality of their cultural and linguistic practices. It is also the case that many global structural economic and political forces which strongly influence the social and spatial patterning of cultural and linguistic diversity in cities lie beyond the control of government institutions engaged in language planning and policy at the national or local level. However, the effects of political and economic globalisation are played out locally in urban environments where a variety of state and non-state actors attempt to manage or influence linguistic diversity. A useful starting point is therefore to distinguish between policies that have been designed for purposes not directly linked to languages or linguistic behaviour, but nonetheless have a rather direct and immediate effect on languages and speakers, and policies and practices that are aimed deliberately at influencing linguistic behaviours or solving language problems. The most important areas with regard to the former are immigration and citizenship policies as well as measures related to the integration and social inclusion of immigrants, while specific language policies can be categorised according to whether they affect the status, the acquisition or the prestige of languages.

Migration and linguistic diversity

When people migrate, they not only bring their labour and skills to new environments, but also their cultural and linguistic practices. People might migrate as individuals or in groups, but after settlement many will seek the company of others with whom they have these practices in common. The formation of sizeable ethnolinguistic communities in the LUCIDE cities are the outcome of more or less recent population movements. As a consequence, policies designed to regulate and control migration and settlement have had and continue to have an important impact on the formation and development of urban linguistic diversity (Baynham, 2011; Duchêne et al., 2013).

The most important principle of migration policy is that sovereign states claim for themselves the right to decide who can lawfully reside in or move into their territories. Migration and citizenship regimes based on sets of differentiated citizenship and immigration statuses allow certain categories of migrants to move relatively freely across national borders, whereas the migration rights of others are severely restricted and their mobility is heavily policed (Castles et al., 2013; Steiner, 2009). In the European context, the most important citizenship and immigration status distinctions are between national citizens, EU citizens and so-called third-country nationals. As mentioned in the previous chapter, the creation of EU citizenship, which is automatically conferred on any person who holds the nationality of an EU

Figure 4.1 Hamburg retirement home (LUCIDE network, 2014)

member state, gives EU citizens the right to move and reside freely in the EU alongside a host of other political and social rights, while so-called third-country nationals are subject to complex sets of entry and residence rules which are specific to each state, although European integration and in particular the creation of the Schengen area of borderless travel have led to some degree of harmonisation. The most important principle followed by all EU member states is to encourage immigration that is considered economically beneficial, while trying to limit or prevent immigration viewed as economically or socially unwanted. Specific sets of rules also exist to regulate migration for educational purposes, family life or reunion, and asylum seeking. Immigration and citizenship policies in Canada and Australia are too complex to be described in any detail here, but they are based on similar principles: the fundamental distinction between citizens and non-citizens; the encouragement of what is considered economically useful immigration, preventing settlement which is considered undesirable, while permitting limited immigration for a number of other reasons (Castles *et al.*, 2013; Paul, 2013).

These migration and citizenship regimes are linked to global divisions of labour and the creation of dual or segmented labour markets in the more affluent Western countries, where so-called unskilled or de-skilled migrant workers have precarious social and political rights and work in the least well-paid and most exploitative sectors of the labour market, while workers needed for higher skilled occupations are granted more secure social and political rights (Castles *et al.*, 2013). Citizenship and migration regimes also have a decisive influence on the socio-economic wellbeing and inclusion of migrants after their settlement in host countries. It is important to note that hierarchies and patterns of social stratification among immigrants are not racially or ethnically 'blind', and that the systematic social exclusion of certain groups of migrants can be explained and analysed in terms of racialisation or 'ethnification': 'practices and forms of exclusion which affect migrants and new ethnic minorities [from] non-OECD countries in particular and which tend to be publicly rationalised and legitimised in ethnic, racial, and cultural terms' (Schierup *et al.*, 2006: 11). These processes also have important repercussions for our discussion of urban linguistic diversity. The systematic socio-economic and political marginalisation of specific communities reduces their ability to engage in political struggles and cultural activities designed to raise the profile and prestige of their linguistic and other cultural practices, while racialisation and ethnification, as well as xenophobic and anti-immigrant sentiments, contribute to discourses which delegitimise the presence of specific 'other' non-European languages and cultures and demand linguistic and cultural assimilation. At the same time, patterns of linguistic differentiation and hierarchies clearly overlap with patterns of socio-economic stratification, as described by Kraus in an article on the multilingual city:

> In the big cities of Western Europe, [...] [t]he upper segments of the staff employed by transnational corporations, IT experts, bankers, as well as people working in research centers or universities often use English as their regular medium of communication. At the other end of the scale, we find the bulk of the immigrants from North Africa, South Asia, Turkey, and other regions of the globe, who continue to use their mother tongues [...]. (Kraus, 2011: 27)

The 'vernacular' European national languages occupy a position of privilege vis-à-vis the languages of minorities, while they increasingly play a subsidiary role in certain domains of the economy and the educational sphere, where English has become dominant, both as an international lingua franca and a specialist language. This connection between patterns of global social stratification and mobility on the one hand, and a hierarchy of languages in terms of perceived usefulness and social prestige on the other, will be further explored when discussing evidence of linguistic hierarchies from the City Reports and other empirical data.

In the last decade or so, linguistic proficiency has also become an important prerequisite for the granting of residence or citizenship rights, and language-testing regimes, ostensibly designed to ensure the acquisition of national majority languages and thereby integration, have become an integral part of the migration and integration policies of most of the states in which the LUCIDE cities are located (Hogan-Brun et al., 2009). This important link between language and migration policies will be discussed under language acquisition policies.

Language Policy and Planning and Urban Linguistic Diversity

The deliberate efforts by policymakers to guide and regulate the linguistic behaviour of individuals and groups who live in multilingual urban environments are an important and central element of language policy and planning (henceforth LPP), an area of public social policy and a field of study which has been defined as the 'deliberate efforts to influence the behavior of others with respect to the acquisition, structure, or functional allocation of their language codes' (Cooper, 1989: 45; Hornberger, 2006). Most classifications distinguish three types of LPP according to whether a policy has been designed to have an effect on the learning of languages (acquisition planning), an effect on how citizens speak or write their language(s) (corpus planning), or an effect on the uses of language(s) in different administrative or social domains (status planning). In addition to these three areas, some writers have added attempts to influence the social esteem of languages (prestige planning; Grezch, 2013), as well as attempts to shape social ideas and discourses about language(s) (discourse planning; Lo Bianco, 2008). For this discussion of language policies in multilingual cities, the most relevant areas of LPP are status and prestige planning as well as acquisition planning outside compulsory state education. Another area closely related to language status and the establishment of institutional languages is translation policy covering institutional rules and practices that regulate the use of translation and interpreting in public domains (Meylaerts, 2011b).

Status planning

In a multilingual urban setting, a primary concern of LPP is the functional relationship between different languages in the public sphere. Decisions about which language(s) to adopt and enforce as official national or regional languages in a given polity are not usually made at the local level (Barbour, 2004; King et al., 2011); and all LUCIDE cities are located in nation states where official national or de facto official national majority language(s), as well as protected regional languages, exist alongside a number of other minority languages. As discussed in the previous chapter, the distinction between majority and minority languages is not only related to the number of speakers in a given polity, but reflects first and foremost the differential political power, privilege and social prestige that is afforded to different languages as a result of the operation of wider historical, social and political forces in a given political territory, and is historically the outcome of the processes that brought about the present configuration of modern polities, chiefly nation building and colonialism (Martin-Jones *et al.*, 2012), as explored in the first chapter of this book.

National languages and linguistic minorities

Following Anderson's and Hobsbawm's ground-breaking work (Anderson, 1983; Hobsbawm, 1992), numerous historians and sociolinguists have stressed the reciprocal connection between the formation of national languages and the development of nation states (Martin-Jones *et al.*, 2012); any description and discussion of contemporary language statuses needs to be put into the historical and political context of nationalism. In the words of Monica Heller (1999: 7), 'linguistic minorities are created by nationalism which excludes them'. As a consequence, any classification of languages has to take into account local political and historical contexts as well as legal frameworks. With regard to the LUCIDE cities, French, for example, can have the status of an official majority language (national in Strasbourg, provincial in Montreal), a recognised and protected national minority language (in Vancouver), or it can be classified as a minority language of migrant communities without official status (e.g. in London or Hamburg), while it is also a highly valued international language which is present as a compulsory language in the education systems of many states. In the present analysis of urban multilingualism at the structural political level, descriptive distinctions will be made between:

- majority national languages that also function as official state languages at national or regional level and thereby 'signal citizenship of a particular state or membership of a specific nation' (Barbour, 2004: 288);
- state-protected minority national languages which enjoy protection vis-à-vis national majority languages (at various levels and to a varying degree) because they are considered indigenous or autochthonous languages that belong to the territory of the nation state; very often these protected minority languages are the national majority languages of neighbouring states (German, for example, enjoys protected status in some regions of Denmark, Belgium and Italy); and
- other non-national minority (immigrant) languages without official recognition or status which are regarded as non-national languages and whose presence goes back to more or less recent migration.

Due to the European integration process and the Europeanisation of national language policies, a fourth language status category comprising the 24 official languages of the EU is becoming increasingly important in all the European LUCIDE cities. Although being an official language of the EU does not confer official status on a language outside EU institutions and the territory of its respective nation state, it does matter considerably in terms of prestige and political support, not least because of the ambitious EU translation policy which ensures that official EU documents are translated into all 24 official languages and guarantees that every EU citizen can communicate with EU institutions in an EU official language. Even if the EU possesses only limited direct influence with regard to national language education policies, since the curricula of educational systems fall under the responsibility of individual member states, a number of EU programmes support language learning and linguistic diversity and therefore exercise considerable influence (Rindler Schjerve & Vetter, 2012).

A fifth category of 'foreign languages' learned in compulsory education reflects the importance and desirability that education policymakers accord to achieving proficiency in a number of widely used international languages. Undoubtedly decisions regarding which languages are part of a compulsory national school curriculum have important repercussions for the status of these languages and for all other languages in a given polity, not least because, as mentioned earlier, some of the prestigious foreign languages can also be important 'non-national' minority languages.

Minority language rights

Some or all of the distinctions between national and non-national majority and minority languages outlined above are recognised in the laws of all nation states to which the LUCIDE cities belong. Taking into account the demolinguistic distribution of languages in the cities under consideration, it becomes clear that the language status legislation in operation in these cities leaves the vast majority of minority languages without specific legal recognition. The position taken by all governments is that no explicit linguistic rights, other than language rights enshrined in general human rights or equality legislation, should be granted to members of ethnolinguistic communities whose presence is a result of more recent migrations (Wee, 2011). These 'tolerance-oriented' language rights – to use a phrase coined by the sociolinguist Heinz Kloss (1977) – would normally include the right to use one's language privately and in public, to establish organisations devoted to the use, promotion and maintenance of one's language, and the right to teach the language in private, for example, in complementary schools. Here the most important principle is that state organs do not prevent minorities from using and championing the use and maintenance of their languages in non-official domains (May, 2011; Wee, 2011). As will be seen below, there is ample evidence in all of the LUCIDE data that such rights are being actively pursued by a variety of NGOs, cultural institutions and community organisations in order to maintain and promote minority cultures and languages.

In addition to 'tolerance-oriented' language rights, states may grant 'promotion-oriented' rights (Kloss, 1977) to ethnolinguistic groups and thereby specifically recognise and protect their languages in public domains. This will usually include the support and promotion of a minority language through its use in official public domains and in political or administrative institutions. It may also involve granting citizens the right to communicate with state officials in their language, granting minority communities the right to receive publicly funded education in their first languages, or the right to broadcast publicly funded TV or radio programmes in the minority language (May, 2011), as described in Chapter 2. An example of such rights includes the legal provision concerning education in national minority languages in Croatia, as mentioned in the Osijek City Report: 'members of national minorities are guaranteed the right to education in their language and script [and] have the opportunity to education in their mother tongue at all levels of education, from pre-school to post-secondary education' (Ministry of Science, Education and Sports, 2013).

In other LUCIDE cities a variety of languages are spoken which enjoy some form of official public protection and/or recognition. Rules and policies concerning translation follow from status policies. In a recent overview article on translational regimes, Meylaerts (2011a: 744) has pointed out that 'there is no language policy without a translation policy'. The very act of institutionalising one or more language(s) as official languages of a given polity must inevitably lead to rules which determine under what circumstances citizens or inhabitants who are not proficient in these languages have a right to translation, while it also necessitates translation into the official language or languages, since documents or messages in other languages will become valid, lawful or legal in a linguistic territory only if they have been translated (Meylaerts, 2011a: 748). In states or institutions that are officially multilingual, reciprocal translation arrangements between official languages also become a legal requirement. This situation is neatly summarised in a response to a question contained in the LUCIDE questionnaire used to elicit data for the City Reports. Asked whether they agreed with the way that Varna approaches the issue of multilingualism, the respondent summarised the administrative workings of a monolingual regime as follows:

> As the only official language of Bulgaria is the Bulgarian language, all documents drafted and issues in relation to performing those services are in this language. In the majority of cases, it is required that all documents presented by the citizens (in case they are originally drafted in another language) are accompanied by their legalised translation. In this sense, most municipal and state official at the local level do not have to use foreign languages in their daily work. (Varna City Report, 2014: 24)

An interesting example of how translation into an official language is enforced for political reasons, even though it is not necessary for comprehension, can be found in the Osijek City Report (2014: 21), where the authors mention that 'many people complain about paying for the translation of [...] documents, requested for various administrative reasons, [from] the neighbouring languages that are understood by everyone anyway (namely, Serbian and Montenegrin)'.

While states legally enforce translation into official languages, individuals' rights to translation into other languages are rather limited. A right to translation is recognised under certain circumstances and especially in legal domains, while in most areas of public life translation is not a legally enforceable right, but something that institutions will provide for the sake of safeguarding understanding and communication in multilingual communities (Wilson et al., 2012).

Acquisition planning

The central aspects of language acquisition policies in multilingual cities belong to the domain of compulsory state education and will be discussed in the next chapter. At the same time, acquisition policies and practices also play an important role outside the educational domain. Rules requiring or guiding citizens towards the acquisition of languages are usually enacted at the national level, but they are implemented at the local level (Liddicoat & Baldauf, 2008). Here a variety of civic institutions play key roles in organising, supervising or funding the learning and maintenance of languages in the LUCIDE cities, both with regard to learning majority national languages and to learning and maintaining minority languages. Moreover, language status policies and language acquisition policies are very closely related and have mutually reinforcing effects. The permanent inhabitants of a city, regardless of their political and immigration status, are expected to be – and usually demonstrate a strong interest in being – functionally competent users of the official national language(s) of their host countries, while the rights conferred on members of national linguistic minorities are usually accompanied by the duty also to learn and use the majority language(s).

In fact, considering the historical development of granting language rights to indigenous or autochthonous ethnolinguistic communities, it is striking that the granting of these rights in Europe generally occurred only after almost all the speakers of these minority languages had developed proficiency in the majority national languages and after many had given up their first language altogether due to the pressures of linguistic assimilation. In this sense, linguistic marginalisation and widespread or complete group bilingualism was the historical prerequisite for the granting of language rights to indigenous linguistic minorities in European nation states (De Witte, 2011). Similar observations can be made with regard to the indigenous languages of Australia and Canada, taking into consideration the historical processes that saw the violent marginalisation and displacement of indigenous communities by European settlers and European colonialism.

Proficiency in the national language also plays a crucial role in the theory and practice of active and participatory citizenship, because proficiency gives citizens and would-be citizens one necessary – but certainly not sufficient – prerequisite for exercising their democratic rights: 'to control the authorities and to communicate with them, to understand the laws taken in their name, to vote, to receive and understand official documents, etc.' (Meylaerts, 2011b: 743). Moreover, proficiency in national languages also holds out the promise of economic and social mobility for individuals, a necessary but by no means sufficient condition for socio-economic integration and success (May, 2011). Given these functions and values of a national, legitimate language, it should come as no surprise that the acquisition of the national majority language, in particular in its standard prestige variety, plays such a central role in language acquisition policy and planning.

Migration and compulsory language acquisition

With regard to migration and settlement, specific language-learning and language-proficiency legislation exists in most of the states in which the LUCIDE cities are located, and LPP has thus become even more deeply embedded in immigration and integration policies. These provisions vary with regard to the proficiency expected from would-be immigrants, residents or citizens, but they all place a legal duty on certain groups of migrants to attend so-called integration or citizenship courses to acquire skills in the national majority language alongside knowledge about the culture of their host country. They also subject certain groups of non-nationals to language proficiency tests that have to be successfully completed to gain admission, residence or citizenship rights and threaten them with punitive measures such as non-renewal of resident rights or even expulsion should they fail to prove that they have attained the requisite level (Hogan-Brun et al., 2009; Little, 2010; Love, 2014).

While individuals seeking full naturalisation and citizenship have, historically, always had to prove some level of proficiency in the majority national language in many European states, the recent wave of language-learning and language-testing legislation linked to migration rights has introduced a new formal regime of compulsory language learning and testing for many non-European and mainly non-Western adult migrants and even would-be migrants. This can be linked to rising anti-immigrant sentiment and xenophobia across Europe and the corresponding shift in public immigration policy, which sees integration no longer as a two-way process but as an individual obligation for which migrants are solely responsible. In Italy the minister responsible for introducing a mandatory Italian language test at level A2 of the Common European Framework of Reference for Languages (CEFR) for migrants seeking permanent legal residency status justified this decision by stating that it guarantees integration: 'I suggest to the foreigner the things to do in order to integrate himself into the community. If he does it, I will give him a *permesso di soggiorno* [a residence permit], if he does not, it means that he doesn't want to integrate' (quoted in Love, 2014: 1–2). The simplistic nature of this kind of argumentation ignores the complexity of successful integration processes which depend on a variety of socio-economic and political factors and certainly not only on migrants' willingness to integrate and their 'achieving a certain linguistic competence or knowledge of the history, laws and customs of the host country' (Little, 2010: 7).

A look at the academic literature and empirical studies suggests that the achievements of compulsory learning in terms of proficiency and communicative competence and the validity of the testing regimes are rather questionable. From this perspective, the regime of compulsory language learning and testing linked to migration and settlement rights is of limited value with regard to improving or measuring linguistic proficiency, while it serves an important gatekeeping function in making it more difficult for certain categories of migrants to enter or settle, in asserting pressure for linguistic assimilation and in shifting the responsibility for successful integration onto individual migrants. In a recent report for the Parliamentary Assembly of the Council of Europe, similar concerns have been summarised as follows:

> Tests may in fact be hindering integration and leading to exclusion, [they] can be an obstacle to family reunification, [and] can prevent [migrants] from enjoying secure residence rights, causing resentment in migrant communities and discrimination against certain groups, […]. There are also concerns that the primary purpose – or at least a predictable consequence – of these tests is to cut down the number of migrants arriving or remaining in the countries concerned. (Council of Europe, 2013)

The limited instrumental value and discriminatory nature of these programmes can also be seen in the context of free intra-EU mobility, which allows EU citizens to settle freely in any member state without being subject to linguistic proficiency tests or compulsory language learning.

Language learning and maintenance is also one of the major fields of activity of urban NGOs, cultural institutions and community organisations which might be supported, at least partially, by state funding. However, while national and state institutional discourses often stress the economic and instrumental value of learning the national majority language and only accord 'sentimental value' (May, 2011: 169) to minority languages, language planning from below, as undertaken by community groups and migrant associations, is characterised by efforts to teach and maintain minority community languages alongside the teaching of the majority national language. These practices clearly refute the idea that the maintenance of minority or heritage languages stands in opposition to the learning of majority national languages, and demonstrate that linguistic integration and linguistic diversity can be fully compatible and complementary goals of LPP.

Prestige planning

The object of language prestige planning is to have a positive influence on the perception and evaluation of a language both by its speakers and by non-speakers and thereby to increase the social esteem and respect accorded to it and its users. The main goals are to campaign for social and political recognition of a language or language variety and to create and project a positive image of the language and the ethnolinguistic group(s) associated with it (Ager, 2005; Grzech, 2013). It is rooted in the desire of individuals and groups for positive linguistic self-identification and in the wish that others acknowledge and recognise this. It is also a response to denigration and discrimination and an attempt to assert one's place in an often hostile and competitive environment, and is thus central to the 'formation, modification, defence and maintenance of the identity of a person, group or state' (Ager, 2005: 3).

At the level of cultural foreign policy the promotion of languages can also be related to the political and economic interests of nation states eager to enhance their 'soft powers', as demonstrated by the activities of numerous national cultural organisations like the Confucius Institute or the British Council, which are controlled and funded by nation states. The central goals related to attempts at enhancing the social prestige and esteem of a language are to increase the number of speakers, to nurture confidence among speakers about using their language and to produce and disseminate texts and other cultural products designed to bolster the image of a language. Evidence from the LUCIDE City Reports and other data show that a variety of state and non-state actors engage in language prestige policy and planning; some examples are given below.

Evidence from the LUCIDE Cities

While most national governments now grant some or all of the 'promotion-oriented' language rights described above to speakers of recognised national minority languages, similar policies and practices vis-à-vis non-recognised linguistic minorities evolve typically at the local level. Here, local government agencies respond to activities, demands and needs originating from local communities and organisations, while they might also take the initiative in order to overcome communication barriers and increase integration. Although these policies and practices do not affect the legal status of languages and do not confer any specific language rights on linguistic communities, they are key instruments in the management of urban linguistic diversity because they recognise and valorise the presence of different languages and their communities within a city, contribute to the learning of other languages and help to overcome language barriers.

The most important language status, acquisition and prestige policies initiated or implemented by civic institutions and/or private organisations and associations at the local level can be grouped under the following headings:

- the use of other languages, including public service interpreting and translation, by public institutions to provide specific information to citizens, inhabitants or foreign visitors who lack proficiency in the city's official national language(s) (informational function), their use to recognise and valorise the presence of other languages and their speakers in the city and to (re)present the city to an international audience (symbolic/representational function);
- the organisation or funding of language learning, both with regard to the acquisition of the official majority language and the maintenance of other languages;
- the organisation or funding of cultural activities or festivals that celebrate the presence of particular languages and cultures in a city or the specific urban mingling of cultures and languages;
- the supply of cultural products (books, audiovisual media) in a variety of languages;
- the adoption of cohesive institutional LPP strategies to support linguistic diversity and integration which specify goals and measures to implement them.

The following sections will provide an overview of these five LPP activities in the LUCIDE cities.

Uses of 'other languages'

Public civic institutions and authorities use languages to communicate with citizens and inhabitants with a view to sharing information with them, to facilitate orientation, to enable participation and to direct their behaviour. Citizens and inhabitants are subjects of governance and, as public service users, they need to communicate with the relevant authorities. Whenever such communication cannot be realised in a common language, public service translation and interpreting (henceforth PSTI) can be used to overcome linguistic barriers between public service providers and public service users. At the same time, urban institutions use language to create messages, narratives and discourses about their cities, usually with the aim of presenting themselves and their cities in the best possible light to citizens, other inhabitants, temporary visitors and to the world at large. Cities have global connections and increasingly see themselves as international players and therefore engage in multilingual communication and image-building strategies to attract foreign visitors and investors.

In many ways the provision of information for foreign visitors is the least problematic and also one of the most obviously developed areas of multilingual public service provision in all of the LUCIDE cities. The obvious economic interests of cities in attracting tourists, as well as the huge involvement of private commercial companies in this area, guarantee that tourist information is available in a range of widely used global and international languages, the most prominent being English, followed by Mandarin, French, Spanish, German, Portuguese, Italian, Russian, Korean and Japanese. The list not only reflects the worldwide number of speakers of these languages, but also correlates with the number of international tourists speaking these languages and the amount of money they spend (UNWTO, 2014). English is always the first and most prominently used language on official tourism portals maintained by LUCIDE cities, but nearly all the reports note both the willingness and the capacity to provide adequate information in other languages. In some cities this can stand in stark contrast to the situation in other areas of public service provision as noted by the authors of the Madrid City Report (2014: 18) who conclude that 'it would appear that the only sector that has made efforts to provide multilingual services is the tourism sector, particularly with regard to public transport. Services and documentation are provided in a range of languages but especially in English'.

Figure 4.2 London, public service interpreting (LUCIDE network, 2014)

The agencies of urban government reviewed here also use other languages (again principally English) on their own official websites and in other official information material geared towards informing an international audience and newly arrived migrants or other citizens or residents lacking proficiency in the majority national language. Apart from Madrid, the official web portals of all non-Anglophone cities provide information in the national majority language and in English. On the website for Rome, the use of English seems to be restricted to basic top-level information, while all other cities make extensive use of English, including, for example, the publication of fairly detailed descriptions of municipal infrastructure projects on the websites of Sofia and Varna. Strasbourg is unique insofar as the city's official website is trilingual and supplies information in French, German and English.

The websites of Melbourne and of the Anglophone Canadian cities of Toronto and Vancouver use English only, but contain prominent, top-level references to the availability of free machine and telephone translation services. The majority francophone city of Montreal has French as its official language and runs a bilingual website in French and English. In Dublin, where Irish is by law the national and first official language of Ireland, the City Council provides an Irish language section on its website (*láthair Ghaeilge*) with a number of subsections that are of direct relevance to Irish and its speakers (i.e. language rights, street names) along with some minimal information on general services. However, the website is not fully, or even mostly, bilingual in terms of allowing users to access the same information on the homepage in both English and Irish. The joint website of the Mayor of London and the Greater London Authority is in English only. This brief synopsis confirms the absolute dominance of English alongside national languages, while the languages of linguistic minorities are largely ignored at this top level of communication by urban institutions with their citizens and other city residents.

Public service translation and interpreting

Policies and practices concerning the use of other languages in the provision of public services to citizens, migrants and other inhabitants vary widely in quality and quantity in the different LUCIDE cities and, very often, civic institutions in the same city observe different rules and practices. To some extent this depends on what these institutions do, i.e. on the kind of service they deliver or the administrative task they are engaged in, but it is also contingent on financial and human resources, national and local political contexts, different legal frameworks and the composition and size of linguistic minorities. Each city and each institution in each city is thus characterised by a unique set of specific practices. Nevertheless, it is possible to identify certain trends and typical behaviours with regard to the use of PSTI.

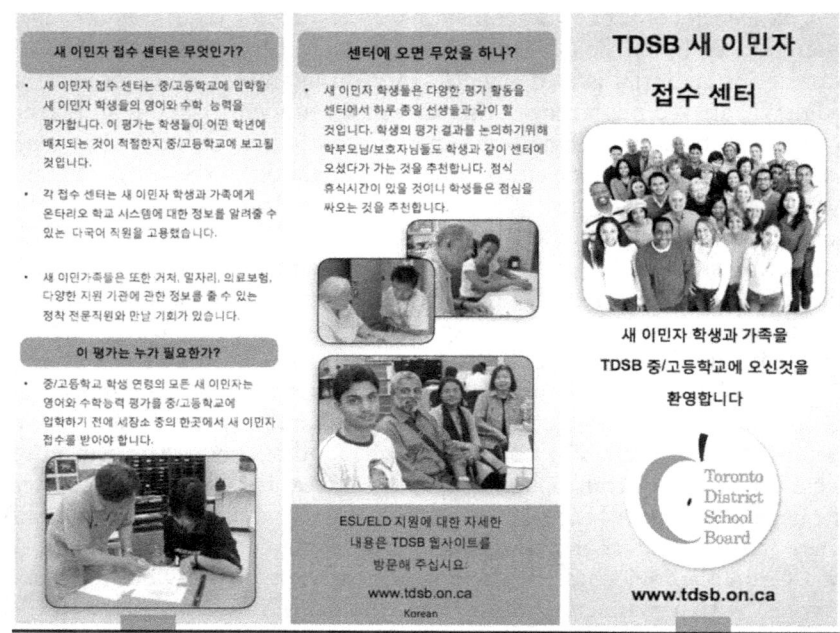

Figure 4.3 Toronto District school board leaflet in Korean (LUCIDE network, 2014)

In line with data published by similar research projects (Extra & Yağmur, 2012), it can be observed that many administrative and public service institutions in all cities, although operating under the general norm of institutional monolingualism, do translate some information into other languages, principally English and other widely spoken European languages. They also use public service interpreting, especially in the provision of legal services, policing, health services and immigration and integration services – areas where many service users enjoy specific legal rights to translation, such as defendants in criminal cases, medical patients in some situations in some jurisdictions, vulnerable adults or children, or asylum seekers seeking protection. Some institutions also possess language or translation policies which specify under what circumstances and for what purposes translation and interpreting should be used. At the same time, the quantity of services (both with regard to the range of languages used and the areas of public services covered) as well as the quality (use of professionally trained interpreters or reliance on informal arrangements) vary considerably from city to city and from organisation to organisation.

Very often speakers with a limited command of the national majority language will struggle to make themselves understood and interlocutors rely on informal interpreting or mediation, language mixing and/or the use of a lingua franca, normally English. On the other hand, explicit PSTI policies do exist to facilitate multilingual encounters. Many of the practices and routines described in the reports can be placed on a continuum of responses to translation and interpreting needs described by Corsellis (2008) and Ozolins (2010), where one end of the spectrum is marked quite simply by neglect, while the other is characterised by explicit planning and regulated practices based on the use of well-trained professional interpreters and public service personnel attuned to the needs of citizens with specific linguistic needs. Considering the historical development of PSTI in countries which can now be considered to have rather comprehensive systems (Australia, Canada and Sweden), it becomes clear that the responses in most host societies evolve from an initial period of almost complete neglect to a phase characterised by makeshift measures and 'muddling through'. At this stage, out of sheer necessity, some institutions, very often the police and public health service providers, start to provide ad hoc interpreting, often through the help of friends, family members and volunteers. In a next phase institutions develop 'generic language services' where, for example, telephone interpreting becomes available and some institutions appoint interpreters as permanent members of staff. A comprehensive stage is reached when the availability of generic and specialist translation and interpreting services based on needs is complemented by certification and quality controls, training programmes for public service interpreters and the widespread adoption of institutional translation policies (Ozolins, 2010: 195).

Looking at the evidence from the City Reports and with the caveat that not all of them cover this area comprehensively, it becomes apparent that the historical development just outlined can be usefully employed to describe the present situation in many of the LUCIDE cities and their public institutions whose translation and interpreting practices can be placed on a continuum ranging from rather limited and inconsistent provision to more fully developed service policies and practices. Employing the scale outlined above, the city of Athens along with Limassol can be positioned at one end of the spectrum characterised by limitations and ad hoc measures, while the cities of Toronto and Melbourne (as well as the other Canadian cities and, with some qualifications, Dublin and London) possess more comprehensive systems and occupy the other end. The evidence from the cities of Rome, Madrid, Hamburg, Utrecht, Strasbourg and Oslo points to the existence of a variety of generic translation and interpreting services, while institutions also seem to make regular use of lay interpreters, as described by the authors of the Utrecht report:

> Translation in the health service, however, is not always ideal. Patients who do not speak Dutch or English sufficiently are frequently asked to bring a relative or friend who can translate for them. If this is not possible or the topics discussed are too personal, a professional translator is consulted, mostly via telephone. (Utrecht City Report, 2014: 21)

Another factor influencing the availability of interpreting services is the relative size of linguistic communities and the duration of their presence. Services in well-established and rather widely spoken community languages are generally more easily available, even in cities where services are otherwise more limited (Turkish in Hamburg), than interpreting services in languages whose speakers have arrived more recently and are smaller in numbers (Lingala in Dublin or Amharic and Tigrinya in London). It should also be noted that some cities face a higher demand for PSTI than others. The fact that the authors of the City Reports for Sofia, Varna and also Osijek do not report extensively on PSTI reflects the relatively smaller number of speakers of other languages in these cities and that many who do belong to a linguistic minority are also proficient in the majority national language. On the other hand, cities with larger groups of linguistic minorities whose presence results from more recent immigration, and especially cities located in countries that have traditionally been characterised by outward migration rather than immigration (Athens, Limassol and even Madrid and Rome) find it more difficult to deal with the linguistic needs of their populations. The authors of the Athens City Report summarise the situation in the city as follows:

> Usually, when it comes to the migrant population that resides in the city, it is not a matter of whether the public servant who comes into contact with an immigrant can speak English or some other language; it is the migrants who actually have to fully adjust themselves to the situation irrespective of whether they have any knowledge of Greek (or English). (Athens City Report, 2014: 13)

They conclude that:

> [a]s far as interpretation services in the public sector are concerned, the situation is far from satisfactory [and] [t]he Greek state on the whole has been unable to respond to and provide for the needs in interpretation services in health care, education, legal matters etc. (Athens City Report, 2014: 16)

If efforts are being made to improve the situation as, for example, in the health sector, initiatives often rely on outside funding and become very vulnerable once this has come to an end. The authors of the Limassol report document the widespread use of English as a lingua franca by institutions; however, they also remark that 'in many cases the English version of the website is not working or is under construction' and point out that 'face-to-face communication in various administrative services [...] is carried out in Greek or [...] English' only (Limassol City Report, 2014: 20), and that no official translation or interpreting services in other languages are available. In Madrid, public services seem to have reached the stage of a general provision of interpreting services in some sectors, notably in public health where a telephone service was established in 2009 'to provide simultaneous translation in hospitals, available on a 24/7 basis in over 50 languages' (Madrid City Report, 2014: 17). At the same time, the authors highlight that '[i]n Spain in general and in Madrid in particular, [...] translation [in] minority languages including sub-Saharan languages and [...] Arabic appear[s] to lack professionalism, perhaps due to limited financial or human resources, or indeed political will' (Madrid City Report, 2014: 17).

The report for London shows that even in a city where translation and interpreting services have reached a comparatively high level of development and are characterised by widespread availability and professionalism in some sectors, the situation can be very uneven, while services can also be affected negatively by changing political considerations. The authors note that 'the degree of commitment as well as the practical arrangements for delivering

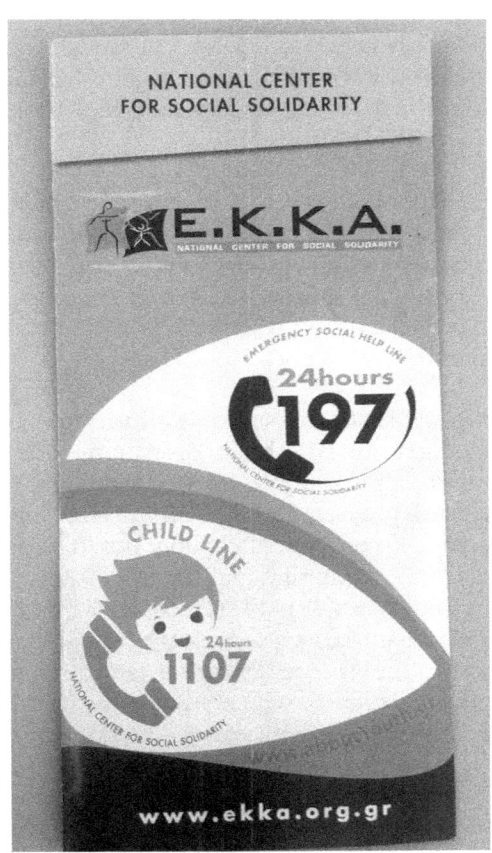

Figure 4.4 Athens, English-language leaflet from EKKA (LUCIDE network, 2014)

multilingual services vary widely from council to council' (London City Report, 2014: 37). Their analysis also demonstrates that some local government agencies consider the provision of translation and interpreting a legal obligation in cases where residents would otherwise be unable to gain access to public services, and therefore commit themselves to a comprehensive provision of PSTI. In contrast, other local government agencies are less committed and have adjusted their policies in line with the stance taken by the UK national government which believes that existing equality legislation does not 'create a legal duty to translate' and considers the provision of translation and interpreting services a disincentive to learning English (London City Report, 2014: 33; cf. Travis, 2013).

The position of the UK central government, which is contradicted by the policies of some local government institutions in London, stands also in marked contrast to the practices in operation in what is probably the most multilingual and multicultural of all the LUCIDE cities, the Canadian city of Toronto. The authors of the Toronto City Report (2014: 8) come to the conclusion that 'although Toronto is officially a unilingual Anglophone city, [...] in many cases, services are provided in languages other than English'. They go on to quote from the multilingual services policy adopted in the city in 2002, which states that:

> The ethnic diversity of our community is a source of social, cultural and economic enrichment and strength [and that] all residents shall be entitled to municipal services and programs which are racially sensitive, culturally and linguistically appropriate, gender appropriate, accommodate disability, and are adequately resourced to ensure equitable access and outcomes. (Toronto City Report, 2014: 11)

The authors also report that '[c]onsiderable efforts are made in Toronto to increase newcomers' access to health services', quoting the example of Language Services Toronto, a programme that 'provides real-time phone interpretation 24 hours a day, seven days a week, in 170 languages, including Aboriginal languages' and conclude that 'public institutions in Toronto seem very sensitive to the issue of multilingualism and the urgent needs of people with limited proficiency in English' (Toronto City Report, 2014: 11).

The local and national factors affecting the provision of translation and interpreting services in the cities under consideration can be summarised by comparing Athens and Toronto, which are the furthest apart in terms of both capability and social and political readiness to offer comprehensive PSTI services. Athens is a city located in a state which has traditionally been a country of emigration and Greece is a society still characterised by a relatively large degree of ethnocentrism where 'multiculturalism is still more of a policy buzzword than a reality' (Faas, 2011: 169). Moreover, the country has also suffered from a severe financial and economic crisis over the last six years, which has polarised the country politically as well as economically, and seen the establishment and considerable electoral success of an openly racist and violent neo-Nazi party, Golden Dawn, alongside an increase in anti-immigrant sentiments and attitudes (Dalakoglou, 2012). On the other hand, Toronto is located in an officially bilingual country with a long history of immigration and a strong multicultural tradition, where the multicultural model of citizenship was pioneered in 1971 and where municipal responses to cultural and linguistic diversity have been characterised as working towards 'successful immigrant settlement, interethnic equity and social harmony' (Good, 2009: 1). Moreover, Canada was one of the economies least affected by the 2008 financial crisis and has been able to develop its multicultural policies in the context of an orderly immigration policy not affected by large-scale unauthorised migration.

Language learning

The acquisition of languages in urban settings has been a main focus of the LUCIDE research programme and the issues of 'foreign' language learning in schools and the linguistic integration of pupils with a home language other than the majority national language are discussed in detail in Chapter 5 of this book. The following focuses therefore on language learning organised by urban government institutions as well as the efforts of private, non-governmental organisations and associations in the areas of linguistic integration (learning the majority national language) and the maintenance of minority languages.

In all LUCIDE cities public institutions focus mainly or exclusively on language and literacy education and training in the majority national language(s), while the maintenance of minority languages, especially of migrant minority languages, is undertaken by a variety of non-state actors who may receive public funding for these initiatives. With regard to learning the majority national language, learning opportunities in the form of more or less formal language classes are provided in all the cities for all or certain categories of newly arrived adult migrants and other residents lacking proficiency in majority national languages. These courses and programmes are usually funded and directly organised by national or regional governments or run by publicly funded quangos or non-state organisations which can apply for public funds. In Greece the coordination and implementation of Greek-language training programmes are the responsibility of local authorities (Athens City Report), while in London the provision of English for Speakers of Other Languages (ESOL) courses has been delegated to a variety of local providers, including the adult education departments of local government councils, which can receive funding for certain eligible groups of learners from a central government organisation (London City Report). In some LUCIDE cities, such as Oslo, Strasbourg and Hamburg, language classes are offered at no cost to all interested learners, while in others free courses are limited to certain categories of eligible learners (e.g. job seekers or migrants on low income). As outlined earlier, new migrants may also be legally obliged to take linguistic proficiency tests in the majority national language or to attend civic integration courses which include training and testing in the majority national language (Council of Europe, 2013). The Oslo report refers to the specific programme in operation in Norway and mentions that '[e]ach learner receives a "salary"' during the time they take part and highlights that it involves learners spending part of their time in workplaces 'in order to obtain "hands-on" language practice' (Oslo City Report, 2014: 14).

At the same time, the availability of free or low-cost formal language training by qualified teachers is not always guaranteed, and there are references in a number of City Reports indicating that the demand for such courses outstrips the existing supply. The authors of the Madrid report describe the provision of publicly funded Spanish language classes for speakers of other languages in the city as 'extremely precarious' and come to the assessment that '[t]he bulk of Spanish language teaching in Madrid seems to be carried out by NGOs, trade unions and some private foundations, often with limited resources' (Madrid City Report, 2014: 18). Similarly, a respondent interviewed for the Athens report remarks that 'there are very few opportunities' for interested learners to acquire Greek, while the prominent involvement of NGOs and volunteer organisations in Rome seems to indicate that professional institutional providers cannot obtain enough funding from the state. In Athens, as in many other cities, the inadequate provision of publicly organised and funded courses has led to numerous efforts by various community organisations and migrant associations to offer free language classes to learners wanting to acquire the national majority language. One example mentioned in the Athens report is the 'Sunday School for Migrants', a volunteer organisation founded by migrant and Greek activists working together to deliver free Greek language classes to migrants and refugees (Athens City Report, 2014: 23). Other examples of private initiatives supporting the acquisition of majority national languages are documented for nearly all LUCIDE cities and feature prominently in the reports for Rome, Hamburg, Madrid and London.

Issues related to the quality of teaching and the outcome of language learning are mentioned in the report for Toronto, where the authors cite the International Adult Literacy and Skills Survey (IALSS), conducted by the OECD and the Canadian Ministry for Statistics, to point out that 'the English or French language proficiency of Canadian immigrants was either poor or weak in 60% of the cases' (Toronto City Report, 2014: 7). They also report research that found the lack of English-language proficiency especially pronounced among middle-aged and older first-generation female immigrants and attributed this to a lack of adequate training programmes (Toronto City Report, 2014: 8). A gender bias in the acquisition of English proficiency is also mentioned in the London City Report.

While most of the LUCIDE City Reports do not mention attainment data for linguistic proficiency in national majority languages among linguistic minorities, other available information highlights differences in linguistic skills between native speakers of national majority languages and speakers with a different first language. The most recent OECD report on adult literacy, numeracy and problem-solving skills, measuring performances in 22 OECD countries, provides an overview of the gap in literacy between native-born, foreign-born adults, foreign-language natives and foreign-language immigrants (OECD, 2013). The conclusion reached by the report is that 'foreign-born and foreign-language adults' are clearly disadvantaged in terms of 'skills needed to succeed in daily life and in work situations involving the host country's language' and the authors stress the likelihood of foreign-language immigrants scoring significantly lower than immigrants whose first language is the same as the majority national language and non-immigrants (OECD, 2013: 127–28). Although the data say nothing about the functional competence of speakers of other languages relative to their work and social life situations, they suggest that significant additional efforts and support structures are needed to provide these speakers with the linguistic skills in national majority languages necessary for social and economic integration. At the same time, it must be stressed that linguistic proficiency in majority national languages is only one of many factors that influence social inclusion.

In most of the LUCIDE cities, language learning to maintain or acquire minority languages without high status is largely left to the initiative of non-state actors and institutions, and all the reports mention an impressive variety of efforts and activities. As noted by the authors of the Hamburg City Report, language acquisition planning by community organisations and linguistic minority groups has usually a strong 'bilingual perspective', where the efforts of linguistic integration through learning the majority language go hand in hand with activities devoted to the maintenance of community and heritage languages. They observe that 'virtually every immigrant community in Hamburg founded a kind of association for the purpose of fostering and promoting their linguistic and cultural heritage' (Hamburg City Report, 2014: 25). The authors of the Osijek City Report (2014: 24–25) mention 'numerous minority institutions and associations' which organise festivals to introduce 'minority culture to the dominant Croatian culture' and provide an opportunity for members of linguistic minorities to meet and speak their languages. Similar observations related to efforts to maintain and strengthen minority languages can be found in all the reports, and the authors of the Utrecht City Report (2014: 23) also point out the importance of such activities in covering 'the gaps [...] in the public sphere'. The Dutch state stopped a public programme designed to maintain heritage and community languages in 2004 'mainly because of its [only] moderate success and the supposed waste of money which was not tolerated in the political climate at that time'

(Utrecht City Report, 2014: 18). Interestingly, a number of reports mention that the activities of community organisations also help speakers of majority national languages to acquire the languages of linguistic minorities (e.g. in Hamburg), while private initiatives aiming to support multilingual families through offering advice and answers to questions related to childhood bilingual language acquisition are reported from some cities (e.g. Vancouver and Utrecht).

The most important exception to the rule that the learning and maintenance of minority languages spoken by migrant communities receives relatively little public endorsement and hardly any public financial support is documented in the Melbourne City Report, which refers to the existence of over 200 community language schools offering language education in 55 languages. These schools are backed by the organisational support of the Ethnic Schools Association of Victoria which in turn receives public support and funding (Melbourne City Report, 2014: 9).

Cultural activities

All the LUCIDE reports refer to numerous cultural activities celebrating the presence of particular languages and cultures in their cities as well as the specific intercultural urban mingling of diverse cultural practices and languages. Some of the larger festivals seem to have gained a decidedly corporate character and can be dominated by commercialism and consumption, such as the 'Maslenitsa Russian Sun Festival' celebrated each year on London's Trafalgar Square (London City Report, 2014: 70), while others are characterised by a local community spirit or a political orientation focused on migrants' rights and grassroots activism. The following quote from the Rome report about a 'Festival of Migrant Culture', celebrated on 29 June, the birthday of Rome, may count as a typical example:

> In Tufello it is a multicultural, multi-racial celebration, it will be a festival of migrant cultures [...] Because the world of today is heterogeneous and multicultural; [...] the mottos [are] *Tufello Meticcio* [multi-racial Tufello], 'to migrate is not a crime' and 'no border, no nation'. (Rome City Report, 2014: 14)

The Rome City Report also mentions that the festival offered 'information stalls, screening of reportages and documentaries [about the situation of migrants and refugees fleeing to Italy and Greece across the Mediterranean], theatrical performances', as well as 'international food stalls, [and an] open mike for free speech and free style/hip hop performances by artists from Tunisia, Mali, Senegal, Egypt' (Rome City Report, 2014: 25). The existence of similar festivals and the pervasiveness and vitality of a specifically urban ethos of multicultural and multilingual tolerance, celebrating the diversity and vitality of urban life, is amply documented in all the reports.

Language Policies and the Politics of Urban Multilingualism 139

The important role of religious organisations in the life of many ethnolinguistic urban communities is highlighted in several accounts of multilingual city life (e.g. in Strasbourg, Hamburg and Rome). The authors of the Dublin report refer to the Dublin Directory of Migrant-Led Churches and Chaplaincies and report that Christian worship in the city is conducted in 28 languages in addition to English and Irish. Other faith groups in Dublin also demonstrate linguistic diversity and the authors mention the translation services provided by the Islamic Cultural Centre between English/Arabic, French/Arabic, French/English, English/Kurdish and Kurdish/Arabic (Dublin City Report, 2014: 30).

It is noteworthy that many of these cultural and religious undertakings are connected to a wider social and cultural activism with an explicit political agenda devoted to protecting and defending the rights of migrant

Figure 4.5 Dublin New Year party (LUCIDE network, 2014)

communities and to improving their socio-economic situation. Here the organisation of and support for the learning of languages and the celebration of cultural practices are accompanied by the provision of legal, psychological or medical advice and aid, and all activities are closely related to the political struggle for equal rights and against social exclusion, racism and xenophobia. Evidence of this type of social activism is especially strong in the reports from Athens and Rome, and can be attributed to the relative weakness of state and municipal institutions with regard to providing services for minority ethnolinguistic groups and also – especially in Athens – to the strong tradition of anti-racist, left-wing activism.

Libraries

The specific role that public libraries play in the lives of speakers of minority languages and in immigrant communities in many cities worldwide has been described and analysed by a number of studies (Luevano-Molina, 2001; Williams, 2014). Public libraries are institutions which provide access to a wide range of information products from linguistic minority and majority cultures and can be particularly useful for newcomers who need to orient themselves in a new environment, providing them with the information necessary to adjust to a new society, while also allowing them to stay in touch with their cultures and languages of origin (Audunson *et al.*, 2011). It is therefore not surprising that all the City Reports mention public libraries that provide access to books and other media in many languages as important centres of cultural and multilingual diversity and exchange, and also as places where languages are learned and speakers of different languages come together.

A particularly noteworthy example from the Rome City Report (2014: 16) is the project *Biblioteche in lingua* (Language Libraries), which aims at 'promoting bilingualism as a value and cultural richness for migrants, and at preserving the language use and culture of the country of origin'. The participating libraries focus on acquiring books and media in the main languages spoken by the largest immigrant communities residing in the Rome area and were selected on the basis of demolinguistic data provided by the municipality of Rome. In Oslo, the city library services include a multilingual library that gives access to books and other media in 57 languages. Indicating the range of the plurilingual repertoires of the users of this service, the report informs us that 'the seven most loaned languages in 2014 were Arabic, Persian, Somali, Spanish, Tigrinya, Chinese, Polish, Russian and Urdu' (Oslo City Report, 2014: 18). The Osijek City Report (2014: 25) highlights the activities of the local City and University Library, which offers resources in a variety of languages and organises festivals to 'stimulate and promote the use of various languages spoken in the city and the region'. Other libraries cater for specific linguistic communities or provide language-learning possibilities. The London report refers to the Westminster Chinese Library, which has a team of four Chinese-speaking staff and provides access to over 50,000 books and films in Mandarin and other Chinese languages, while the authors of the Dublin City Report highlight the role the Open Learning Centre at Dublin's Central Library plays in providing language-learning possibilities for English, Irish and other languages.

Multilingual language policies

The survey used by the LUCIDE researchers who compiled the City Reports contained one question which respondents in many cities found rather difficult to answer, namely the question of whether they agreed 'with the way that [their city] approaches the issue of multilingualism'. Usually respondents took this as an opportunity to comment on specific aspects of multilingualism, such as educational policies concerning the learning of languages, translation or interpreting services or the use of other languages on websites or municipal signs, as, for example, in the Dublin report. At the same time, quite a few respondents simply stated that they were not aware of such an approach, as the summary of answers provided in the reports for London, Strasbourg and Osijek demonstrate. In London the majority of respondents were not able to answer the question either because they were not aware of the city's policies on multilingualism, or 'because they thought that there was not an identifiable coherent approach towards the issue' (London City Report, 2014: 43). A recurrent theme was the adverse effects of recent cuts in the budget for local government agencies on the provision of English classes and on translation and interpreting services. Respondents also identified 'a lack of serious effort with regard to multilingual policies' and criticised the fact that translation and interpreting were often viewed negatively and that not enough emphasis was put on the learning of foreign languages (London City Report, 2014: 43). In Rome, answers highlighted the activities of non-state organisations, while another respondent found that the issue is often 'approached through specific restricted projects' rather than as a city policy (Rome City Report, 2014: 45). Another interviewee believed that there was 'too much confusion' around the issue and 'not enough awareness' and criticised the lack of cooperation between city authorities and immigrant associations (Rome City Report, 2014: 46).

In the cities where linguistic diversity is primarily the result of the presence of autochthonous minorities whose languages enjoy official recognition and support (Sofia, Varna and Osijek), the reports point to the existence of these national policies and mention the role that municipal agencies have in implementing these programmes.

The difficulties that respondents had in identifying an approach by their city to the issue of multilingualism are summarised and explained in the report for Utrecht. Although the city of Utrecht has developed a cultural diversity policy which mentions multilingualism as a positive asset that the city wishes to exploit, the authors point out that this policy is not 'widely known' and that respondents commonly stated that 'they were unaware of it'. The authors explain this convincingly by the simple fact that, although the city has a strategy with regard to cultural diversity in general:

> [it] does not have an explicit policy with respect to multilingualism/ plurilingualism. Multilingualism-related matters are fragmented and belong to different departments, such as youth, education, internationalization [or] globalization or culture. There is no such thing as a [city] '(sub-) department of linguistic or multilingual matters'. (Utrecht City Report, 2014: 20)

If we accept this observation and explanation for the relative underdevelopment of urban policies related to linguistic diversity as valid, a number of conclusions might be drawn. On the one hand, cities as local political entities usually lack competences in the different policy areas and arenas related to multilingualism, and initiatives in this field probably need the coordinating power of central governments. Secondly, a lack of public awareness might also suggest that urban government agencies may not be very good at demonstrating their efforts and expertise in the management of cultural and linguistic diversity. On the other hand, the apparent lack of coherent political approaches to multilingualism at the city level might also confirm that the ways in which multilingualism is constructed conceptually by academic researchers simply do not correspond to the political arena where policies are mostly influenced by public discourses, debates and ideologies and above all political interests. This raises the general problem of how the knowledge gained by socially committed research can be translated into policies and practices. It also confirms the deeply political nature of all LPP and demonstrates, in the words of a recent observer, that 'linguists need to be more strategic about how they position themselves as participants in language ideological debates' (Wee, 2011: 21). Some of the language ideological debates which have a profound effect on how multilingualism is viewed and managed by policymakers and members of the public will be the subject of the concluding section of this chapter, which concerns the politics of urban linguistic diversity.

The Politics of Urban Linguistic Diversity

If LPP is about achieving certain objectives with regard to linguistic behaviours, language politics is related to normative decisions and to certain interests which define these outcomes as desirable in the first place. A look at the discussions and ideological debates surrounding urban multilingualism, and the political responses to it, can illuminate whose interests are at stake and whose interests prevail.

One area in which ideological notions about the value of linguistic diversity and the legitimacy of languages come to the forefront concerns the hierarchical relationship between languages and their visibility in the public realm of the city. A central hypothesis formulated and empirically tested during the research programme that preceded the writing of the LUCIDE City Reports was the assumption that 'some languages are more visible than others in city life'. The outcomes of the LUCIDE City Reports, as discussed in the two preceding chapters, broadly confirmed the hypothesis of a differential visibility of languages, demonstrating the widespread inequality of languages and the existence of a number of linguistic hierarchies in terms of more highly and less highly valued languages. As mentioned in Chapter 3, the authors of the Utrecht City Report (2014: 6) use the concept of 'prestigious and plebeian multilingualism' to describe the linguistic hierarchies they found in their city and explain that,

> prestigious plurilingualism refers to forms of plurilingualism among higher educated people who have two or more European languages in their repertoire [whereas] plebeian plurilingualism is mainly found among urban migrant communities. The languages [...] are usually home languages, learned informally as mother tongues and economically less valued. (Jaspers & Verschueren, 2011)

Along similar lines, the authors of the Hamburg City Report (2014: 15) comment on the 'fragile status of immigrant languages' in the city state's education system and observe that while 'the learning of 'foreign languages' including English is highly appreciated, the immigrants' heritage languages receive only desultory support'. The authors of the London City Report (2014: 74) conclude that 'speakers of languages which are perceived as high status – either because of their current economic value or historical circumstances – experience London in a fundamentally different way to those who speak less prestigious languages'. For the city of Madrid, the authors mention the 'poor visibility of immigrant languages in the city' and find that a 'linguistic ideology which perceives diversity as a threat to the nation's political and economic objectives is reflected in the recent promotion of bilingualism in schools, largely oriented towards the learning of English'. They contrast 'the enormous effort put into this task [...] with the indifference or neglect [shown towards] other languages that inhabit the shared space of the city as well as varieties which are co-official languages in other parts of the country' (Madrid City Report, 2014: 16). The authors of the report for Limassol (2014: 27) state that 'the wide use of English [...] and the neglect of other languages is one of the key themes that has emerged from the data'.

The City Reports also contain evidence of defensive language ideologies which confirm the hierarchies of languages and reflect the internalisation of

144 The Multilingual City

'values speakers associate with the linguistic differences they recognise' (Gal, 2012: 30) as well as the deeply embedded notion that the citizens of a nation state ought to use a single shared language (cf. Martin-Jones *et al.*, 2012: 3). The following extracts from the Strasbourg City Report highlight and contrast attitudes towards the use of Turkish and German in France held by the same respondent.

> *J'étais à la banque, à ma banque personnelle à Brumath qui est une petite ville. Au guichet, il y avait une dame assistante turque, et elle parlait avec une cliente devant en turc. Ça m'a choquée. Je ne suis pas d'accord avec ça. On est en France. On parle en français. J'étais derrière. Je comprenais pas qu'est-ce qu'elle disait. J'avais l'impression de me retrouver en Turquie. Je trouvais ça … on est en France. On parle en français, mais on ne parle pas une autre langue.*

> I was at the bank, my own bank in the small town of Brumath. At the counter, there was a Turkish female member of staff, and she was talking with the customer in front in Turkish. That shocked me. I don't agree with that. We are in France. We speak French. I was behind. I didn't understand what she was saying. I had the impression that I had been transported to Turkey. I found that … we are in France. We speak French, but we don't speak another language. (Strasbourg City Report, 2014: 46)

Later in the same interview the respondent recounts a further experience involving use of a language other than French:

> *J'étais à Strasbourg. J'ai acheté un pantalon pour [mentions child's name]. Il y avait des Allemands à côte de moi et la vendeuse, la caissière n'arrivait pas à parler un seul mot en allemand. Donc, c'est moi qui ai fais l'interprète. Ça me faisait bizarre. J'étais là en train d'acheter et j'ai fait l'interprète parce que la cliente elle voulait un renseignement et ni le caissière ni la vendeuse ne parlait absolument pas un seul mot en allemand et pourtant on est à coté de la frontière.*

> I was in Strasbourg. I bought a pair of trousers for [mentions child's name]. There were some Germans beside me and the shop assistant, the cashier couldn't manage to speak a single word of German. So, it was me who interpreted. It felt strange. I was there in the middle of buying something and I acted as an interpreter because the customer wanted information and neither the cashier nor the shop assistant spoke a single work of German and yet we are beside the border. (Strasbourg City Report, 2014: 47)

As is the case with many ideological convictions held deeply by individuals, the respondent is not aware of the obvious contradiction in their position. It might be possible to dismiss this as a rather crude, but ultimately not very important position, if related ideologies characterised by defensive monolingualism were not also in evidence in the formulation of official language policies. In May 2011, the council of the borough of Newham, one of London's ethnically and linguistically most diverse local government areas, decided to remove 'foreign language newspapers from its libraries' (BBC, 2011). The mayor of the borough justified the decision with the argument that removing the papers would 'encourage people to speak and learn English.' (BBC, 2011).

Supporting multilingualism through policy and practice

The overall picture which emerges from the LUCIDE City Reports is a situation where international prestige languages, first and foremost English and other larger European languages, occupy the top positions in the cities' linguistic hierarchies, whereas the languages of national and immigrant minorities are considered as less important and worthy of political support. These inequities between languages with regard to status and prestige principally reflect differences in the political status of speakers and their differential positions and integration into global, national and local polities and socioeconomic structures. These worldwide patterns of social stratification, labour division and mobilisation are replicated locally and are linked to the complex processes of urban ethnolinguistic differentiation observable in all of the LUCIDE cities.

The often contradictory and inconsistent multilingual policies and practices described in this chapter are simultaneously shaped from above, as politicians and policymakers try to manage and reconcile different interests and ideologies, and from below, as communities struggle for the recognition of their needs and interests. The politics of denial and recognition of other languages and their speakers, of integration and exclusion, are played out against the background of fiscal austerity and an increasingly xenophobic public discourse against immigration, characterised by the defensive revival of nationalist and racist ideologies. In a political environment where immigration is tolerated mainly for economic reasons, but the diversity associated with it is seen as a potential threat to an imagined national cohesion, multilingualism will not be welcomed as a cultural value as such. At the level of national politics and discourses, the evidence from LUCIDE's research points towards the continued force of what has been described as 'the linguistic ideology of the nation' alongside 'the linguistic ideology of the economy' (Jaffe, 2011: 83). While the former prescribes essentially monolingual linguistic assimilation, the latter sees multilingualism in terms of market value and employability and ranks languages accordingly. Another related development is the instrumentalisation of language and linguistic skills in debates about integration in which 'it is often a rhetorical trick of the powerful to play the language card in ways that shift attention from more challenging and difficult-to-fix social issues of structural inequality and exclusion of which language is often an intractable part' (Baynham, 2013: 310).

At the same time, city governments and local public service providers – responding to the logic of a multilingual urban reality, to the pressure and needs articulated by communities from below and the distinctly multicultural outlook that many of their citizens have adopted – often implement policies and practices which recognise the needs of local populations and acknowledge diversity as a positive public good and cultural value. Indeed, our data suggest that, in many cities, there is a potential disconnect and contradiction between municipal policies recognising, accommodating and supporting urban multilingualism, and national policies and political interventions which are characterised either by a narrow economic appreciation of multilingualism or the defensive rejection of linguistic diversity and the advocacy of integration through monolingual assimilation. In the next chapter we will consider how at city and community level diversity can be both accorded and valued in the all-important domain of education.

Public education is usually funded by central government, and schools are mostly required to follow national curricula. Multilingual cities nevertheless have a direct impact on public education, partly because the linguistic profile of their population determines the number of languages present in their schools and the proportion of pupils whose home language is not the language of schooling, and partly because policy implementation is always influenced by local context. According to the Common European Framework of Reference for Languages, the goal of language education should be the development of fully integrated plurilingual repertoires. In order to achieve this goal, schools must: ensure that all pupils become fully proficient in the official language of schooling; provide appropriate language support for pupils whose home language is not the language of schooling; as far as possible foster the literacy development of such pupils in their home language; and help all pupils to acquire communicative proficiency in the foreign language(s) of the curriculum. The chapter addresses each of these dimensions of language education in turn, mostly taking the LUCIDE City Reports as its starting point, and concludes by suggesting some ways in which schools might more effectively help their pupils to develop integrated plurilingual repertoires.

5 Languages at School: A Challenge for Multilingual Cities

David Little

> *Wer fremde Sprachen nicht kennt, weiß nichts von seiner eigenen.*
> *You come to know your own language by learning other languages.*
> Johann Wolfgang von Goethe

This chapter is concerned with languages and language teaching and learning in publicly funded education; its focus, in other words, is on what Chapter 4 defined as 'acquisition planning', the efforts that education systems make to develop the plurilingualism of the children and adolescents for whom they are responsible. In matters of education, cities are subject to national, state or provincial policies and legal instruments, and funding mostly comes from central government rather than the municipality. It might thus seem that education is an issue on which cities can have little direct impact. Nothing could be further from the truth, however, for two reasons. First, cities differ greatly in their multilingual fabric. This is partly a function of size: there are many fewer languages in Osijek and Varna than in Hamburg, Madrid and London. It is also a consequence of history: the number and range of languages in London and Madrid is in some measure due to the colonial histories in which the two cities played a central role, while the minority languages in Varna and Osijek are an inheritance of the porous internal borders of the Austro-Hungarian and Ottoman empires. Geographical position also plays a role: Limassol serves as a hub for shipping in the Mediterranean; the flow of immigration to Melbourne is predominantly from South and East Asia; and although Vancouver has a similar proportion of immigrants to Toronto, Montreal and Ottawa, its distance from Quebec means that it has very few French speakers. This infinite variation in multilingual fabric gives the school-going and immigrant populations of each city their own distinctive character, which generates a unique range of challenges. The second reason why cities have a direct impact on education arises from the inescapable fact that implementation is always a local phenomenon. It takes place in institutions whose character derives in large measure from the social, cultural and economic context in which they operate. In education, individual learning experience and achievement always depend on what happens in the individual classroom, which is shaped in part by the ethos of the individual school, which in turn is shaped in a multitude of ways by the city context in question.

The language of instruction in publicly funded schools is usually the national language, and one or more foreign languages are included in most curricula. But especially in multilingual cities, other languages are also present: the languages of minorities with legal status; 'heritage' languages that are not officially recognised but continue to play a role in the lives of minority communities; and the home languages of recent immigrants. According to the *Common European Framework of Reference for Languages* (CEFR), the goal for each pupil should be a fully integrated plurilingual repertoire, 'a communicative competence to which all knowledge and experience of language contributes and in which languages interrelate and interact' (Council of Europe, 2001: 4). In order to achieve this goal in a context of linguistic and cultural diversity, education systems must: give all pupils access to literacy and the language skills required for effective academic study in the official language of schooling; provide appropriate language support for pupils whose home language is not the language of schooling; as far as possible foster the literacy development of such pupils in their home language; and help all pupils to acquire communicative proficiency in the foreign language(s) of the curriculum. This chapter discusses each of these aspects of language education in turn, and concludes by suggesting some ways in which schools might more effectively help their pupils to develop integrated plurilingual repertoires.

The Language of Schooling

The role of language and communication in the educational process has been a major preoccupation of curriculum and pedagogical theory in the English-speaking world for many decades. One thinks, for example, of the Bullock Report, *A Language for Life* (Bullock, 1975), and the work of James Britton (e.g. Britton, 1970; Britton *et al.*, 1975) and Douglas Barnes (e.g. Barnes, 1976) in England; of Jerome Bruner's preoccupation with the language of education in the United States (e.g. Bruner, 1966, 1986); of Jim Cummins' work on informal and academic language proficiency in Canada (see the collection of his work edited by Baker & Hornberger, 2001); and the work of David Rose and J.R. Martin on discourse genres in Australia (e.g. Rose & Martin, 2012). These references are chosen more or less at random and could be multiplied many times over. What they share is an acknowledgement that there can be no learning without communication, and that our knowledge is inseparable from the language that we use to express, store and access it.

It is worth pursuing this thought further with reference to one of the sources just cited, Douglas Barnes' (1976) book, *From Communication to Curriculum*, which laid the foundations for much subsequent research into classroom communication. In this book Barnes has two complementary aims: to illustrate 'some ways in which children use speech in the course of learning, and to indicate how this depends upon the patterns of communication set up by teachers in their classrooms'; and to argue that 'since the learner's understandings are the *raison d'être* of schooling, an adequate curriculum theory must utilise an interactive model of teaching and learning' (Barnes, 1976: 9). According to Barnes, what is taught at school too often remains external to the learner: 'We partly grasp it, enough to answer the teacher's questions, but it remains someone else's knowledge, not ours. If we never use this knowledge we probably forget it' (Barnes, 1976: 81). The key challenge facing teachers is to find ways of exploiting the 'action knowledge' learners bring with them to the classroom so that 'school knowledge' (curriculum content) can build on what they already know:

> In so far as we use knowledge for our own purposes [...] we begin to incorporate it into our view of the world, and to use parts of it to cope with the exigencies of living. Once the knowledge becomes incorporated into that view of the world on which our actions are based I would say that it has become 'action knowledge'. (Barnes, 1976: 81)

The classroom experiments that Barnes describes sought to promote the incorporation of 'school knowledge' into learners' 'action knowledge' via the exploratory talk required to complete problem-solving activities carried out in small groups. Clearly, the success of such activities depends on the degree to which they connect with and exploit the learners' 'action knowledge'. For Barnes, exploratory talk was at once communication and thought, the medium but also the substance of learning: 'what [pupils] learn can hardly be distinguished from the ability to communicate it' (Barnes, 1976: 20). Almost every page of his theoretical chapters expands on this idea in one way or another. For example, control of metalinguistic and metacognitive resources allows the learner to manage the reflective and evaluative processes of exploratory talk: 'The more a learner controls his own language strategies, and the more he is enabled to think aloud, the more he can take responsibility for formulating explanatory hypotheses and evaluating them' (Barnes, 1976: 29). Language is not only a medium of communication but a means of managing learning: 'If we consider language solely as a communication system this could be taken to relegate the learner to a passive role as the recipient of socialisation; if we consider language as a means of learning we regard the learner as an active participant in the making of meaning' (Barnes, 1976: 31). And if language is a means of managing learning, that is because it is the tool we use to give reflective shape to our experience: 'Teachers have become so habituated to thinking of language in terms of communication that many have ceased to consider that it also performs important subjective functions, since it is the major means by which we consciously organise experience and reflect upon it' (Barnes, 1976: 84). Language, in other words, is the means by which we control and shape all aspects of our learning: 'Speech, while not identical with thought, provides a means of reflecting upon thought processes, and controlling them. Language allows one to consider not only what one knows but how one knows it, to consider, that is, the strategies by which one is manipulating the knowledge, and therefore to match the strategies more closely to the problem' (Barnes, 1976: 98).

Barnes' distinction between 'school knowledge' and 'action knowledge' and his interest in the use of informal modes of spoken interaction gradually to appropriate concepts and knowledge that belong to more formal registers seem to anticipate Cummins' celebrated distinction between 'basic interpersonal communication skills' (BICS) and 'cognitive academic language proficiency' (CALP; see, for example, Cummins, 1979), later simplified to 'conversational' and 'academic' language proficiency (Cummins, 1991). Conversational language, typical of informal communication in the world outside the classroom, is context embedded: comprehension and production of meaning are supported by paralinguistic cues (intonation, gesture, eye contact, feedback, etc.) and by features of the physical situation (persons and objects in focus, the sunshine that is pleasantly warm, the rain that is making you wet, etc.). Communication of this kind is a precondition for child language acquisition and informal acquisition of second and foreign languages; it is also what produces our 'action knowledge'. The language used to mediate curriculum content in classrooms and other academic contexts, on the other hand, tends to be context reduced: cues to meaning are primarily linguistic, contained in the spoken or written text we seek to understand or produce. Also, different areas of study have their own terminology and discourse genres that generate discipline or subject-specific dialects; knowledge of subject content necessarily includes familiarity with appropriate terminology and discourse conventions. Academic language is not confined to education, of course; it is used in a multitude of contexts in the world outside the classroom or lecture theatre, which means that mastery of it is an important life skill.

These matters are not explicitly in focus in any of the LUCIDE City Reports, but they provide an essential preliminary to discussion of a concern that is present in many of them – the linguistic integration of pupils whose home language is not the language of schooling.

Integrating Minority Language Pupils

The challenge

Educational underachievement by pupils from immigrant backgrounds is not a new phenomenon, but it has been brought into especially sharp focus by the OECD's Programme for International Student Assessment (PISA) surveys, carried out in 2000, 2003, 2006 and 2009/2010 (for details see www.oecd.org), which show that in most countries immigrant pupils lag behind their non-immigrant peers. The surveys are motivated by the assumption that in a knowledge-based society national development and economic performance depend crucially on educational outcomes. Countries that underperform in comparison to other countries are vulnerable to the charge that they are making less of their human capital than they should.

As the Toronto City Report points out, immigrant pupils often come from countries with low standards of education and so have gaps in their knowledge, and they may have low levels of literacy in their home language. Also, immigrant pupils are more likely than others to be living in poverty, which affects their educational progress; poverty may mean that they are susceptible to a high rate of mobility, which leads to discontinuities in their schooling, and they are at higher than average risk of dropping out, which results in unemployment and dependency on benefits. At the same time, it is important to recognise that the term 'immigrant' applies not only to those who are socio-economically deprived but also to newcomers with a wide range of educational qualifications and skills; as recent research has shown, an immigrant background does not automatically lead to educational underachievement. Australian-born pupils from East Asian families, for example, significantly outperform their Australian-heritage peers in the maths component of PISA (Jerrim, 2014). This is likely to be due to multiple factors, including East Asian parents' attitudes to education and their own levels of educational achievement, but language seems not to be an issue: 'there is very little difference in average PISA maths test scores between second-generation East Asian immigrants who speak English in the family home and those who do not' (Jerrim, 2014: 11).

In any case, as Cummins (2013: 7) points out, immigrant students' performance tends to be better in countries like Canada and Australia, which have encouraged immigration, developed a coherent infrastructure to support integration, and favour immigrants with strong educational qualifications. Even in those countries, however, integrating pupils whose home language is not the language of schooling can be problematic, and the nature of the linguistic challenge is almost infinitely variable. As the Vancouver report notes, children from linguistic minorities tend to be concentrated in certain schools, which means that the task of integration is not shared evenly across the system. Immigrant pupils may also come from a wide range of different language backgrounds, and the relationship between their linguistic repertoires and the language of schooling is subject to great variation. According to the Madrid report, for example, approximately 50% of immigrant pupils speak one of the South American varieties of Spanish – Ecuadorian, Dominican, Peruvian, Colombian or Cuban. They are obviously in a very different situation from the 26% of immigrant pupils who come from European countries, especially Romania, Bulgaria, Poland and Russia. According to the Toronto City Report, immigrant pupils there come from more than 100 countries and speak more than 70 languages; translations into more than 20 languages are needed for school–home communication. The situation in London is still more diverse.

Interestingly, in two of the smaller LUCIDE cities, Varna and Osijek, the integration of immigrant pupils is not reported as a problem. The Varna City Report tells us that immigrants mostly come from neighbouring countries whose languages are closely related to Bulgarian, so their children have no difficulty 'picking up' the language of schooling. The Osijek report mentions that there is no support available to help teachers to cope with immigrant pupils; on the other hand, numbers are small and the report mentions the city librarian's impression that immigrant children master Croatian very quickly. This may well be the case. If immigrant pupils are a rarity it is entirely possible that they receive a level of attention, from their teachers and their peers, that accelerates their linguistic and social integration.

Approaches to integration in the LUCIDE cities

The integration of immigrant pupils is mentioned as a major educational challenge in the LUCIDE reports from AAK/Athens, Dublin, Hamburg, Limassol, London, Madrid, Ottawa, Toronto and Vancouver. All but one of these reports state that special measures are in place to meet the challenge, although it is beyond their scope to provide detailed information on structures and teaching approaches. Broadly speaking, there are three ways of providing for the development of immigrant pupils' proficiency in the language of schooling: by teaching them separately from the mainstream; by assigning them to mainstream classes but organising separate instruction in the language of schooling; and by providing them with language support in the mainstream classroom. In principle, the three modes can be used in sequence, the first in an initial phase of reception, the second in a period of transition, and the third when immigrant pupils are deemed capable of participating fully in mainstream education, even though they still need language support. In practice, most countries tend to emphasise one or other of the modes in their policy documents, although the boundaries between them may not be firmly fixed. At the end of the 1990s, Ireland, for example, adopted the practice of providing each pupil whose home language was neither English nor Irish with two years of English language support.

The Department of Education and Skills expected that this support would be delivered to immigrant pupils outside their mainstream class but insisted that the responsibility for immigrant pupils' educational progress lay with class teachers in primary schools and subject teachers in post-primary schools. According to the OECD (2006), most countries favour the third organisational mode, immersion in the mainstream, although it acknowledges that systematic language support is not always provided. In any case, school size, the number and proportion of immigrant pupils in the school, the range of ethnicities and home languages present, and many other local factors combine to produce large variations in practice, not just from country to country but from school to school within the same city.

The Madrid, Dublin and London reports mention that language support for immigrant pupils has been badly affected by funding cuts arising from the economic crisis of recent years. In London teaching assistants have been appointed instead of specialist teachers, while in Dublin English language support has become closely associated with learning support, which is provided for pupils with learning difficulties. This may seem to confirm the already widespread 'deficit view' of migrant pupils, according to which having a home language other than the language of schooling is seen as something to be 'remediated'. According to the educational leaders and teachers interviewed for the London report, this view persists in their city, along with the belief that the presence in schools of large numbers of pupils whose home language is not English somehow disadvantages monolingual English-speaking pupils. This belief may help to explain the invisibility of pupils' home languages in many schools. As one of the London interviewees observed: 'There are 76 languages spoken by children in my school and we operate an English only rule on site. All these languages are invisible apart from Spanish and German as [modern foreign languages]' (London City Report, 2014: 30). The report also notes a tendency to place bilingual children in low ability sets and a general failure to recognise the skills that they have in their own language. A further problem mentioned in several reports is that teachers rarely enter the profession equipped to deal with multilingual classrooms; the London report also points out that there is no special training for head teachers and school leadership teams.

In contrast to these largely negative views, the Hamburg City Report tells us that there has been a recent improvement in the provision of support to develop migrant pupils' proficiency in German and to involve their parents more effectively in their education. This is due in no small measure to two projects of the University of Hamburg – FörMig and LiMA – which are discussed in the next section.

Supporting integration: Three examples

The OECD report, *Where Immigrant Students Succeed*, found that 'policies to help immigrant students attain proficiency in the language of instruction have common characteristics but vary in terms of explicit curricula and focus' (OECD, 2006: 10). This consideration, together with the generally rather bleak view of integration presented by the City Reports, prompts the question: What forms of language support should be provided? In this section we describe some research activities undertaken and tools and approaches developed by universities in LUCIDE cities. Their relevance to the larger argument of this chapter is that they begin to offer ways of breaking down the barriers between the languages involved in the education process. Two of the three examples refer to English as an additional language, which reflects the large amount of research and development Anglophone countries have undertaken in this area. On the other hand, the most ambitious and wide-ranging projects we discuss were carried out in Germany.

The English Language Support Programme

According to the argument with which we began this chapter, educational success depends on mastery of academic language, which is inseparable from mastery of academic content. In other words, the educational integration of immigrant pupils ultimately depends on how effectively language is brought into focus in the different curriculum subjects. This requires the language-across-the-curriculum perspective that is one of the central concerns of the Council of Europe's Languages of Schooling project (www.coe.int/lang). But it is one thing to offer general descriptions of academic language, quite another to develop practical tools that teachers can use in their classrooms. That was the task undertaken by the English Language Support Programme (ELSP), which was part of Trinity College Dublin's Trinity Immigration Initiative (2007–2010).

The ELSP set out to describe the language of six core curriculum subjects – English, geography, history, CSPE (civic, social and political education), mathematics, and science – in the first three years of Irish post-primary schooling, the so-called junior cycle. It did so by carrying out a corpus linguistic analysis of the most commonly used textbooks and recent public exam papers in each subject. This approach was chosen because textbooks are the principal source of disciplinary knowledge, underpinning teacher talk in the classroom and the spoken and written production required of pupils, and the academic language used in exams reflects the language of textbooks.

Once the various corpora had been compiled, the first task was to compute the type:token ratio for each corpus, that is, the ratio of the total number of different words to the total word count. It was striking that the English corpus contained significantly more types and tokens than any of the others – English textbooks contain more words and have a richer vocabulary than textbooks for other subjects. On the other hand, although the maths corpus was larger than the corpora for history and geography, its lexicon was much smaller, thus confirming one's intuitive sense that maths operates with a specialised but limited vocabulary.

The next task was to compute the most frequent content words for each subject, which gives a general sense of lexical and semantic links across the curriculum while revealing that there are very different kinds of pattern within the different subjects. This became clearer still when the top 10 subject-specific keywords were computed (that is, words around which significant amounts of information cluster). 'Ireland' is the most frequent content word in the history corpus, 'Irish' comes fourth and 'British' seventh. But when the focus shifts to keywords, 'British' comes fourth, 'Ireland' comes fifth, 'Irish' goes down to ninth and 'Hitler' creeps in at number 10. The frequency counts of content words and keywords provided a basis for the extensive array of subject-specific learning materials that are available on the ELSP website (www.elsp.ie) – materials that have been accessed from many different countries.

Further analysis of the corpora yielded a wealth of more detailed insights. For example, for each corpus it was possible to identify the most frequently occurring nouns. In the English corpus the singular forms 'story' and 'poem' occur many more times than their plural forms, whereas there is no significant difference between the frequency of 'question' and 'questions', 'character' and 'characters'. Further analysis focused on the distribution of word classes across subjects, subject-specific collocations and the top five grammatical and semantic categories in each corpus. It was also possible to identify subject-specific semantic fields and sort the words within them by frequency. Three semantic fields fairly obviously define the chief concerns of CSPE, for example: 'belonging to a group', 'government' and 'green issues'. It was also possible to explore semantic links across the different corpora. For instance, the semantic field 'paper documents and writing' cropped up in all six subjects, 'cause/effect-relations' only in geography, history, CSPE and science, 'people' and 'places' in English, geography, history and CSPE, and 'substances and materials' in geography, history, CSPE and science. These and other results of the corpus analysis remain largely unexploited: by the time they were available, the funding had run out and the economic crisis had arrived. For a fuller account of this project, which could be replicated for any language of schooling, see Kostopoulou (2011, 2013) and Lyons (2013).

Cummins' Literacy Engagement Framework

The London report makes the point that, in schools where between them the pupils may speak as many as 40 languages, those languages are likely to be invisible, as though they have no contribution to make to pupils' developing mastery of the language of schooling. Cummins' Literacy Engagement Framework (Cummins, 2013: 18) is based on the opposite belief, claiming that literacy engagement, which presupposes free access to books and other printed materials, directly determines literacy achievement. Cummins bases this claim on the findings of empirical research, pointing out that the PISA studies have 'consistently reported a strong relationship between reading engagement and reading achievement among 15-year-old students in countries around the world' (Cummins, 2013: 18). The framework specifies four instructional dimensions that Cummins argues are critical to enabling all pupils, but especially immigrants, to engage actively with literacy from an early stage of their schooling: (1) their ability to understand is scaffolded in a variety of ways; (2) instruction connects to their lives outside school by activating and building on prior knowledge (which may be encoded in their home language); (3) instruction affirms their identity – academic, linguistic and cultural – by enabling them to showcase their literacy achievements in their home language as well as the language of schooling; and (4) a variety of techniques are used to extend their knowledge of and control over language across the curriculum. As this description should make clear, Cummins' Literacy Engagement Framework is a practical restatement of the Council of Europe's ideal of plurilingual education (see, for example, Coste et al., 2009). Activities like the production of dual-language texts, in which immigrant pupils use their L1 writing abilities as a stepping stone or scaffold to writing in the language of schooling, their L2, further affirm their identity (see also Cummins & Early, 2011). This engagement of learners' identity and prior knowledge in their learning recalls Douglas Barnes' argument that learners use their 'action knowledge' gradually to appropriate 'school knowledge'. It is a point to which we shall return when we consider two further issues – the role that home languages can play in immigrant pupils' education, and innovative approaches to foreign language learning.

The FörMig and LiMA projects of the University of Hamburg

The FörMig project (Förderung von Kindern und Jugendlichen mit Migrationshintergrund [Support for children and adolescents from migrant backgrounds]; www.blk-foermig.uni-hamburg.de) was funded for five years, from 2004 to 2009, involved 10 of the 16 German federal states, and brought together expertise from across the country to address questions of learning and education in linguistically and culturally heterogeneous settings. The project was particularly concerned to develop measures that would support children and adolescents from migrant backgrounds at key points of transition in the education system: from kindergarten to primary, from primary to secondary, and from secondary to vocational training. Coordinated by the University of Hamburg, FörMig involved a range of institutions engaged in language education – family, school, daycare, libraries, clubs and societies, companies and businesses – helping them to collaborate in the development of language support schemes. One of the project's central concerns was to foster close links between schools and the surrounding community. Accordingly, it implemented a network of 'developmental partnerships' comprising a 'basic unit' (for example, local schools, a municipal daycare centre, a parents' initiative and the town administration) and 'strategic partners' (for example, the public library, the local education authority, the educational psychology service, a centre for early child development and a medical association).

FörMig's principal research-lead activities were in diagnostics and integrated language education. It helped to develop and test tools to support the diagnosis of individual language development and inform the design and implementation of individualised language support plans (Gogolin et al., 2005; Reich et al., 2007). The work on integrated language education adopted a language-across-the-curriculum approach, a major concern being to promote cooperation between the different language areas of the curriculum and subjects traditionally thought not to have a language focus. A separate strand was devoted to the competences and resources young people need if they are to make a successful transition into vocational and workplace training (Ohm et al., 2007). Each of the 10 participating *Länder* had its own project dealing with language support and/or diagnostics.

In 2010 the FörMig-Kompetenzzentrum was established (www.foermig.uni-hamburg.de), a centre of expertise the purpose of which was to engage in research that could inform educational practice, policymaking and public perceptions regarding matters of bi- and multilingualism. It came to an end in 2013, to be succeeded by new research activity.

The Research Cluster LiMA (Linguistic Diversity Management in Urban Areas; www.lima.uni-hamburg.de) was funded from 2010 to 2014. Its purpose was to bring together expertise in multilingualism (linguistics and education sciences) at the University of Hamburg and focus it on the investigation of migration-induced multilingualism as found in urban centres worldwide. In particular, it sought to explore ways of translating migration-induced multilingualism into advantages for individuals and society and benefits for the cultural and economic development of urban centres. LiMA's core research activities comprised a panel study and three interdisciplinary research networks. The panel study investigated the plurilingual development of individuals over time, periodically assessing them in the two languages in which they were most proficient, and collected data on the individual and social conditions that help to shape plurilingual development. As well as pursuing its own research agenda, the panel study served a transversal function for the research cluster as a whole, applying standard instruments to the measurement of potentially significant variables, taking on specific research questions from other LiMA projects and providing them with data for further analysis.

The nature of school instruction has largely been ignored in research that explores the relation between plurilingualism and academic achievement. The first of the interdisciplinary research networks, the LiMA video study, set out to remedy this lack, analysing video-recordings of lessons in order to identify ways of orienting instruction to the specific needs of plurilingual students, especially as regards the development of their proficiency in academic language at the point of transition between lower and upper secondary education. The second interdisciplinary research network, 'Multilingual communication in urban spaces', was concerned with the societal relevance of multilingualism from linguistic, ethnological and urban sociological perspectives. It addressed questions like: Which social contexts reveal the potential as well as the challenges of multilingualism? Which strategies are most likely to allow us to deal efficiently with multilingualism, responding to its challenges and exploiting its potential? And how are we to understand multilingualism empirically as well as theoretically? The third interdisciplinary research network, 'Language contact, language variation and language acquisition', addressed the fact that, whereas studies of language contact have long focused on the interaction of two language systems, in today's urban areas contact between more than two languages is rapidly becoming the norm. Within each research network there were a number of individual research projects, details of which will be found on the LiMA website.

LiMA provided training for postgraduate students, organised summer schools and a series of public lectures, and was responsible for a large number of publications, among them three edited books that include contributions from outside Germany: Siemund *et al.* (2013), Duarte and Gogolin (2013) and Grommes and Hu (2014).

The FörMig and LiMA projects have stimulated the development of a new culture of language education in Germany and established the University of Hamburg as a major international centre for the interdisciplinary study of multilingualism. Their particular strength derives from the strong links they forged not only between universities and schools but also between educational institutions and their wider administrative and social contexts. In this respect in particular, they provide an example that could usefully be followed in other multilingual cities.

Minority Languages in Education

Minority languages with official status

Irish is the first official language of Ireland, and French has equal status with English in Canada. Thus in a legal sense neither is a minority language, although each is the first language of a minority of the national population. Dublin has Irish-medium primary and post-primary schools, French is the language of schooling in Quebec, and other Canadian provinces offer French immersion schooling. In addition, Irish is an obligatory school subject for the English-speaking majority in Ireland, and French is the principal 'foreign' language taught in English-medium schools in Canada. According to the Vancouver report, English-speaking parents see it as an advantage to enrol their children in French immersion programmes; some parents of English-speaking children in Ireland have the same view of Irish immersion programmes.

In Canada, Aboriginal (or First Nations) children are entitled to receive educational support in their heritage languages, and some Canadian provinces provide kindergarten and early primary schooling in those languages. The Toronto report tells us that, according to the Aboriginal Peoples Survey, 'parents of 60% of Aboriginal children in non-reserve areas believed it was very important or somewhat important for their children to speak and understand an Aboriginal language' (Norris, 2007: 24); also the Canadian Council on Learning (2009) has emphasised that the educational outcomes of Aboriginal pupils are significantly worse than those for non-Aboriginal pupils. The Vancouver report notes that British Columbia's First Peoples' Heritage, Language and Culture Act is meant to 'support and advise ministries of government on initiatives, programs and services related to Native heritage, language and culture' (First Peoples' Heritage, Language and Culture Council, 2010).

Two other City Reports mention provision for linguistic minorities with legal status. In Varna, schools are required to offer elective mother tongue courses for members of four recognised ethnic minorities: Armenian, Turkish, Hebrew and Roma. However, these courses have not been taken in recent years because they are taught at the same time as subjects like mathematics, history and foreign languages, which are more important for success in exams. The Osijek report explains that Croatia offers three models of minority language education: (A) education through a minority language; (B) bilingual education in Croatian and a heritage language; and (C) elective modules in a minority language. The report cites two examples of model A in the city (involving Serbian and Hungarian) and five examples of model C (involving German, Hungarian, Albanian, Slovakian and Macedonian). In the Croatian context, model A leads to segregation, as one of the pupils at the Serbian school complained to the authors of the report (other pupils, however, believed that immersion schooling gave them membership of two communities); while model C, with a maximum of six lessons a week, may fail to achieve significant language-learning outcomes, especially if pupils are not already proficient in their heritage language. The report mentions that it is not always possible to recruit qualified teachers for model C courses. It is striking that there are no examples of model B, which avoids the charge of segregation, at least in terms of language, while in principle making the heritage language in question available to pupils from outside the heritage community. Two Slovakian-speaking pupils interviewed by the authors of the Osijek report explained that they had chosen to take model C courses in Slovakian in order to improve their final grades, which play an important part in enrolment in secondary schooling. As the authors point out, this raises an important issue of motivation.

Support for languages without legal status

Most of the home languages present in the LUCIDE cities' schools do not have official status, which means that schools are not obliged to teach them.

In Strasbourg, pupils at all levels of schooling, regardless of their nationality or cultural background, can enrol in any of the optional heritage language classes provided free of charge by the region and supervised by an inspector from the Ministry of Education. The teaching of heritage languages is also supported by bilateral agreements between France and Algeria, Spain, Italy, Morocco, Portugal, Serbia, Tunisia and Turkey.

Especially in larger cities, minority and immigrant communities may organise their own 'community', 'complementary' or 'supplementary' schools, which operate outside regular school hours, especially at weekends. Such schools, which may or may not receive funding and/or other forms of official support, aim to develop literacy in home languages and maintain awareness of minorities' cultures of origin; they may also provide pupils with support in mainstream curriculum languages and content learning. The London City Report refers to research carried out by London Metropolitan University in 2010 that identified more than 1000 supplementary schools in England, which operate apart from mainstream schools, although they may use their premises and on occasion collaborate with them. Kenner and Ruby (2012), for example, report on action research in two London schools that showed how mainstream and complementary teachers can work together to exploit the plurilingual repertoires of pupils from minority communities to their educational advantage.

In some cities, community initiatives are developed collaboratively with the educational authorities. For instance, the Toronto report mentions a joint project of the Greek community and the Toronto District School Board that offers speakers and non-speakers of Greek a Greek language and culture programme in schools around Toronto. This is by no means an isolated example; in 2005, nearly 40% of the schools in Toronto were offering 57 different heritage and international language classes to their students (Basu, 2011). In Melbourne, where about 25% of pupils complete schooling with a second language qualification, more than 200 community schools offer courses in 55 languages. The City Report notes that the state of Victoria has been especially responsive to languages other than English, which explains the large-scale provision of community-based courses as well as the fact that qualifications in some 50 languages are accepted for university admission scores. Currently 150 language communities in Melbourne benefit from state support. In Canada the *Commission Scolaire de Montréal* funds the *Programme d'enseignement des langues d'origine* (PELO), which teaches children their mother tongue as well as French at school. In place since 1978, the programme helps immigrant pupils to maintain and improve their skills in their home language; it is also open to other interested pupils. In the last 20 years, approximately 6500 pupils have benefited annually from this programme, chiefly in Montreal's elementary schools.

For the most part, however, publicly funded schools in the LUCIDE cities make few concessions to the languages of minority and immigrant communities. For example, in AAK/Athens there is no official policy to help immigrants maintain their home language; in Limassol, where the school-going population is increasingly diverse, the implementation of intercultural education (an official aim) is constrained by the rigidity of the official curriculum; in Madrid there are few initiatives designed to help immigrant pupils maintain their home language; and in Utrecht migrant languages have little place in the school system, although the Netherlands previously had schemes to teach migrant pupils in their home language. There seems to be a widespread tendency to concentrate exclusively on the language of schooling. The Madrid report tells us that teachers tend to promote exclusive use of Spanish as the best route to immigrant pupils' integration, while the Dublin report notes that immigrant parents are often encouraged to speak English with their children at home, and some post-primary schools discourage the use of home languages outside lessons.

Although the Irish system makes no provision to teach immigrants' languages, it offers school-leaving (Leaving Certificate) exams in 15 EU languages that are not part of the curriculum: Bulgarian, Czech, Danish, Dutch, Estonian, Finnish, Modern Greek, Hungarian, Latvian, Lithuanian, Polish, Portuguese, Romanian, Slovakian and Swedish. In order to take the exam in one of these languages pupils must come from another EU country, speak the language in question as a first language, be following a general programme of study leading to the Leaving Certificate and be entered for the Leaving Certificate exam in English. Although aimed at native speakers, these exams are modelled on the first foreign language final written paper of the European Baccalaureate. It is tempting to conclude that they serve little purpose other than to provide candidates with easy points for university entrance; as one of the Dublin interviewees pointed out, 'students can get up to 100 points towards going to third level for reading and writing their first language' (Dublin City Report, 2014: 42). Compare this with the comment from the two pupils in Osijek who were taking a model C course in Slovakian (see page 159 above).

Cummins' interdependence hypothesis

Cummins formulated his interdependence hypothesis to counter the common-sense view that time spent teaching literacy in a 'minority' language would be better spent improving literacy skills in the language of schooling. The hypothesis proposes that:

> To the extent that instruction in Lx is effective in promoting proficiency in Lx, transfer of this proficiency to Ly will occur provided there is adequate exposure to Ly (either in school or environment) and adequate motivation to learn. (Cummins, 1981: 29)

For example:

> [In] a Spanish-English bilingual program in the United States, Spanish instruction that develops Spanish reading and writing skills is not just developing Spanish skills, it is also developing a deeper conceptual and linguistic proficiency that is strongly related to the development of literacy in the majority language (English). In other words, although the surface aspects (e.g. pronunciation, fluency, etc.) of different languages are clearly separate, there is an underlying conceptual proficiency or knowledge base that is common across languages. This common underlying proficiency makes possible the transfer of concepts, literacy skills, and learning strategies from one language to another. (Cummins, 2008: 52)

According to this hypothesis, whatever benefits accrue from education in a 'minority' language need not be bought at the cost of underachievement in the 'majority' language. By now there is a large body of empirical research that supports this view (for reviews, see, for example, August & Shanahan, 2006; Genesee et al., 2006). More research is needed in order to explain in detail why bilingual programmes achieve their goals, but it is already clear that the more languages the individual can use fluently, the better. In particular, research into the advantages of bilingualism shows that access to literacy in two languages benefits cognitive development (Allen, 2004; Bialystok, 2001; Bialystok et al., 2005). Thus the home language skills of immigrant pupils should be fostered by whatever means are practically available, partly as a matter of human rights and partly in order to increase society's linguistic and cultural capital. The development of literacy skills is especially important since it is a prerequisite for extensive mastery of any language and the possibility of using that language in professional life. The interdependence principle also implies that it makes sense to encourage the use of home languages to understand and internalise key concepts that underlie the different curriculum subjects. In addition, use of the home language at school affirms the migrant pupil's identity and helps to counteract any tendency to stigmatise him or her for membership of a group that is perceived as being linguistically inferior. In a comprehensive research review, Schofield and Bangs (2006: 93) conclude that 'the threat of being judged and found wanting based on negative stereotypes related to one's social category membership, can seriously undercut the achievement of immigrant and minority students'.

An alternative to bilingual education

Assuming that there is a readiness to accommodate and fund initiatives designed to exploit and further develop immigrant pupils' home language skills, the kind of programmes that can be offered depend on two factors: the concentration of speakers of particular languages in particular areas and schools, and the availability of qualified teachers who are proficient speakers of those languages. These factors are evidently present in the case of Chinese in Vancouver where, as the City Report tells us, some schools offer English/Chinese bilingual programmes. Such programmes are likely to be feasible in large cities where immigrant communities are substantial and tend to live in the same general area. London provides an extreme example: Polish, Bengali and Gujarati have more than 100,000 speakers each; French, Urdu, Portuguese, Turkish, Spanish, Arabic, Tamil and Panjabi have between 68,000 and 84,000 speakers each; and Somali, Chinese languages and Italian have around 50,000 speakers each. Of course, providing bilingual programmes for immigrant populations of this size may be politically impossible if indigenous pupils have no interest in learning immigrant languages and there is a general hostility to immigration and the linguistic and cultural diversity that it brings.

In any case, arrangements of this kind cannot be put in place when immigrant communities are dispersed or schools are educating pupils from a large number of different language backgrounds. What can be done in these circumstances to exploit and further develop immigrant pupils' home language skills? One possibility is to promote 'functional multilingual learning' (Sierens & Van Avermaet, 2013: 217), which entails that teachers encourage immigrant pupils to use their home language when performing collaborative tasks, even though the teacher does not know that language. This is one of the characteristics of an approach described in the Dublin City Report:

> The work of the Principal of Scoil Bhríde Cailíní in Blanchardstown, Dr Déirdre Kirwan, and her colleagues can be cited as an example of good practice in supporting pupils learning English, as well as valuing all 40 home languages of those pupils – more than 70% of pupils are from a non-English-speaking background. The languages pupils bring with them to school are seen as resources which can support the learning of English and Irish – represented visually on the school's walls as the roots of 'language trees', roots which must also be nurtured and watered [Figure 5.1]. Above these 'home language roots', pupils stick on leaves of language-learning accomplishments, creating a colourful and growing image of the interconnectedness of linguistic repertoires and a reminder that language learning does not happen in isolation [Figure 5.2]. Pupils are encouraged to draw on their linguistic knowledge to make guesses, for example, about the meanings of new words and how words are connected across languages. They are free to use their home languages to communicate with other pupils as well as pupils from neighbouring language families, and they are indeed encouraged to reflect on why and how, for example, some of them can understand aspects of other

language varieties when spoken slowly, without having learned them. The school's journey of encouraging multilingualism as a way of encouraging the successful acquisition of English as an Additional Language is demonstrated in the girls' homework projects, for example, through creative writing where pupils use each of their languages (e.g. English, Irish, French and Urdu) to recount parts of a story, or through small translation projects. Most of these pupils initially enrolled at Scoil Bhríde Cailíní without any English, yet the language tree and supporting 'proofs' of homework, demonstrate how English as an Additional Language can be supported through multilingual language learning and sustained language awareness initiatives which receive whole-school support. (Dublin City Report, 2014: 15–16; see also Kirwan, 2013 and, for an account of similar work in France, Auger, 2013)

Figure 5.1 Our language tree (LUCIDE network, 2014)

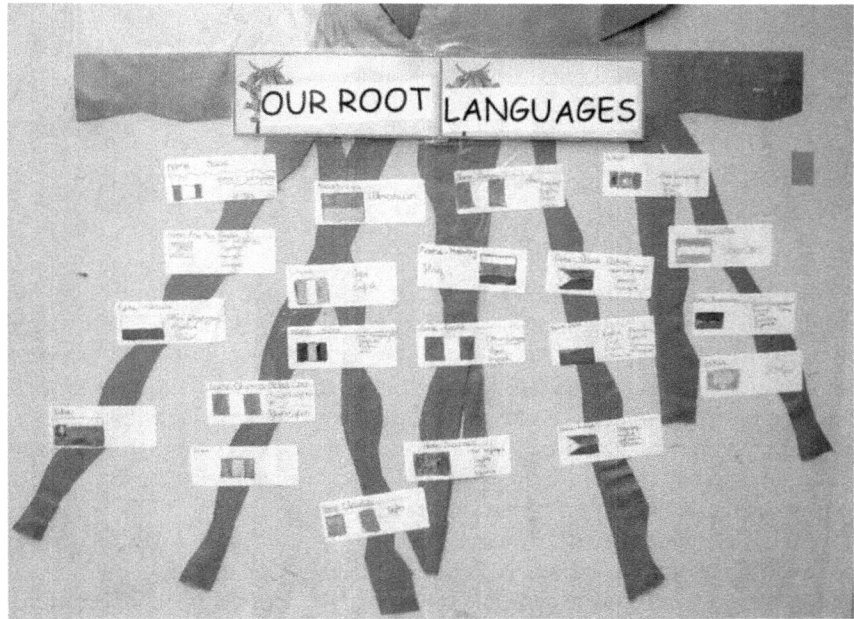

Figure 5.2 Our root languages (LUCIDE network, 2014)

More generally, the Utrecht City Report emphasises the importance of home language maintenance for the educational success of pupils from migrant backgrounds, citing the example of a primary school in Schiedam, near Rotterdam:

> In this school parents are strongly involved: they are informed about language development and how they can stimulate this at home. Special attention is paid to Dutch as a second language and at the same time teachers and parents are aware of the positive effect on children's identity of home language maintenance. Parents realise how important it is for their children to have a positive attitude towards their home languages. This school in Schiedam has significantly higher scores on cognitive tests than other schools with a comparable population. (Utrecht City Report, 2014: 31)

Similarly, the Hamburg City Report quotes a Turkish-speaking teacher who finds that using Turkish phrases in her German-speaking classroom is an effective teaching strategy even for those students who do not speak Turkish:

> My students like that. They laugh and even integrate those phrases into their everyday language. They realise that their teacher is bilingual. In the

beginning I was concerned about the reaction of the German parents, but they don't mind. At least they haven't complained. They tell me that they now hear Turkish words at home. (Hamburg City Report, 2014: 14–15)

Foreign Language Learning

What the LUCIDE City Reports tell us

All but one of the LUCIDE City Reports give some account of foreign language learning in their schools. The exception is the London report, which concentrates on English as an additional language for pupils from minority communities, although the business people interviewed by the authors of the report regretted the decline of foreign language learning in English schools. In Canada the most widely taught second languages are English in Quebec and French in the other provinces; according to the Montreal report, Spanish may also be taken at secondary schools in the city. In the non-English speaking LUCIDE cities the first foreign language is always English. Other languages offered tend to be one or more of: French, German, Spanish, Italian or Russian. Sometimes individual schools offer courses in less commonly taught languages – Chinese, Japanese and Arabic, for example, in some schools in Sofia. The introduction of new foreign languages is not always welcomed; in Utrecht one school's plan to teach Turkish to all first-year pupils was blocked by political protest.

Foreign language learning is an obligatory part of schooling in all the LUCIDE cities apart from Dublin. There, however, Irish is compulsory from the beginning of primary to the end of post-primary schooling, and the four university colleges that make up the National University of Ireland require a school-leaving qualification in a foreign language for matriculation. Again in the non-English-speaking cities, foreign language learning typically begins in primary school. In AAK/Athens pupils start to learn English in Grade 3 and French or German in Grade 5; in Utrecht English is learnt in the last two years of primary school; in Strasbourg pupils begin to learn their first foreign language (German) at the age of seven, their second foreign language (usually English) at the age of 11, and (optionally) a third foreign language at the age of 14; in Sofia and Varna the first foreign language is introduced in Grade 2, the second foreign language in Grade 4 and a third foreign language may be taken after Grade 8.

One indicator of the importance that educational systems – and parents – attach to foreign language proficiency is the introduction of language learning at kindergarten, which is mentioned in the Sofia and Osijek City Reports. The benefits that this brings can be undermined, however, by discontinuity in language learning from kindergarten to primary school. One of the stakeholders interviewed by the authors of the Osijek report, for example, complained that children who begin to learn German in kindergarten may not be able to continue with the language at primary school. Parents decide which foreign language their children will take at primary school; most opt for English, and that weakens demand for German and may in due course lead to a reduction of the number of German teachers in the system.

Another indicator of the importance attached to foreign language proficiency is the introduction of bilingual programmes that deliver the official curriculum partly in the official language of schooling and partly in a foreign language. Bilingual education (usually with English) is gaining ground in Utrecht and is available to 10% of primary pupils in Strasbourg. There are bilingual high schools in Sofia and Varna – in the latter city there are four such schools that between them offer programmes in English, German, French, Spanish, Russian and Italian. Schools in Madrid offer bilingual programmes under the rubric of content and language integrated learning (CLIL), introduced via a partnership project involving the Ministry of Education and the British Council. Well known among language education specialists, this project has greatly strengthened the position of English in Madrid schools.

Learning outcomes

No doubt the foreign language learning achievements of many pupils in LUCIDE cities are eminently satisfactory, especially if they are enrolled in a bilingual programme. Yet the EU and the Council of Europe continue to emphasise the need for countries to do better. The Barcelona European Council Conclusions of 2002 called for 'action to improve the mastery of basic skills, in particular by teaching at least two foreign languages from a very early age', while the first chapter of the CEFR declares that Council of Europe language policy aims to 'equip all Europeans for the challenges of intensified international mobility and closer co-operation not only in education, culture and science but also in trade and industry' (Council of Europe, 2001: 3).

In 2012 the European Commission's European Survey on Language Competences (www.surveylang.org) confirmed that the educational systems of most EU member states are still some way from meeting these aspirations. The survey collected information on the proficiency of pupils in their first and second foreign language in the last year of lower or first year of upper secondary education. Tests of listening, reading and writing were prepared in five languages – English, French, German, Italian and Spanish – and the results were reported using the first four proficiency levels of the CEFR: (A1) 'a basic user who can use very simple language, with support'; (A2) 'a basic user who can use simple language to communicate on everyday topics'; (B1) 'an independent language user who can deal with straightforward, familiar matters; and (B2) 'an independent language user who can express herself clearly and effectively' (European Commission, 2012: 4). Altogether approximately

54,000 pupils were tested. B1 or B2 was achieved by 42% of the sample in their first and by 25% in their second foreign language; at the other end of the proficiency scale, 14% of participants failed to achieve A1 in their first and 20% failed to achieve A1 in their second foreign language.

Seven of the countries that took part in the survey had cities participating in the LUCIDE project: Bulgaria (Sofia and Varna), Croatia (Osijek), France (Strasbourg), Greece (AAK/Athens), the Netherlands (Utrecht), Spain (Madrid) and UK/England (London). Of the pupils surveyed in Bulgaria, France, Spain and England, 20% or more failed to achieve A1 in their first foreign language. In the league table for first foreign language, the Netherlands, Croatia and Greece were in the top eight, while Bulgaria, Spain, France and England were in the bottom eight (France and England occupied the last two places). In the league table for second foreign language, only the Netherlands and Spain were in the top eight, while Bulgaria, Croatia, France, Greece and England were in the bottom eight.

In addition to the language tests, the survey administered background questionnaires to participating learners and their teachers. One finding is worth mentioning here: there was little evidence that teachers and learners were using the target language as the preferred medium of their teaching and learning. This may help to explain why a number of the interviewees cited in the City Reports described themselves as monolingual even though they had learnt one or more foreign languages at school (see, for example, Dublin City Report, 2014: 35, 55; Varna City Report, 2014: 25; Oslo City Report, 2014: 75). If the experience of learning a foreign language at school does not include frequent spontaneous use of that language, it is unlikely to become a vital part of the individual learner's plurilingual repertoire.

An alternative approach: Learner autonomy

Some of the LUCIDE City Reports refer to the CEFR's proficiency levels, but none of them mentions either its broader purpose or its companion piece, the European Language Portfolio (ELP). Part of the CEFR's broader purpose is to 'promote methods of modern language teaching which will strengthen independence of thought, judgement and action, combined with social skills and responsibility' (Council of Europe, 2001: 4), while the ELP was designed to promote learner autonomy, intercultural awareness and plurilingualism (Council of Europe, 2011). Although the CEFR stops short of advocating any particular language teaching method, its 'action-oriented' approach to the description of language proficiency implies that target language use should play a central role in language learning. What is more, it argues that '[a] utonomous learning can be promoted if "learning to learn" is regarded as an integral part of language learning, so that learners become increasingly aware of the way they learn, the options open to them and the options that best suit them' (Council of Europe, 2001: 141).

In practical terms this entails developing an approach that is shaped by three principles. First, within the framework provided by the official curriculum objectives, pupils set their own goals, choose their own learning activities and materials, monitor the learning process, and evaluate learning outcomes. Secondly, language learning is seen not only in individual and cognitive terms but also as a social phenomenon grounded in interaction and collaboration; group work is indispensable, and the developing proficiency of each member of the class is a resource available to all other members. Thirdly, from the beginning the target language is as far as possible the principal medium of classroom communication: discussing and agreeing on learning goals, selecting and carrying out learning activities, evaluating learning outcomes. (For a detailed description and discussion of this approach, see Little, 2007, 2009.) It is no accident that this approach first took shape in Denmark under the impact of Douglas Barnes' work: learner autonomy implicates the learner's identity (knowledge, skills and interests) and thus his or her 'action knowledge' (see Dam, 1995). We shall return to this theme in the last part of the chapter.

Towards Integrated Plurilingual Repertoires

Since the publication of the CEFR in 2001 the Council of Europe's language education policy has assigned a central role to the human capacity for plurilingualism. According to the CEFR:

> the plurilingual approach emphasises the fact that as an individual person's experience of language in its cultural contexts expands, from the language of the home to that of society at large and then to the languages of other peoples (whether learnt at school or college, or by direct experience), he or she does not keep these languages and cultures in strictly separated mental compartments, but rather builds up a communicative competence to which all knowledge and experience of language contributes and in which languages interrelate and interact. (Council of Europe, 2001: 4)

From this perspective, the aim of language education is to help pupils develop the fully integrated plurilingual repertoires to which we referred at the beginning of this chapter, taking account of the fact that some languages are learnt informally ('action knowledge'), while others are learnt formally ('school knowledge'). Of course, besides inviting a reconceptualisation of language education, the plurilingual ideal has important political implications, especially in Europe:

> Plurilingualism forms the basis of communication in Europe, but above all, of positive acceptance, a prerequisite for maintaining linguistic

diversity. The experience of plurilingualism also provides all European citizens with one of the most immediate opportunities in which to actually experience Europe in all its diversity. (Beacco & Byram, 2007: 10)

The LUCIDE City Reports offer little evidence to suggest that education systems are making substantial progress towards realising this ideal. For the most part the various languages of the curriculum and the other languages present in the school remain in their separate boxes and, as we have seen, those who learn a foreign language sometimes retain an image of themselves as monolingual. One possible way forward, at least for Europe, is set out in *A Rewarding Challenge: How Language Diversity Could Strengthen Europe*, a report delivered to the European Commission in 2008 by an international group chaired by Amin Maalouf. The report argues for a sense of European identity based on linguistic and cultural diversity:

While most of the European nations have been built on the platform of their language of identity, the European Union can only build on a platform of linguistic diversity. This, from our point of view, is particularly comforting. A common sense of belonging based on linguistic and cultural diversity is a powerful antidote against the various types of fanaticism towards which all too often the assertion of identity has slipped in Europe and elsewhere, in previous years as today. (European Commission, 2008: 5)

How is such diversity to become a reality? According to Maalouf and his colleagues, immigrants should learn the language of their host country, and Europeans should learn non-European languages (which overlooks the fact that in many countries immigrant languages are European), so that in linguistic terms integration becomes a two-way process:

Just as immigrants would be encouraged to fully adopt the language of the host country and the culture it carries, it would be fair and useful for the immigrants' languages of identity to also be part of the languages which Europeans themselves would be encouraged to adopt. We have to gradually get out of this one-way relationship in which people from elsewhere are getting better and better at learning European languages, while very few Europeans take the trouble to learn the languages of the immigrants. (European Commission, 2008: 11)

This recalls Madie's (2012) argument, noted in the Vancouver City Report, that in Canada language education should reflect the linguistic composition of society rather than the official French/English bilingualism policy. It also reminds us of the shift in focus from European to East Asian languages in Australian language education in recent decades.

The Maalouf report argues that Europeans should learn at least two new languages, one a language of international communication and the other a 'personal adoptive' language (European Commission, 2008: 7). This proposal is not worked out in any detail, and it seems fanciful of the authors to suppose that it could be successfully implemented simply on the basis of advocacy and encouragement from the EU. But some version of the proposal is eminently achievable within the walls of an individual school, always provided that the concept of plurilingualism is appropriately understood. As defined by the Council of Europe, plurilingualism is based on the assumption that we use the different languages in our repertoires in different contexts and for different purposes, that we are able to do things in one language that are beyond us in another, and that language learning is sometimes informal and sometimes formal. The plurilingual approach explicitly rejects the traditional assumption that the ultimate goal of all language learning is to achieve native-speaker proficiency. Consider the following description of the languages used by a London-based academic in a typical day:

> [He] generally begins his day in London (UK) in a mixture of Gujarati and Swahili while buying English language newspapers from his local newsagent who is of Indian origin and who was brought up in Kenya. He then orders an espresso and discusses some of the football news in Italian with the owner of the Venetian café opposite, before going to the gym where a Colombian receptionist registers his entry in Spanish, and a Brazilian trainer takes him through the exercise routines in Portuguese. On his way to the School of Oriental and African Studies [SOAS, University of London], he stops in at the bank where a Sikh teller processes his bills while extolling the virtues of having visited the holy Golden Temple during her last visit to Amritsar (India) in Punjabi. The security guard at the university entrance gate checks his identity card while conversing in Polish, evoking the usual mixed response in Polish and English from our colleague. This multilingual start to the day continues for him at work given the large number of languages spoken by the staff and students at SOAS specifically, and London generally. (Sachdev et al., 2012: 391)

Our academic may have acquired two or three of these languages as a child, one or two others he may have learnt at school, and the rest will have been acquired informally in social interaction. As regards these latter languages, acquisition was no doubt supported at a macro level by a favourable societal context and at a micro level by strong personal motivation. He may be capable of fluent conversation in all the languages mentioned in this quotation, although it is likely that his range varies somewhat from language to language and unlikely that he is functionally literate in all of them. As an academic, he operates in English.

The first step in any attempt to implement plurilingual education, obviously enough, is to articulate and enact a school policy of linguistic, cultural and ethnic inclusivity. This entails that all home languages present in the school are explicitly acknowledged, perhaps by introducing multilingual signage and displays (it requires creativity, ingenuity and a great deal of negotiation to accommodate the 40 or more home languages that are often present in schools in multilingual cities). The next step is to create regular 'social spaces' in the school day in which minority language pupils use their home language in ways that involve majority language pupils. Minority language pupils develop informal proficiency in the language of schooling partly through social contact and engagement with their majority language peers. Following the line of argument we derived from Douglas Barnes, this informal proficiency is an extension of the 'action knowledge' that they acquired via their home language. The same is true of whatever informal proficiency majority language pupils are able to acquire in a minority language by interacting with speakers of that language. They might, for example, learn how to use the language to play a game, or be shown how to pick their way through a simple illustrated story, or be introduced to straightforward online communication. Precisely because such learning is socially embedded, it has the potential to be spontaneous and unselfconscious, which increases the likelihood that fragments of the language will become part of majority language pupils' action knowledge.

The European Survey on Language Competences found that informal learning greatly benefits learners' language proficiency and identified the internet as an important source of such learning (European Commission, 2012: 53–56). In a lecture he gave in 2010, David Crystal argued that the internet provides our best hope of promoting plurilingualism:

> Once an attractive online multilingual presence is established, we can forget about the need to persuade young people to explore it. They will do so, of their own accord. ... We need to work towards presenting children with an enticing online multilingual experience, with plenty of age-appropriate material – an experience where good role models (the celebrities they admire) affirm that languages are cool, where characters in their favourite games act out their roles in different languages, where forums happily switch between different languages, where code-mixing is seen to be expressively enriching, where errors are thought of as natural and not criminal, and, in short, where all the good things we have noted as good practice in European linguistic decision-making are seen enacted online in Facebook forums, on Twitter, in YouTube videos, and

in Second Life. These are the domains whose gates we need to unlock, and the route whereby we create 'the best future for language learning'. (cit. King *et al.*, 2011: 39)

It might be even more beneficial to promote the development of overtly multilingual online games in which participation would entail communication in more than one language, and progression from one level to the next would depend on the acquisition of certain communicative resources. A suite of such games, all making use of a number of languages and each designed for a different age group, would be likely to do a great deal more for the development of plurilingualism than traditionally conceived online language courses.

As we pointed out in our discussion of the language of schooling, the task of education is to help pupils gradually master curriculum content and the various dialects of academic language that it entails by exploiting their 'action knowledge' and the language proficiency that is integral to it. This is a challenge for indigenous as well as immigrant pupils and requires a pedagogical approach rooted in reflective interaction (see again Barnes, 1976; see also Bruner, 1986). If minority languages are explicitly acknowledged and play a role in informal interaction between pupils, there should be no difficulty in drawing on them in mainstream subject classrooms to contribute to the exploration of new concepts as they arise in the language of schooling (we have given an example of how this is done in one Irish primary school; see page 163 above).

When it comes to foreign languages we must use procedures of formal learning associated with the acquisition of 'school knowledge' to frame and implement a process that seeks to engage pupils' identities (their knowledge, skills and interests) in ways that 'recode' elements of their action knowledge in the target language. That is what the 'learner autonomy' approach entails (see page 168 above). Once learners have developed a basic proficiency in their target language and are able to use it spontaneously to plan, implement, monitor and evaluate their learning, they should easily be able to cope with one or another version of CLIL.

The implementation of the various elements of plurilingual education is likely to be greatly facilitated if they are brought together in a single framework. A school that is serious in its pursuit of the plurilingual ideal could usefully develop its own version of the European Language Portfolio, embracing the language of schooling, home languages and the foreign languages of the curriculum – a process in which pupils as well as teachers should have a role to play.

Large-scale educational reform is notoriously difficult to implement successfully, especially when a top-down approach is followed. On the other hand, much can be achieved by individual schools, whether working on their own or in local networks. The path sketched in this concluding section of the chapter is one that schools in multilingual cities might consider following if they wish to exploit the linguistic capital in their midst to the educational and cultural benefit of all pupils and, by extension, their families, their communities and society as a whole. The initiative should not be left entirely with schools, however. Multilingual cities have an interest in doing all they can to promote educational success and social cohesion, and should thus be prepared to lend their support in a variety of ways to schools that decide to pursue the goal of plurilingual education.

The city is widely regarded as a driver of change in modern society. What is sometimes overlooked is that this is part of a historical process which has developed over centuries and also that cities are connected to their hinterlands, which in the 21st century may have expanded across the globe. The multilingualism which has always been a part of the city story thus becomes more, not less important; this contrasts with the monolingual assumptions of modern nationalism. These factors are outlined in the last chapter of our city story. Urban multilingualism is described in its diverse manifestations, relating to a broad typology of cities and different lived experiences of languages, including those languages which are less visible and regarded as less 'valuable'. People's feelings and reactions to this urban diversity are summarised, as too are the threats to the vision of 'unity in diversity'. We conclude with some proposals for both research and policy development which support a more optimistic future for the vitality of urban multilingualism.

6 Multilingual Cities and the Future: Vitality or Decline?

Lid King

> *Chris sat silently watching the city of Scranton, Pennsylvania, preparing to take off, and sucked meditatively on the red and white clover around him. It was the first time for each of them. Chris had known since he had been a boy [...] that the cities were deserting the Earth, but he had never seen one in flight. Few people had, for the nomad cities, once gone, were gone for good.*
> James Blish, A Life for the Stars

Aficionados of science fiction may recognise this extract from the second of the novels in the *Cities in Flight* series. In this dystopian vision of the future, the only salvation for humanity is quite literally to take flight: through a marvel of engineering, the Spindizzy, the whole city can detach itself from its environment and find a new resting place beyond the solar system, where the city and its inhabitants can prosper, exploiting the resources of a new planet, in ways as yet unimagined. It is a fantastic and rather terrifying image of the future. But the premise that cities can be separated in this way from their contexts – the hinterland, the national or collective space – perhaps finds echoes in some contemporary thinking about the onward march of the city towards a new utopia where mayors can 'rule the world' (Barber, 2013; and see Chakrabarti & Foster, 2013; Katz & Bradley, 2013).

City and Hinterland: A More Historical Perspective

The LUCIDE project itself began from a premise that cities, and specifically multilingual cities were, if not the spaceships of our salvation, at least significant indicators of future possibilities:

> a microcosm of what is to be, and a powerful generator of ideas, both for understanding what is, and for driving what is possible in the future.

As we outlined at the start of this book, we identified a number of reasons for this:

- Cities are a working model of the future. They are places where new policy discourse can be created and can act as a mode of persuasion.
- They are places where the constraints of national policies and limitations of national discourse can be modified or overcome.
- The city (as a multicultural therefore multilingual reality) is the locus for multilingualism in all its functions – learning and using – and in all its contexts – institutional, commercial, educational, and governmental.
- Cities also link to other cities, and provide the space where the articulate young in particular are creating their new reality (cit. King et al., 2011: 39; also used as part of the rationale for the LUCIDE project).

In the preceding chapters, using the data and the stories from our LUCIDE cities, we have considered the extent to which these supposed factors for change are actually influencing the lived reality of urban life and we have attempted to analyse the nature of that reality in some key domains, whether objective (policy, education) or subjective and affective (the sense of the city and identity formations). In this concluding part of the city story, we will draw some perhaps tentative conclusions and also look forward – not indeed to a life of disconnected cities in outer space – but to where we think we may be headed while still rooted to our own earth.

Triumph of the city?

A first and probably uncontroversial conclusion must be that cities are the places where change happens, and to that extent they can be seen as models of the future. Many observers have pointed to the apparently paradoxical phenomenon that there have been critical times in history when a given city or cities seem to attract particular kinds of talent and to create unprecedented levels of creativity, whether in literature (Athens in 5th century BC, Elizabethan London), art (15th-century Florence, 19th-century Paris), music (18th-century Vienna), political thought (17th-century Amsterdam), architecture (early 20th-century Chicago) or even financial services (contemporary London, New York) (for example, Glaeser, 2011: 8). In fact this is not paradoxical at all, as talent and opportunities for expression attract other talents that flourish through proximity and face-to-face interaction. Despite the potential for virtual communication offered by the internet, this phenomenon has continued and even intensified in the 21st century; it has given rise to a new concept – 'agglomeration' economies, described as the 'role that density can play in speeding the flow of ideas' (Glaeser & Gottlieb, 2009: 2).

Where we diverge from the certainties of some of the contemporary champions of urbanism (see in particular, Barber, 2013) is in the assumption that this dynamism is a largely modern phenomenon, very often based on a US liberal model of a city, and also that in some sense the city can be separated from its hinterland or context. At the LUCIDE final conference in London, Joe Lo Bianco criticised this pervasive worldview as one which imagines 'a global network of cities disconnected from ethnic and national hinterlands and connected to each other through communication density technology' (Lo Bianco, 2014).

As Lo Bianco has also pointed out, in this worldview 'they talk about cities as though the kind of pluralism that they embody is new'. A more historical perspective (see Chapter 1) would show that this cultural diversity has been a characteristic of the city since its origins and one which has developed over time rather than being an invention of modern urban sociologists. Moreover, cities have never been isolated from their surroundings, except in the case of the imagined 'cities in flight' of science fiction. Cities have always been part of a place – a hinterland – whether the countryside of Attica and the colonised islands or the farms of Latium and Etruria and eventually the provinces of Empire. The same is true of the cities in the embryonic nation states of western Europe or the urban centres of the vast multilingual empires in eastern and central Europe, and indeed Asia and Africa. What this underlines is the fact that the city has rarely, if ever, been a stable and unchanging place (Manent, 2013); it is a pole of attraction for peasants and for freemen, for those seeking to make a better life, for artists and philosophers and political refugees. It is this mobility, this perpetual motion and movement of people (and so of ideas and of different ways of thinking) that underpinned the vitality of Athens, of Florence and Venice, of the Dutch cities of the golden age, of 19th-century Paris and of modern Mumbai – these 'cosmopolitan cities' which 'bring together a critical mass of diverse minds, and (whose) nooks and crannies can offer places for Mavericks to seek refuge. The Ages of Reason and Enlightenment were also an age of urbanisation' (Pinker, 2011: 215).

On the other hand, as the contributors to this volume have pointed out from their different perspectives, there has also been a persistent underestimation of the importance of linguistic diversity as a catalyst for such creativity and change. How, after all, does Pinker's cosmopolitanism and diversity arise? It has not merely been the size and intensity of the city which generate change but the vitality created out of cultural (and therefore language) diversity. Even the champion of city triumphalism, Edward Glaeser, seems to get it:

> During the millennia since Athens attracted the finest minds of the Mediterranean world, cities have grown by attracting people from diverse cultures. The most successful cities today – London, Bangalore, Singapore, New York – still connect continents. Such cities attract multinational

enterprises and international expatriates. Immigrants are often a vital part of their economic model, both at the top and bottom ends of the pay scale. ... (Glaeser, 2011: 251)

The argument is not, however, developed further.

City, languages and the nation state

This brings us to another important historical factor, which is the interrelation of city and nation, and the connection between nation, national language and diversity. As we outlined in Chapter 1, in the pre-nationalist era linguistic diversity and linguistic tolerance tended to be the norm. This was usually the case in ancient Greece and Rome (although some languages enjoyed higher status than others) (Mullen & James, 2012) and in the Roman Empire. As the LUCIDE City Report from Sofia (2014: 6) states, such tolerance was even inscribed in law by the Sofia-born Emperor Galerius (Edict of Toleration, 311). The great empires of Europe and Asia were also multilingual until the growth of nationalist movements with their drive for single national markets and languages. According to Lo Bianco (2014) it is easy to forget that multilingualism is historically the norm and that national monolingualism has been of relatively short historical duration: 'The reason we talk about pluralism in the city as though it is disrupting something is because we have normalised the idea of that "something" being the national state.'

Even in the 19th-century western European states, monolingualism was far from the normal experience of most citizens. In his account of the modernisation of rural France in the late 19th and early 20th centuries, for example, Eugene Weber describes how few French citizens spoke French, and how different sectors of the rural population – masons from the Creuse, woodcutters from the Tarn, plumbers from the Livradois – were driven to the city for a better life, working and living 'together as fellow countrymen in little communities, their only goal that of supporting the family farms back home. Yet without meaning to they fell under the city's sway' (Weber, 1976: 300–301).

> Despite the emigrants' remarkable isolation from the urban environment that employed them, they nevertheless spread its germs among their fellows at home. An Auvergnat writing on the eve of the Great War noted how quickly migrants returned to local usages as soon as they were back home. Yet, though almost impervious to strange ideas, they brought different manners with them. ... They sent back letters, tracts and newspapers; they suggested new practices and tastes; they sent home parcels containing all sorts of curious sweets, spices and fabrics. ...They were the first to use dishes at the table, to show off a bicycle, to paint their house

or install lighting. **First also in many places to speak French as part of their 'city dress' ... [using] ... 'French words that they do not know too well'.** (Weber, 1976: 288, our emphasis)

Despite the nationalist belief in the inevitability and normality of single language groups in single national units, we can see here that even the creation of the nation state was a far more complicated affair. If the 19th century was a high point in Europe for the creation of the nation state with a single national language, a great deal of the history of the 20th century has involved not only the oppression of linguistic minorities within states, but the creation of conflict and division around this nationalist monolingual construct. In his diaries, Harold Nicholson, then a young diplomat, describes how after the Great War the old Empires of Europe were divided up to create new nations, and how every time they drew a line on the map they created a new national minority:

February 23. A disheartening job. How fallible one feels here! A map – a pencil – paper. Yet my courage fails at the thought of the people whom our errant lines enclose or exclude, the happiness of several thousands of people. How impossible to combine speed with examination. (cit. Woodward, 2009: 426; see also Andelman, 2008: 10; Phelps, 2013: 264)

In his fascinating account of the 20th century in Europe, envisaged as a year's journey from city to city at the turn of the 20th century, Geert Mak, the Dutch journalist and historian, describes the end of the Austro-Hungarian Empire – 'a crazy quilt of nationalities bound together by an elderly emperor' (Mak, 2004: 52) – and the end of the linguistic diversity of the Ottoman Empire.

It was nineteenth century nationalism that put an end to the tolerance of the Ottoman Empire, and by the start of the twentieth century the tension had risen to breaking point in Anatolia. But it was only under Ataturk that ethnic cleansing was adopted as government policy. His modern Turkey was to form a single national and ethnic unit, he considered the Ottomans' multinationalism sentimental and obsolete. (Mak, 2004: 495; and for the intensification of this process after World War II see Judt, 2005: 27)

So, far from 'natural', the creation and the imagining of the monolingual national state may be seen as the product of particular economic and political conditions, and one which, rather than resolving conflicts, has been a continuing basis for discord even in the 21st century. From our own modest LUCIDE investigations we can say that issues relating to language and national identity are particularly sensitive and difficult to resolve in areas of conflict and new nation building (City Reports from Osijek, Limassol) and also, as we explore below, a source of internal contradiction and intolerance over the rights of minorities, particularly new arrivals from other linguistic groups (for example, Athens, Strasbourg, London).

As a final observation about the connections between city, state, nation and language, we would suggest, however, that fundamentally there has been a history of continuity and development rather than a modernist break with the past (the separate cities in flight). The historical process of population movements from the country to the city characteristic of the centuries of European expansion is still continuing. This is happening not only in the new cities of Asia and Africa and Latin America – it has been said that over 10,000 people arrive in Mumbai every week (BBC, 2014) – but also in the old cities of Europe. It is estimated that between 2012 and 2013 the population of London grew by 108,000 to reach 8.42 million and by 2050 it is set to reach 11 million (ONS, 2014). This is nothing but an intensification of the process that began with the growth of the first city states. But now instead of the centrifugal attraction of the city being confined to the immediate hinterland or even to a single country, it is a global phenomenon (Saunders, 2010: 81). The importance of language diversity, of the vitality of multilingualism, therefore becomes not peripheral but a fundamental aspect of urban realities.

Our City Stories: Some Conclusions From the Reports

So what have we learned from our journeys through 18 cities? Are there any common themes which might indicate the next phases in the story? Or does every city tell a different tale? Despite the homogenisation associated with globalisation, diversity is indeed one striking characteristic of our urban world. History, geography, economics and the less tangible but still powerful influences of place and memory all contribute to making London specifically London, Madrid definitely Madrid, and Osijek unmistakably Osijek (see Chapter 3). In his European journey, Geert Mak paints a vivid picture of the specificity of European cities in space and time. He also – and his book itself is a striking testament to this phenomenon – demonstrates the historical links between cities and their common sense of belonging through a kind of shared diversity: 'Europe's weakness, its diversity,' he writes, 'is also its greatest strength' (Mak, 2004: 834).

This idea of 'unity in diversity' has also been a central theme of EU political thought, certainly until very recent times (Pantel, 2005: 46ff.), and it may provide the most helpful framework for understanding the common threads which bind our multilingual cities together. As the previous chapter has already mentioned, one of the most eloquent statements about both the complexity and the importance of this diversified European identity is that of Amin Maalouf *et al.*'s (2008) report as Chair of the Group of Intellectuals for

Intercultural Dialogue, entitled *A Rewarding Challenge: How the Multiplicity of Languages Could Strengthen Europe*:

> While most of the European nations have been built on the platform of their language of identity, the European Union can only build on a platform of linguistic diversity. This, from our point of view, is particularly comforting. A common sense of belonging based on linguistic and cultural diversity is a powerful antidote against the various types of fanaticism towards which all too often the assertion of identity has slipped in Europe and elsewhere, in previous years as today. (European Commission, 2008: 5)

This leads us logically to the first of our general conclusions.

Present-day urban linguistic diversity is itself diverse

We will not begin to understand the complexity or the significance of the multilingual cities of the 21st century if we expect to find one single and simple model. We have already seen how the weight of history – including the sense of place – influences present-day realities. If we add to this the effects of current economic and political tensions and the social and cultural consequences which ensue, then the model is not one of 'the multilingual city', but of a more complex typology of cities, which share some common characteristics, but which are essentially distinct and rooted in particular landscapes.

One obvious result of this 'diversity in diversity' is that political and social priorities across our multilingual cities may vary significantly. In what Joe Lo Bianco (2013) has characterised as the 'Cosmopolis'[1] – the cities which we have also categorised as 'built on immigration' (Chapter 1) and which others have called hyper-diverse – the major linguistic issues concern, on the one hand, the impacts of immigration and settlement and the consequent diversity of languages used in the urban context and on the other hand, the demands of the global market in relation to trade and exchange. This will also involve a significant interest in 'temporary' migrants such as tourists and students, who now constitute a major part of the city's ecology and economy. These issues have an effect both on language policy planning – in health, public services and above all education and also on peoples' attitudes to what we have called the image of the city, whether positive or negative.

In other cities the linguistic priority may be to prepare for globalisation through developing increased plurilingual competence among the indigenous population, and creating better conditions for welcoming visitors to the city, whether for trade or tourism. In these cases policy may be directed first towards language education at school and university, in particular in relation to the major languages of international communication – the supercentral

Figure 6.1 Oslo convenience store (LUCIDE network, 2014)

languages of de Swaan's (2001) 'constellation' of languages, and secondly towards the provision of multilingual services and information for these temporary visitors (often using English as the recognised hypercentral language).

The languages of immigrants may remain largely invisible, even though they are usually present. Indeed in a number of cities, in particular those which until relatively recently were cities of emigration rather than immigration (Athens and Oslo, for example), there may be no systematic response to the linguistic challenges of immigration or the needs of new migrants since immigration is still regarded as a temporary phenomenon which might pass.

> The Greek state, along with Greek society, has appeared reluctant to accept the fact that immigrants are here to stay (at least a large number of them, those with legal documents) and that immigration is not a temporary phenomenon. Until due regard is given to the issue of immigration, policymaking will not be done with an eye on the longer term. (Athens City Report, 2014: 22)

Another noticeable variant in the diversity spectrum is the importance for some cities – in particular those close to national borders – of the position of long-term minorities within the city and its hinterland and of the languages of close neighbours. Such concerns may be a result of a historical juxtaposition of language groups, predating the growth of 19th-century nationalism, for example in the multilingual Ottoman Empire, or they may be consequences of 20th-century wars, population displacement and the redrawing of borders. Policy in this domain is not only a matter of equity and equal access to information and resources, but very importantly about the maintenance of national or ethnic identity and the resolution of conflicts, including quite recent ones. In comparison with the ambiguous and rather lukewarm attitudes of most nation states and international institutions towards supporting immigration and 'migrant languages', and perhaps in recognition of the sins of our fathers, support for these 'national minority languages' is quite explicit and widespread (Council of Europe, 1992; see also Extra & Yağmur, 2012: 8, 12), although as pointed out in Chapter 2 such support is often not much more than lip service.

It should again be emphasised that these are not solid and impermeable categories of city types. For example, many of the characteristics we have mentioned in relation to the Cosmopolis are also relevant for other, smaller 'globalising' cities. In some cases it is a matter of degree. Nonetheless there are important variations between our cities and these variations lead to different degrees of visibility for languages (and so institutional/legal support) and different views on the vitality of multilingualism.

This in turn leads to a second general proposition.

Multilingualism takes different forms and has different meanings

As discussed in our introductory chapter, definitions of 'multilingualism' can be tricky. The term can be applied to people who have competences in a number of languages or to places where many languages are used. In LUCIDE we have preferred the distinction between multilingualism as the characteristics of a place – city, society, nation state – and plurilingualism as the attribute of an individual who therefore has a 'plurilingual repertoire' (Council of Europe, 2007). Even this more focused definition has its problems. This, for example, is a fairly typical (and positive) description of multilingualism in another English city (Manchester):

> Manchester's language and cultural diversity is one of its outstanding assets: Over 150 languages are spoken in the Greater Manchester area. Some two-thirds of secondary school pupils in inner Manchester have a heritage and family language other than English. A large proportion of Manchester's work force have excellent foreign language skills enabling them to communicate directly with business partners from Europe, the Middle East, South Asia, East Asia and Africa. [...] Manchester's many ethnic and language minorities are here to stay, and multilingualism is a

permanent part of our urban landscape in public signs and public services, in businesses, markets, and cultural centres. (Multilingual Manchester website, n.d.)

In this narrative, multilingualism is about the number of languages spoken and used in the city, the linguistic background of school children, the workforce's competence in foreign languages (aka plurilingualism), the use of languages for trade and in business and the diverse appearance of the urban landscape. As a working definition this could well apply to the main perspectives discussed in the LUCIDE City Reports.

However, the realities that we uncovered – both objective and attitudinal – are rather more nuanced. The starting point for many descriptions of the multilingual city, as in the Manchester example, is the number of languages spoken or commonly used in the city. Leaving aside the point that there is something faintly hypocritical about this 'celebratory discourse' when it comes from politicians, as though the number of languages spoken in a city was in some way a result of their progressive and far-sighted policies (see Chapter 1), this is also misleading in another sense. Is this headcount of languages a convincing indicator of what we have called the vitality of multilingualism? It could be part of the answer, but at best it is a blunt measure. Even in the major cities described in LUCIDE – this celebrated 'multilingualism' often means multiple separate bilingual (or in some cases even monolingual) communities. A more valid test of the vitality of multilingualism is likely to include the extent to which there is interaction between linguistic communities, the degree of public acceptance of and support for linguistic diversity, and critically the ways in which this 'multilingual capital' is part of the political and economic infrastructure including in the all-important area of education. Multilingualism is not just a question of numbers.

That this is not merely a semantic difference may be more clearly demonstrated by a third proposition.

Some kinds of multilingualism are more visible than others

It would appear that a great deal of a city's multilingualism is often invisible to many people. A large number of languages are used in the family or the community (the private sphere) and emerge in public only on special occasions, in celebrations such as Chinese New Year or Diwali. Then they may indeed become a part of the lived urban experience of many people including those from other linguistic groups. As we have suggested, this kind of symbolism can be very positive in developing an ethos of multilingualism as not only accepted but valued by significant parts of the urban community.

In other ways, too, citizens experience multilingualism almost unconsciously in their daily lives, particularly in global cities including large numbers of different language groups. The most ubiquitous example of this is

Figure 6.2 Ottawa Little Italy (LUCIDE network, 2014)

commercial – as in the local shops run by different language communities (Indian, Bengali, Turkish, Kurdish, Chinese, Polish, Italian) and serving the whole local community, increasingly indeed as a preferred outlet to the global supermarket (Orr, 2014), There are many other local and community initiatives (cultural, sporting, educational and religious) which constitute practices driven by needs of various kinds which grow from below and become an accepted and essential part of the daily fabric of urban life. The nature and extent of this 'mushroom' growth also varies from city to city, and is a powerful indicator of vitality – even when there is little overt political endorsement or administrative support.

Another, definitely less positive distinction in people's understanding of multilingualism is the distinction between 'valued' and 'non-valued' languages. With some exceptions (Melbourne is probably the most striking example), these invisible, non-valued languages still tend to be the languages of recent immigration, which are seen as 'different' and less-valued than the supercentral languages of communication such as French, German or indeed Mandarin Chinese. In some of our cities 'multilingualism' tends to be interpreted as having a population that knows or uses the national language plus one or two major languages learned in school. In the public sphere as well, the provision of multilingual services can often mean the use of the national language with English alternatives, on the assumption that most tourists will speak English. Even in the more developed multilingual communities

Figure 6.3 London Korean restaurant (LUCIDE network, 2014)

Figure 6.4 London Japanese community noticeboard (LUCIDE network, 2014)

there are ambiguities. On the one hand there is, as we have seen in Chapter 4, a degree of normalisation and public support for linguistic diversity in some spheres. On the other hand, there are limitations and conditions related to the perceived usefulness of a given language. In our multilingual cities not all languages are equal.

This leads us to a fourth broad conclusion, about the image of the multilingual city and how people see it.

People interpret multilingual realities in different ways

Just as the realities of the multilingual cities described in the City Reports are diverse, so too are the images of those cities. If these images are 'combinations of what the city is and what it wants to be' (Chapter 3), then the aspiration to a form of multilingual identity as a marker of global vitality is a strong one in most LUCIDE cities. It is not, however, universal. Some cities – again the more recent arrivals at the globalised table – are not considered by their city-zens to be multilingual in the same way as more typically diverse cities such as London, New York or Melbourne. For them, multilingualism is mainly about individual citizens' competences in the national language and learned languages of communication (especially, but by no means exclusively, English).

For most of the LUCIDE cities, however, an image as multilingual is seen as highly desirable. Utrecht, for example, presents itself as a 'multilingual hotspot', where individuals speak more languages than anywhere else in Europe and the administration of the city presents this as a positive thing and a sign of a better way of life. Melbourne, as home to people from more than 140 countries, presents itself as a richly multicultural city, whose history, economy and current identity are intimately connected to migration. This image is vividly articulated in the Sandridge Bridge development in the city centre which illustrates the history of all of the nations and people who have shaped the city (and state's) current identity, 'a physical representation of our City's diversity and tolerance' (Figure 6.5; City of Melbourne, 2015).

These are but two examples of many which show the importance attached by city authorities to the multilingual, multicultural brand. Most of the LUCIDE cities say something similar, although, as the examples of Utrecht and Melbourne indicate, they may actually be talking about rather different phenomena – on the one hand the plurilingual capabilities of the population and, on the other, the diverse linguistic and cultural make-up of the city. It is, however, undoubtedly significant that most cities now claim to promote some degree of multilingualism as a positive factor in a globalised world.

If this is the kind of positive image (however varied and imprecise) that the city authorities wish to put forward, it also seems to be the case that individual inhabitants have a less settled view. To take the most emblematic

Figure 6.5 Sandridge Bridge, Melbourne (Vincent Quach, 2007, Wikimedia Commons)

example of a European Cosmopolis, London: for many people it is the quintessential vibrant, cosmopolitan, creative city of over 200 languages. It is the place where they want to live, and language diversity plays a part in that choice. For others, however, it is an uncomfortable place.

> Does that make me slightly awkward? Yes it does. (...) I don't feel very comfortable in that situation. (...) This is not the kind of community we want to leave to our children and grandchildren. (Nigel Farage quoted by Sparrow, 2014)

Mr Farage, a nationalist politician, was undoubtedly making political mischief for his own political ends, and was widely ridiculed in the press, especially as his own children are half-German. Such attitudes, however, are not isolated ones, and they find many echoes in the City Reports. What this underlines, perhaps, is that while the massive and rapid effects of globalisation – new mobility, new communication modes, new ways of working – have often been accepted and welcomed by many as creating an exciting and dynamic space for working and living, for other city dwellers the very speed of change has been a rather more disturbing phenomenon. This applies to the newcomers who feel 'lost in the cities that would not pause even to shrug' (Ali, 2004, *Brick Lane*), as well as to the older inhabitants for whom change has come too rapidly and who find diversity disconcerting. At a time of economic crisis like the present, such feelings of loss and uncertainty are also fuelled by the simplistic promises of nationalism and extremist politicians of various kinds.

It is this which brings us to a fifth general conclusion.

The ideals and practices of multilingualism are under threat

As the Farage quotation illustrates, and as Maalouf presaged, the economic crisis is encouraging more extreme forms of nationalism and insularity and attacks on the very idea of positive multilingualism or, in broader terms, multiculturalism. Such attacks are no longer confined to overtly xenophobic parties and groups. In recent years the British Prime Minister and the German Chancellor, both said to be moderate politicians of the centre right, have criticised multiculturalism as a failed policy. According to Angela Merkel:

> At the beginning of the 60s, our country called the foreign workers to come to Germany and now they live in our country ... We kidded ourselves a while, we said: 'They won't stay, sometime they will be gone', but this isn't reality. And of course, the approach [to build] a multicultural [society] and to live side-by-side and to enjoy each other ... has failed, utterly failed. (BBC News, 2010)

Such views are by no means the terrain solely of politicians of the moderate and extreme right. As we mention in Chapter 4, social democratic parties, even in multilingual London, share this concern that diversity is a threat to cohesion. Such a retreat to what is in effect a modern variant of the 'one nation, one language, one culture' ideologies of the 19th century (Chapter 1) is given added weight by recent debates and discussion in both the social and academic spheres (see, for example, Alexander, 2013; Bosetti, 2011; Habermas, 2006). Politicians of all colours have joined a chorus of concern about the consequences of globalisation and have stressed the need to reaffirm national identities. Statements such as those of Merkel and Cameron, along with the more strident comments of nationalist politicians in most parts of Europe, and indeed North America and Australia, constitute the dog whistles which encourage intolerance, focused in particular on ever more explicit opposition to immigrants, asylum seekers and minorities more generally. Anyone with a memory or even a sense of the conflictual history of Europe in the 20th century will rightly be concerned about the increased polarisation of the current climate.

This has an effect, not only on the discourse of politics but also on the realities of national policy. Just as there has been a perceptible shift in the language used about multiculturalism and the value of diversity, so too, certainly in Europe, has policy shifted from the optimistic view of the future so trenchantly described by Amin Maalouf. Many of the accepted liberal consensual views about the value of diversity and the role of the state, particularly in promoting inclusive education, are being called into question. Access to support or learning of 'mother tongues' is, for example, no longer the norm in countries where this has long been a tradition, and in general there has been a move at both national and European level away from valuing, respecting and supporting immigrant languages towards more single-minded concentration on learning the national language of the various states (Chapter 5). At European level, the Council of Ministers and the Commission have pulled back from more overtly liberal statements of support for migrant languages and cultures, preferring to stress the importance of national rather than immigrant languages. This new or revived conservatism is paralleled in the nation states, which have developed a more overtly nationalistic focus linked to debates about single national identities and the search for national certainties (see Chapters 3 and 4; King *et al.*, 2011: 27–28). Perhaps significantly the latest discourse of anger is not confined to the languages of Asia and Africa, but includes the languages of recent arrivals from other European countries. The emphasis at political level now is on assimilation rather than any kind of unity in diversity.

There is, however, a counterbalancing tendency, rooted in practice, and this brings us to our sixth and final generalisation.

Policy and politics can be changed from below: The power of vitality

Despite the negative discourse of politicians, and the even more dangerous activities of extremists, there is an inescapable logic to reality, especially in the more or less democratic and open cities of our LUCIDE network. National policy or the dominant political narrative may be one of exclusion – quotas, restrictions, finding ways to keep people out. It may favour assimilation over community cohesion, whether through language priorities in education or through restricting public access to non-majority languages. However, as pointed out in Chapter 4, local authorities and local and community institutions need to respond to local populations and enable their communities to function. This means that they are less concerned with ideological positioning than with solving actual problems for real people ('fixing the sewers', in a phrase which has been attributed many times to the former Mayor of New York, Fiorello La Guardia). Whereas all of our LUCIDE cities are dependent to a greater or lesser extent on national policies and funding, they also – even those in the most difficult circumstances – find space to develop pragmatic solutions for their citizens (electors). One consequence of this is that local authorities are more orientated towards inclusion and integration than the dominant political rhetoric would suggest.

Cities are also places where community action and interventions by NGOs can have a major impact. One striking example is the growth of 'complementary schools' in London – the schools set up by local communities

Figure 6.6 Athens convenience store (LUCIDE network, 2014)

mainly to enable children to develop language skills in their home or heritage language and to maintain and increase their understanding of the cultures of the various communities. These initiatives have at times received some degree of official support, but they are essentially self-funded and resourced. Generally we have seen that, although there can be city-wide coordination or at least endorsement of such endeavours (see the Utrecht City Report), more often there is no such explicit policy but a more pragmatic approach of 'getting by' in response to local needs and aspirations, whether this is implemented by local authorities and agencies, by community organisations or by city-zens themselves. This 'mushroom' growth has a major impact, in the first instance on the cityscape (Chapter 2), often unnoticed by the inhabitants until it becomes a normal and unexceptional part of the multilingual urban fabric. This in turn affects the political discourse, the attitudes and expectations of all the city-zens and the visibility of languages in a given area.

This is something which we see happening in all or nearly all of our LUCIDE cities. One only has to see a newsreel of any of our cities from even 35 years ago (never mind 50) to see the change that has taken place, almost organically and beneath our feet (hence the image of the mushroom). It brings us to a final point, which is also a question: is urban linguistic diversity becoming a permanent, or at least stable, feature of our societies? According to the Hamburg City Report:

> research and observations lead us to conclude that migrants' heritages are now much more stable than they were in historical periods of migration. There are a number of reasons for this development, such as the new dynamics of migration in globalisation and the development of new communication technologies and techniques. Today, migration is conceptualised as an open process. Transmigrant communities emerge for whom the heritage languages are the main, if not the only, means of communication. The rapid pace of technological developments adds to the vitality of heritage languages in migrant communities. (Hamburg City Report, 2014: 42–44; see also Gogolin & Pries, 2004; McMonagle, n.d.)

The authors go on to argue that these new factors are leading to a change in the general climate, whereby linguistic diversity is accepted as a normal reality and the civic authorities support its further development.

> Multilingualism is presented as an asset of the Free and Hanseatic City of Hamburg [...] visitors are welcomed in many languages at the airport or on the city's official 'Welcome' portal; multilingual competences are sought by employers in the public and private sectors; in public media we find many languages from all over the world. We can report of a kind of affirmative action concerning the employment of young people with a migrant background in Hamburg's administration.

Of particular significance may be the observation that:

> A number of migrants' heritage languages are taught in the general school system, and many semi-private or private initiatives are also engaged in the fostering of these languages. It may be taken as an indicator of growing acceptance of language diversity that migrants' heritage languages are also learned by members of the majority community. (Hamburg City Report, 2014: 29)

This positive description is not surprisingly counterbalanced with concerns about the status of different languages and about the provision of resources. Nonetheless it is a striking example, mirrored in other LUCIDE cities to different degrees, of how the vitality and consequent growth of language diversity (from below) has influenced city policy and public attitudes. The report also gives important pointers to the reasons behind this new stability, linked to the major characteristics of globalisation as we have described them in our Introduction to this book. It is this which leads us – albeit tentatively – to conclude that as far as the multilingual city is concerned we have indeed crossed some kind of Rubicon. We will not, barring the kind of cataclysm described in *Cities in Flight*, go back to a pre-global, pre-digital existence. Diversity, mobility, multilingualism are here to stay in our cities. It is the negative reaction to them which belongs in another era.

Some Reflections on the Future of our Cities

If our present is one of complexity and challenge, leavened with the optimism of this change from below, what of the future? What will be the next chapter in the city story? In looking to that future we are of course mindful of the limitations of our current narrative. As we said in our Introduction, there are gaps in our data. Not only that, but our story has revolved around cities in Europe, with Canada and Australia as points of reference; the larger epic of world cities, many of which are speeding even more quickly to an imagined future, is something for another day.

We should also beware of certainties. One of the characteristics of this continent, perhaps particularly in the last 100 years, has been one of change and transience. We do not need to invoke the memory of Percy Shelley's *Ozymandias* to remind ourselves that empires fall and cities change their nature:

> My name is Ozymandias, king of kings
> Look on my works, ye Mighty, and despair!
> Nothing beside remains. Round the decay

Of that colossal wreck, boundless and bare
The lone and level sands stretch far away.

A striking example of this change in more recent times is given by Geert Mak, who argues that the end of Ottoman rule has had a major impact on the nature of Istanbul:

> It is a city which [...] is losing its cosmopolitan character and is in the process of becoming, in spirit, a provincial city. The Jews have left for Israel, the Greeks for Greece, the country's political power has moved to Ankara, the merchants have been scattered across the face of the earth. (Mak, 2004: 496)

Even so, the current of history seems clear. Individual cities may decline or change, or be left behind, but for the future that we can imagine the direction seems to be set, if not to the stars, to a world of cosmopolitan diversity. Istanbul itself is rediscovering a different kind of cosmopolitan identity, with the arrival of populations from the East and South and the growth of mass tourism (the transitory migrants described in Chapter 3) (see also Saunders, 2010: 169–196).

The challenge, as we have described it, is not whether globalisation will continue to affect our city dwellers, but how. Will they and we move in the direction of assimilation or of cooperation and mutual learning? Of conformity to an imagined past ideal or of embracing the more demanding delights of diversity? What choice will be made between 'inclusion and exclusion; between learning by exchange and learning by introspection and self-absorption; the joy of curiosity and the safety of home' (Hans Sakkers, cit. King et al., 2011)?

For on the one hand the multilingual, multicultural city is a driver of progress. In the Cosmopolis, ideas are exchanged and creativity flourishes: the open city is a city of solutions and invention, of cultural richness, economic growth and communication with the world. It looks outwards to other cultures and cities. It is above all a powerful, democratic and progressive force, respectful of the views and aspirations of its diverse populations and building a genuine unity in diversity. On the other hand, there are global and national factors inimical to such a future. The current world economic situation of long-term crisis is giving rise to social and political tensions in which many people take refuge in ancient, if illusory, certainties – holding on to what they have, looking to an imagined past of national or religious uniformity, rejecting the 'Other'. The growth of xenophobic, nationalist and anti-immigration politics and ideologies since the late 2000s, in particular, have become a major block to cosmopolitan progress. Even the more understandable fears of many people that life is becoming difficult and uncertain and that resources are limited can exacerbate existing challenges to the rational organisation of diversity – so undermining our vital multilingualism. It becomes easier to justify the lack of planning and organisation for universally accessible social and civic services, to reduce educational and interpreting provision for immigrant adults and to cut back on the all-important school educational opportunities when 'difficult choices' have to be made.

Despite such obstacles, which are described in all of the LUCIDE City Reports, our conclusion remains a positive one. Those factors which underpin the major changes in the ways we live and in the operation of our cities – new kinds of work, mass mobility, electronic communications – belong to our foreseeable future. What then is to be done? As our history will tell us, for such optimism to be translated into reality human intervention and a response to some identifiable challenges will be required. In part, these concern our understanding of the complexities that we have uncovered which need further investigation – challenges in the field of research and also in the articulation and dissemination of that research. There are also major requirements in the policy sphere, challenges which are essentially political, in the broadest sense.

Further research in urban multilingualism

We have already mentioned the need for a more systematic gathering of data about our multilingual cities and a broadening of the scope of enquiry to the great cities of the world. Even within Europe there are some aspects to our story which we have of necessity only briefly told. In particular, there is more to be understood and more to be said about the divisions between East and West, North and South, the impact of the last great empire, the Soviet Union, and of the latest conflicts of the late 20th and early 21st centuries on current realities and perceptions.

One shortcoming highlighted in our narrative has been the relative lack of interest among researchers of urbanism in the multilingual Cosmopolis. This is something to be addressed in the future, through further collaboration between linguists, sociolinguists and urban economists. Some unresolved issues that we have identified have been about the relative status of languages in the city – the questions of visibility and invisibility, of linguistic 'legibility' and the ways in which this affects the perceptions of different population groups. There is also more to be understood about the social identities of the inhabitants of the multilingual city and the extent, for example, to which they develop new allegiances to the city group rather than to a particular nation or ethnicity. Related to this is the need for better understanding of the reasons for the resurgence, in times of crisis, of different kinds of group identity, linked to the imagined community of the nation, and the persistence of language/nation dichotomies even in the Cosmopolis. There are doubtless other areas for reflection in all of the fields described and analysed – the cityscape and city identity, city policy and politics and the nature of education for plurilingualism.

But the challenge is not exclusively, or perhaps even mainly, a challenge in the realm of research and understanding. In parallel we need to reshape our policies in and for the diverse city. And just as our descriptions – the city stories in this book – show no unique model of diversity, so too these political solutions will vary according to place and circumstance. Variance does not, however, mean randomness. There are common threads and common solutions which can strengthen the vitality of multilingualism, creating a more holistic paradigm of 21st-century diversity.

Validating multilingualism: Endorsement of the cityscape

The strength of urban multilingualism is first and foremost in the initiatives and structures which grow up from the ground (the mushroom-like growth). These happen because of need and in response to community aspirations. At policy and political levels, multilingual vitality will be maintained and will flourish in cities which allow freedom and give support to these communities, rather than seeking to suppress or homogenise growth and diversity. As the examples of Hamburg, Utrecht and Melbourne suggest, the city's role will be – through existing and newly invented political structures – to provide coordination and resources, building on many individual but often small-scale and fairly invisible citizen initiatives, and to welcome the diverse manifestation of cultures as part of its own city identity.

Developing urban policies for multilingual societies

Successful cosmopolitan cities will also initiate procedures to facilitate multilingual communication as an intrinsic part of civic life – in health, in social services, in law and public services in general. This will include the provision of interpreting services and of adult education for both the national language and languages of the community. There is no single blueprint for this as circumstances differ, but there are a range of existing effective examples of what is being and what can be done in the LUCIDE cities (for instance, the multilingual toolkits created by the LUCIDE project). New technologies will play a major role in supporting communication within the city and between the city and other cities. The successful cities of the future will enable all citizens to participate equally in civic life, while valuing their specificities and identities.

Education for plurilingualism

Of critical importance for the future of the multilingual city is the state of language education in the compulsory school system. It is here, above all, that citizens of the future acquire not only their language competences but their understanding of and appreciation of diversity and their intercultural understandings. As argued in Chapter 5, the development of a coherent educational offer for plurilingualism is key to this process (see page 169 above). It is one field where indeed the researchers and educators have a major role to play, alongside policymakers and administrators. The frameworks to make such an offer possible already exist, in particular through the work of the Council of Europe. What are needed are resources and also political clarity and will, since a plurilingual approach to education challenges and undermines some of the traditional certainties of exclusive monolingualism and a narrow national form of education (Stern, 1964). A more inclusive approach is already thriving in individual schools and communities. It must be a priority to build on such approaches, pointing out that this is critical for social cohesion and mutual understanding and also essential for the linguistic competence of a city community and its continuing growth and prosperity. Writing about the Australian experience in 2009, Joe Lo Bianco described the importance of articulating 'the public "donation" of bilingualism offered by minority communities with the focused and instructed language skills produced in public institutions'. Although speaking in general of the whole nation, his words apply even more pertinently to the multilingual city, for if this were to be done we could ...

> generate a widespread, effective and less wasteful distribution of bilingual human capital. Combining the largely untapped resource of community bilingualism with the expertise of education institutions would refine, extend and apply latent bilingual skills to the national repository. Such an approach is both possible and necessary. (Lo Bianco with Slaughter, 2009: 4)

Promoting a positive message about city diversity

In support of such specific policy developments, an overarching objective, of researchers and policymakers alike, must be that of articulating a rationale for multilingual vitality and of promoting an inspirational message about the value and strength of the diverse city. Some models for such a rationale already exist, as we have discussed in our story, but we should and must go further if we are to counter the simplistic blandishments of monocultural nationalism or global uniformity. We are said to live in an era of individualism, of cynicism and of political apathy where citizens are not inspired by ideas. Reality and experience suggest that this is not necessarily the case and that maybe the messages need to be framed in different ways, so that they catch the imagination – in modern parlance, 'go viral'.

Many of the obstacles to a more positive vision of our multilingualism are attributed to peoples' 'attitudes'. And attitudes, even irrational ones, are based on some kind of reality, particularly at times of crisis, when we seek the comfort of the familiar. Offering new kinds of inspiration or a different worldview can, as we have seen, appear threatening. But it can also provide solutions. We know also that these rather imprecise attitudes change. In Europe, the last half-century, even the last 20 years, has seen massive changes in the way that people view their environments and identities, in what they regard as normal and acceptable and even 'comfortable'. Change has been so rapid that it is easy to forget how different were the cityscapes of our parents and grandparents, and how much those parents and grandparents have themselves changed. Most of that change has been towards a more tolerant view of other people, more inclusive ways of living and greater mutual understanding, which is not to say that intolerance does not flare up given combustible conditions and the application of petrol to the fire. But despite the obstacles and despite the uncertainties of where our cities and societies are heading next, we can take some confidence from this optimistic view of humankind. We can look forward to a future city where the city-zens are not disturbed by people speaking other languages on the train, but where their lives are more like the rich experience of the plurilingual inhabitant of London described in Chapter 5, in a place where diversity becomes normal.

Our cities will never take flight from this earth, since they are irretrievably bound to a multicultural, multilingual, multicoloured world. To return to the biblical image with which we began our story – the Babel myth apparently demonstrating that multilingualism was a punishment from God – Blanc (2008) concluded his discussion of ancient multilingualism with an opposing image which negates the story of Babel, and points instead to an acceptance and validation of speaking in tongues as a gift of God and a triumph of humankind. The vitality of urban multilingualism.

> And there appeared unto them cloven tongues, like as of fire, and it sat upon each of them. And they were all filled with the Holy Ghost, and began to speak with other tongues, as the spirit gave them utterance. And there were dwelling at Jerusalem Jews, devout men, out of every nation under heaven. Now when this was noised abroad, the multitude came together and were confounded, because that every man heard them speak in his own language. And they were all amazed. (*Acts of the Apostles*, Chapter 2, Verses 3–7 (King James Translation)

Note

(1) The term was first coined by Leonie Sandercock (1998) but with a rather different emphasis and less focused on language than other forms of diversity. See also Sandercock (2003).

LUCIDE City Reports

Alba Pastor, C., Casado Casado, J., López Escribano, C., Zubillaga del Río, A., Menéndez Alba, E., Blanco García and M. (2014) *Multilingualism in Madrid*. London: LSE Academic Publishing.
Brasileiro, I., Nortier, J. and Ridder, J. (2014) *Multilingualism in Utrecht*. London: LSE Academic Publishing.
Carson, L. McMonagle, S. and Murphy, D. (2014) *Multilingualism in Dublin*. London: LSE Academic Publishing.
Carson, L., McMonagle, S. and Skeivik, A. (2014) *Multilingualism in Oslo*. London: LSE Academic Publishing.
Ellyson, C., Andrew, C., Lemoine, H. and Clément, R. (2014) *Multilingualism in Ottawa*. London: LSE Academic Publishing.
Ellyson, C., Andrew, C., Lemoine, H. and Clément, R. (2014) *Multilingualism in Montreal*. London: LSE Academic Publishing.
Ellyson, C., Andrew, C., Lemoine, H. and Clément, R. (2014) *Multilingualism in Vancouver*. London: LSE Academic Publishing.
Ellyson, C., Andrew, C., Lemoine, H. and Clément, R. (2014) *Multilingualism in Toronto*. London: LSE Academic Publishing.
Evangelisti, P., Menghini, M., Fazio, A. and Serratore, B. (2014) *Multilingualism in Rome*. London: LSE Academic Publishing.
Gogolin, I., Duarte, J., Hansen, A. and McMonagle, S. (2014) *Multilingualism in Hamburg*. London: LSE Academic Publishing.
Hélot, C., Caporal Ebershold, E. and Young, A. (2014) *Multilingualism in Strasbourg*. London: LSE Academic Publishing.
Kolenić, L. and Bilić Meštrić, K. (2014) *Multilingualism in Osijek*. London: LSE Academic Publishing.
Lo Bianco, J. (2014) *Multilingualism in Melbourne*. London: LSE Academic Publishing.
Mehmedbegović, D., Skrandies, P., Byrne, N. and Harding-Esch, P. (2014) *Multilingualism in London*. London: LSE Academic Publishing.
Papadima-Sophocleous, S., Nicolaou, A., Boglou, D. and Parmaxi, A. (2014) *Multilingualism in Limassol*. London: LSE Academic Publishing.
Politov, A. and Lozanova, D. (2014) *Multilingualism in Sofia*. London: LSE Academic Publishing.
Sierra, E. (2014) *Multilingualism in Athens*. London: LSE Academic Publishing.
Tankova, E., Karagyaurova, D., Klimov, B. and Hubcheva, K. (2014) *Multilingualism in Varna*. London: LSE Academic Publishing.

Note

Originally published online in 2014, the current online editions are referenced as 2015 http://www.urbanlanguages.eu/cityreports.

References

Introduction

Aronin, L. and Singleton, D. (2012) *Multilingualism*. Amsterdam: John Benjamins.
Blommaert, J. (2013) *Ethnography, Superdiversity and Linguistic Landscapes: Chronicles of Complexity*. Bristol: Multilingual Matters.
Butter, S. (2013) Witamy* to Hillingdon (*that's 'welcome' in Polish). *London Evening Standard*, 31 January. See www.standard.co.uk/lifestyle/london-life/witamy-to-hillingdon-thats-welcome-in-polish-8475046.html (accessed 23 October 2014).
Cadier, L. and Mar-Molinero, C. (2012) Language policies and linguistic super-diversity in contemporary urban societies: The case of the City of Southampton, UK. *Current Issues in Language Planning* 13 (3), 149–165.
Castells, M. (2000) Toward a sociology of the network society. *Contemporary Sociology* 29 (5), 693–699.
Castles, S, de Haas, H. and Miller S. (2013) *The Age of Migration: International Population Movements in the Modern World*. Basingstoke: Palgrave Macmillan.
Clément, R. and Andrew, C. (2012) *Cities and Languages: Governance and Policy*. Ottawa: Invenire Books.
Cochrane, A. (2006) *Understanding Urban Policy: A Critical Approach*. Oxford: Blackwell.
Collins, N. (2010) Local councils spend nearly £20m in a year translating documents. *Daily Telegraph*, 16 January. See www.telegraph.co.uk/news/uknews/6995845/Local-councils-spend-nearly-20m-in-a-year-translating-documents.html (accessed 23 October 2014).
de Swaan, A. (2001) *Words of the World: The Global Language System*. Cambridge: Polity Press.
Extra, G. and Yağmur, K. (eds) (2004) *Urban Multilingualism in Europe. Immigrant Minority Languages at Home and School*. Clevedon: Multilingual Matters.
Extra, G. and Yağmur, K. (eds) (2011) Urban multilingualism in Europe: Mapping linguistic diversity in multicultural cities. *Journal of Pragmatics* 43 (5), 1173–1184.
Fishman, J.A. (1991) *Reversing Language Shift: Theoretical and Empirical Foundations of Assistance to Threatened Languages*. Clevedon: Multilingual Matters.
Gottdiener, M. and Budd, L. (2005) *Key Concepts in Urban Studies*. London: Sage.
Hutchinson, R. (ed.) (2010) *Encyclopedia of Urban Studies*. London: Sage.
King, L., Byrne, N., Djouadj, I., Lo Bianco, J. and Stoicheva, M. (2011) *Languages in Europe: Towards 2020. Analysis and Proposals From the LETPP Consultation and Review*. London: The Languages Company.
Kraus, P.A. (2011) The multilingual city. The cases of Helsinki and Barcelona. *Nordic Journal of Migration Research* 1 (1), 25–36.
Mac Giolla Chríost, D. (2007) *Language and the City*. Basingstoke: Palgrave Macmillan.
Mac Giolla Chríost, D. and Thomas, H. (2008) Linguistic diversity and the city: Some reflections, and a research agenda. *International Planning Studies* 13 (1), 1–11.

Marcuse, P. and van Kempen, R. (eds) (2002) *Of States and Cities: The Partitioning of Urban Space*. Oxford: Oxford University Press.
Otsuji, E. and Pennycook, A. (2010) Metrolingualism: Fixity, fluidity and language in flux. *International Journal of Multilingualism* 7 (3), 240–254.
Sassen, S. (2005) The global city: Introducing a concept. *Brown Journal of World Affairs* xi (2), 27–43.
Sassen, S. (2006) *Territory, Authority, Rights: From Medieval To Global Assemblages*. Princeton, NJ: Princeton University Press.
Schäffner, C. (2008) Behindert Übersetzung die Integration? In G. Vorderobermeier and M. Wolf (eds) *Meine Sprache grenzt mich ab … Transkulturalität und kulturelle Übersetzung im Kontext von Migration* (pp. 169–188). Vienna: LIT.
Sibley, D. (1995) Gender, science, politics and geographies of the city. *Gender, Place and Culture* 2 (1), 37–50.
Simmel, G. (1903) The metropolis and mental life. In G. Bridge and S. Watson (eds) (2002) *The Blackwell City Reader*. Oxford and Malden, MA: Wiley-Blackwell.
UN (2014) *World Urbanization Prospects: The 2014 Revision, Highlights* (ST/ESA/SER.A/352). New York: United Nations, Department of Economic and Social Affairs, Population Division.
Wirth, L. (1938) Urbanism as a way of life. *American Journal of Sociology* 44 (1), 1–24.

Chapter 1

Adams, J.N. (2003) *Bilingualism and the Latin Language*. Cambridge: Cambridge University Press.
Anderson, B. (1983) *Imagined Communities: Reflections on the Origin and Spread of Nationalism*. London: Verso.
Austin, P.K. and Sallabank, J. (eds) (2011) *Cambridge Handbook of Endangered Languages*. Cambridge: Cambridge University Press.
Billows, R. (2005) Cities. In A. Erskine (ed.) *A Companion to the Hellenistic World*. Malden, MA: Blackwell Publishing.
Blackledge, A. (2000) Monolingual ideologies in multilingual states: Language, hegemony and social justice in Western liberal democracies. *Estudios de Sociolingüística* 1, 25–45.
Blanc, M. (2008) Multilingualism in the Ancient Near East. Paper presented at Conference to Honour Professor Michel Blanc, Birkbeck College, University of London. Unpublished manuscript.
Brown, J. (2013) 200 languages: Manchester revealed as most linguistically diverse city in western Europe. *The Independent*, 13 August. See www.independent.co.uk/news/uk/home-news/200-languages-manchester-revealed-as-most-linguistically-diverse-city-in-western-europe-8760225.html (accessed 26 September 2014).
CSO (2012) *Census 2011 Ireland and Northern Ireland*. Cork: Central Statistics Office. See www.cso.ie/en/census/census2011irelandandnorthernireland/.
Edwards, J. (1994) *Multilingualism*. London: Routledge.
Elwell, V.M. (1982) Some social factors affecting multilingualism among Aboriginal Australians: A case study of Maningrida. *International Journal of the Sociology of Language* 36, 83–104.
Extra, G. and Yağmur, K. (2012) *Language Rich Europe: Trends in Policies and Practices for Multilingualism in Europe*. Cambridge: Cambridge University Press.
Giles, H., Bourhis, R.Y. and Taylor, D.M. (1977) Towards a theory of language in ethnic group relations. In H. Giles (ed.) *Language, Ethnicity and Intergroup Relations*. London: Academic Press.

Government of Ireland (1937) Bunreacht na hÉireann (Constitution of Ireland). See www.irishstatutebook.ie/constitution.html (accessed 12 November 2013).

Gregoriou, P., Kontolemis, Z. and Matsi, Z. (2010) Immigration in Cyprus: An analysis of the determinants. *Cyprus Economic Policy Review* 4 (1), 63–88.

Institut National de la Staistique et des Etudes Economique (2012) Populations Legales 2012. See http://www.insee.fr/fr/ppp/bases-de-donnees/recensement/populations-legales/ (accessed 20 August 2015).

Kreindler, I. (1982) The changing status of Russian in the Soviet Union. *International Journal of the Sociology of Language* 33, 7–39.

MacLennan, H. (1945) *Two Solitudes*. Toronto: MacMillan Company of Canada.

Martin, T. (2001) *The Affirmative Action Empire: Nations and Nationalism in the Soviet Union, 1923–1939*. Ithaca, NY: Cornell University Press.

Mullen, A. and James, P. (eds) (2012) *Multilingualism in the Graeco-Roman Worlds*. Cambridge: Cambridge University Press.

Redder, A. (2013) Multilingual communication in Hamburg. In P. Siemund, I. Gogolin, M.E. Schulz and J. Davydova (eds) *Multilingualism and Language Diversity in Urban Areas: Acquisition, Identities, Space, Education*. Amsterdam: John Benjamins.

Rochette, B. (2011) Language policies in the Roman Republic and Empire. In J. Clackson (ed.) *A Companion to the Latin Language*. Oxford: Wiley-Blackwell.

Roussopoulos, D. and Benello, C.G. (eds) (2005) *Participatory Democracy: Prospects for Democratizing Democracy*. Montreal and New York: Black Rose Books.

Sachdev, I. (1995) Language and identity: Ethnolinguistic vitality of Aboriginal Peoples in Canada. *London Journal of Canadian Studies* 11, 16–29.

Sachdev, I. and Bourhis, R.Y. (1993) Ethnolinguistic vitality and social identity. In D. Abrams and M. Hogg (eds) *Group Motivation: Social Psychological Perspectives*. Hemel Hempstead: Harvester Wheatsheaf.

Sachdev, I., Arnold, D.Y. and Yapita, J.D (2006) Indigenous identity and language: Some considerations from Bolivia and Canada. *BISAL* 1, 107–128, London: Birkbeck College.

Sachdev, I., Giles, H. and Pauwels, A. (2012) Accommodating multilinguality. In T.K. Bhatia and W.C. Ritchie (eds) *The Handbook of Bilingualism and Multilingualism* (2nd edn). Chichester: John Wiley.

Stavrianos, L.S. (1958) *The Balkans Since 1453*. New York: Rinehart.

Tasan-Kok, T., van Kempen, R., Raco, M. and Bolt, G. (2013) *Towards Hyper-Diversified European Cities: A Critical Literature Review*. Utrecht: Faculty of Geosciences, Utrecht University. See www.urbandivercities.eu/wp-content/uploads/2013/05/20140121_Towards_HyperDiversified_European_Cities.pdf (accessed 26 September 2014).

Turin, M. (2012) New York, a graveyard for languages. *BBC News Magazine*, 16 December. See www.bbc.co.uk/news/magazine-20716344 (accessed 26 September 2014).

UN (2014) *World Urbanization Prospects: The 2014 Revision, Highlights* (ST/ESA/SER.A/352). New York: United Nations, Department of Economic and Social Affairs, Population Division.

Vertovec, S. (2007) Super-diversity and its implications. *Ethnic and Racial Studies* 30 (6), 1024–1054.

Chapter 2

An Coimisinéir Teanga (Language Commissioner) (n.d.) *Protecting Language Rights*. See www.coimisineir.ie (accessed 12 January 2013).

Ball, R. (1989) The French retail trade versus the English language. *Modern Languages* 70 (4), 196–201.

Bogatto, F. and Hélot, C. (2010) Linguistic landscape and language diversity in Strasbourg: The 'Quartier Gare'. In E. Shohamy, E. Ben-Rafael and M. Barni (eds) *Linguistic Landscape in the City* (pp. 275–291). Bristol: Multilingual Matters.

Bouchard B. (2008) *Les entreprises de 11 à 49 employés: Portrait de leur réalité linguistique.* Montréal: Office Québécois de la langue française.

Buckley, S. (2010) Third pillar of media pluralism: Community broadcasting in the UK and Europe. Paper presented at the Conference of the Media, Communication and Cultural Studies Association (MECCSA), London School of Economics and Political Science, 6–8 January. See www.lse.ac.uk/media@lse/events/MeCCSA/pdf/papers/SteveBuckley.pdf (accessed 1 September 2014).

Carson, L. and Extra, G. (2010) Multilingualism in Dublin: Home language use among primary school children, report on a pilot survey. Dublin and Tilburg: Trinity College and Tilburg University.

Cenoz, J. and Gorter, D. (2006) Linguistic landscape and minority languages. *International Journal of Multilingualism* 3 (1), 67–80.

Cheshire, J., Kerswill, P., Fox, S. and Torgersen, E. (2011) Contact, the feature pool and the speech community: The emergence of multicultural London English. *Journal of Sociolinguistics* 15 (2), 151–196.

Clyne, M. (2000) Lingua franca and ethnolects in Europe and beyond. *Sociolinguistica* 14, 83–89.

Coluzzi, P. (2012) The linguistic landscape of Brunei Darussalam: Minority languages and the threshold of literacy. *South East Asia: A Multidisciplinary Journal* 12, 1–16.

Cronin, M. (2004) Babel Átha Cliath: The languages of Dublin. *New Hibernia Review* 8 (4), 9–22.

De Tona, C. (2006) But what is interesting is the story of why and how migration happened. *Forum: Qualitative Sozialforschung/Forum: Qualitative Social Research* 7 (3), Art. 9.

Dietz, A. (2011) *Dimensions of Belonging and Migrants by Choice: Contemporary Movements Between Italy and Northern Ireland.* Münster: Waxmann Verlag.

Dimova, S. (2007) English shop signs in Macedonia. *English Today* 23, 18–24.

Dorleijn, M. and Nortier, J. (2012) Bilingualism and youth language. In C.A. Chapelle (ed.) *The Encyclopedia of Applied Linguistics* (pp. 480–487). Oxford: Wiley-Blackwell.

European Parliament (2008) European Parliament resolution of 25 September 2008 on Community Media in Europe (A6–0263/2008). See http://www.europarl.europa.eu/sides/getDoc.do?pubRef=-//EP//TEXT+TA+P6-TA-2008-0456+0+DOC+XML+V0//EN (accessed 20 August 2015).

Government of Ireland (1937) Bunreacht na hÉireann (Constitution of Ireland). See www.irishstatutebook.ie/constitution.html (accessed 12 November 2013).

Government of Ireland (2012) Gaeltacht Act 2012. See www.irishstatutebook.ie/2012/en/act/pub/0034/print.html#sec1 (accessed 2 September 2014).

Hall, S. (2012) *City, Street and Citizen: The Measure of the Ordinary.* London: Routledge.

Hill, D. (2013) The real roots of multicultural London English. *The Guardian*, blog post, 6 February. See www.theguardian.com/society/davehillblog/2013/feb/06/paul-kerswill-multicultural-london-english (accessed 10 October 2014).

Hult, F.M. (2009) Language ecology and linguistic landscape analysis. In E. Shohamy and D. Gorter (eds) *Linguistic Landscape: Expanding the Scenery* (pp. 88–104). London: Routledge.

Jacobs, J. (1961) *The Death and Life of Great American Cities.* New York: Random House.

Kallen, J. (2009) Tourism and representation in the Irish linguistic landscape. In E. Shohamy and D. Gorter (eds) *Linguistic Landscape: Expanding the Scenery* (pp. 270–283). London: Routledge.

Kallen, J. (2010) Changing landscapes: Language, space, and policy in the Dublin linguistic landscape. In A. Jaworski and C. Thurlow (eds) *Semiotic Landscapes: Language, Image, Space* (pp. 41–58). London: Continuum.

Kallen, J. and Ní Dhonnacha, E. (2010) Language and inter-language in urban Irish and Japanese linguistic landscapes. In E. Shohamy, E. Ben-Rafael and M. Barni (eds) *Linguistic Landscape in the City* (pp. 19–36). Bristol: Multilingual Matters.

Keung, N. (2013) Toronto's Chinatown, Greektown and Little Italy now resemble tourist landmarks, while new immigrant enclaves sprout in suburbs. *The Toronto Star*, 7 May. See www.thestar.com/news/immigration/2013/05/07/torontos_immigrant_enclaves_spread_to_suburbs.html (accessed 12 December 2014).

King, R. and Reynolds, B. (1994) Casalattico, Dublin and the fish and chip connection: A classic example of chain migration. *Studi Emigrazione* 31 (115), 398–426.

Kotsinas, U.B. (1988) Immigrant children's Swedish: A new variety? *Journal of Multilingual and Multicultural Development* 9 (1–2), 129–140.

Lamoureux, S.A. and Clément, R. (2012) En guise d'introduction: Politique linguistique et bilinguisme en milieu urbain – débats situés. In R. Clément and C. Andrew (eds) *Villes et Langues: Gouvernance et Politique* (pp. 1–12). Ottawa: Presses de l'Université d'Ottawa.

Landry, R. and Bourhis, R.Y. (1997) Linguistic landscape and ethnolinguistic vitality: An empirical study. *Journal of Language and Social Psychology* 16 (1), 23–49.

McMonagle, S. (2012) Gaeltacht Thuaisceart an Oileáin Úir: Post-territorial Irishness and Canadian multiculturalism. *Irish Studies Review* 20 (4), 407–425.

Monnier, D. (1989) *La langue d'accueil et la langue de service dans les commerces à Montréal*. Notes and documents 70. Québec: Conseil de la langue française.

Mottiar, Z. and Walsh, L. (2012) Leisure space reflecting changing city demography: Tracking the phase of an international quarter development in Parnell Street East, Dublin. *Leisure Studies* 31 (1), 21–32.

Nortier, J. and Dorleijn, M. (2008) A Moroccan accent in Dutch: A sociocultural style restricted to the Moroccan community? *International Journal of Bilingualism* 12 (1–2), 125–142.

Nortier, J. and Dorleijn, M. (2013) Multi-ethnolects: Kebabnorsk, Perkerdansk, Verlan, Kanakensprache, Straattaal, etc. In P. Bakker and Y. Matras (eds) *Contact Languages: A Comprehensive Guide* (pp. 237–270). Berlin: De Gruyter.

O'Carroll, S. (2012) Clondalkin could be Dublin's first official Gaeltacht. *TheJournal.ie*, 9 February. See www.thejournal.ie/clondalkin-could-be-dublins-first-official-gael tacht-350427-Feb2012/ (accessed 12 November 2014).

Reynolds, B. (1993) *Casalattico and the Italian Community in Ireland*. Dublin: Foundation for Italian Studies, UCD.

Rosenbaum, Y., Nadel, E., Cooper, R.L. and Fishman, J.A. (1977) English on Keren Kayemet Street. In J.A. Fishman, R.L. Cooper and A.W. Conrad (eds) *The Spread of English: The Sociology of English as an Additional Language* (pp. 179–196). Rowley, MA: Newbury House.

Scarvaglieri, C., Redder, A., Pappenhagen, R. and Brehmer, B. (2013) Capturing diversity: Linguistic land- and soundscaping in urban areas. In J. Duarte and I. Gogolin (eds) *Linguistic Superdiversity in Urban Areas: Research Approaches* (pp. 45–73). Hamburg Studies on Linguistic Diversity 2. Amsterdam: John Benjamins.

Schlick, M. (2003) The English of shop signs in Europe. *English Today* 19 (1), 3–17.

Scollon, R. and Scollon, S.W. (2003) *Discourses in Place: Language in the Material World*. London: Routledge.

Tulp, S.M. (1978) Reklame en tweetaligheid: Een onderzoek naar de geografische verspreiding van franstalige en nederlandstalige affiches in Brussel. *Taal en Sociale Integratie* 1, 261–288.

Wiese, H. (2009) Grammatical innovation in multiethnic urban Europe: New linguistic practices among adolescents. *Lingua* 119 (5), 782–806.

Chapter 3

Ali, M. (2004) *Brick Lane*. London: Black Swan.
Anderson, B. (1983) *Imagined Communities: Reflections on the Origin and Spread of Nationalism*. London: Verso.
Arel, D. (2002) Language categories in censuses: Backward- or forward-looking? In D. Kertzer and D. Arel (eds) *Census and Identity. The Politics of Race, Ethnicity and Language in National Censuses*. Cambridge: Cambridge University Press.
Aristotle (1946) Boom VII, Chapter 4.4-14. In E. Barker (ed. and trans.) *The Politics*. New York: Oxford University Press.
Bauman, Z. (1998) *Globalization: The Human Consequences*. Cambridge: Polity Press.
Broeder, P. and Mijares, L. (2004) *Multilingual Madrid. Languages at Home and at School*. Amsterdam: European Cultural Foundation.
Castells, M. (2000) *The Information Age. Economy, Society and Culture* (2nd edn). Oxford and Malden, MA: Blackwell.
Castles, S. and Miller, M.J. (2009) *The Age of Migration: International Population Movements in the Modern World* (4th edn). Basingstoke: Palgrave MacMillan.
Cresswell, T. and Merriman, P. (2011) *Geographies of Mobilities: Practices, Spaces, Subjects*. Farnham: Ashgate.
Deutsch, K. (1942) The trend of European nationalism: The language aspect. *American Political Science Review* 36 (3), 533–541.
Eurobarometer (2004–2014) *Standard Eurobarometer No. 61-82*. Brussels: Commission of the European Union.
Eurobarometer (2013) *Flash Eurobarometer 366. Quality of Life in Cities. Perception Survey in 79 European Cities*. Brussels: Commission of the European Union.
Eurostat (2011) *European Cities – Demographic Challenges*. See http://ec.europa.eu/eurostat/statistics-explained/index.php/Archive:European_cities_-_demographic_challenges.
Gellner, E. (1983) *Nations and Nationalism*. Ithaca, NY: Cornell University Press.
Gogolin, I. (1994) *Der monolinguale Habitus der multilingualen Schule*. Münster and New York: Waxmann.
Hall, P. (1984) *The World Cities* (3rd edn). London: Weidenfeld and Nicolson.
Hall, P. (1996) Globalization and the World Cities. UNU/IAS Working Paper No. 12. UN University Institute of Advanced Studies.
Honneth, A. (1992) *The Struggle for Recognition: The Moral Grammar of Social Conflicts*. Cambridge, MA: MIT Press.
Jaspers, J. and Vershueren, J. (2011) Multilingual structures and agencies. *Journal of Pragmatics* 43 (5), 1157–1160.
King, E., Byrne, N., Djouadj, I., Lo Bianco, J. and Stoicheva, M. (2011) *Languages in Europe Toward 2020*. London: The Languages Company.
Lakhous, A. (2008) *Clash of Civilisations Over an Elevator in Piazza Vittorio*. New York: Europa Editions.
Lynch, K. (1960) *The Image of the City*. Cambridge, MA: Technology Press and Harvard University Press.
Marcuse, P. and van Kempen, R. (eds) (2000) *Globalizing Cities: A New Spatial Order?* London: Blackwell.
Marcuse, P. and van Kempen, R. (2002) *Of States and Cities: The Partitioning of Urban Space*. Oxford: Oxford University Press.
Pinder, D. (2011) Cities: Moving, plugging in, floating, dissolving. In T. Cresswell and P. Merriman (eds) *Geographies of Mobilities: Practices, Spaces, Subjects*. Farnham: Ashgate.
Sampson, R.J. (2009) Disparity and diversity in the contemporary city: Social (dis)order revisited. *British Journal of Sociology* 60 (1), 1–31.

Sassen, S. (2001) *The Global City: New York, London, Tokyo*. Princeton, NJ: Princeton University Press.
Sassen, S. (2005) The global city: Introducing a concept. *Brown Journal of World Affairs* xi (2), 27–43.
Sennett, R. (1970) *The Uses of Disorder: Personal Identity & City Life*. New York: Vintage.
Sennett, R. (2009) Urban disorder today. *British Journal of Sociology* 60 (1), 57–58.
Smith, A. (1991) *National Identity*. Reno, NV: University of Nevada Press.
Taylor, C. (1992) The politics of recognition. In A. Gutmann (ed.) *Multiculturalism: Examining the Politics of Recognition* (pp. 25–73). Princeton, NJ: Princeton University Press.
Urry, J. (2007) *Mobilities*. Cambridge: Polity Press.
Wirth, L. (1938) Urbanism as a way of life. *American Journal of Sociology* 44 (1), 1–24.

Chapter 4

Ager, D. (2005) Image and prestige planning. *Current Issues in Language Planning* 6 (1), 1–43.
Anderson, B. (1983) *Imagined Communities: Reflections on the Origin and Spread of Nationalism*. London: Verso.
Audunson, R., Essmat, S. and Aabø, S. (2011) Public libraries: A meeting place for immigrant women? *Library & Information Science Research* 33 (3), 220–227.
Barbour, S. (2004) National language and official language. In K. Mattheier, U. Ammon and P. Trudgill (eds) *Sociolinguistics/Soziolinguistik. An International Handbook of the Science of Language and Society* (2nd edn) (pp. 288–295). Berlin: De Gruyter.
Baynham, M. (2011) Language and migration. In J. Simpson (ed.) *The Routledge Handbook of Applied Linguistics* (pp. 414–427). London: Routledge.
Baynham, M. (2013) Postscript. In A. Duchêne, M. Moyer and C. Roberts (eds) *Language, Migration and Social Inequalities: A Critical Sociolinguistic Perspective on Institutions and Work* (pp. 309–314). Bristol: Multilingual Matters.
BBC News (2011) Newham's libraries remove foreign language newspapers. *BBC News*, 10 May. See www.bbc.co.uk/news/uk-england-london-13352845 (accessed 23 October 2014).
Castles, S, de Haas, H. and Miller, S. (2013) *The Age of Migration: International Population Movements in the Modern World*. Basingstoke: Palgrave Macmillan.
Cooper, R.L. (1989) *Language Planning and Social Change*. Cambridge: Cambridge University Press.
Corsellis, A. (2008) *Public Service Interpreting: The First Steps*. Basingstoke: Palgrave Macmillan.
Council of Europe (2013) *Integration Tests: Helping or Hindering Integration?* Strasbourg: Parliamentary Assembly. See www.assembly.coe.int/CommitteeDocs/2013/amdoc11_2013TA.pdf (accessed 8 November 2014).
Dalakoglou, D. (2012) Beyond spontaneity: Crisis, violence and collective action in Athens. *City: Analysis of Urban Trends, Culture, Theory, Policy, Action* 16 (5), 535–545.
De Witte, B. (2011) Language rights: The interactions between domestic and European developments. In A.L. Kjaer and S. Adamo (eds) *Linguistic Diversity and European Democracy* (pp. 167–188). Farnham: Ashgate.
Duchêne, A., Moyer, M. and Roberts, C. (eds) (2013) *Language, Migration and Social Inequalities: A Critical Sociolinguistic Perspective on Institutions and Work*. Bristol: Multilingual Matters.
Eckert, P. (2006) Communities of practice. In K. Brown (ed.) *Encyclopedia of Language and Linguistics* (pp. 683–685). Amsterdam: Elsevier.
Extra, G. and Yağmur, K. (eds) (2012) *Language Rich Europe. Trends in Policies and Practices for Multilingualism in Europe*. Cambridge: Cambridge University Press.

Faas, D. (2011) Between ethnocentrism and Europeanism? An exploration of the effects of migration and European integration on curricula and policies in Greece. *Ethnicities* 11, 163–183.

Gal, S. (2012) Sociolinguistic regimes and the management of 'Diversity'. In M. Heller and A. Duchene (eds) *Language in Late Capitalism: Pride and Profit* (pp. 22–37). London: Routledge.

Good, K.R. (2009) *Municipalities and Multiculturalism: The Politics of Immigration in Toronto and Vancouver.* Toronto: University of Toronto Press.

Goodin, R.E., Rein, M. and Moran, M. (2008) The public and its policies. In M. Moran, M. Rein and R.E. Goodin (eds) *The Oxford Handbook of Public Policy* (pp. 4–36). Oxford: Oxford University Press.

Grzech, K. (2013) Planning language, planning identity: A case study of Ecuadorians in London. *SOAS Working Papers in Linguistics* 16, 291–309. See www.soas.ac.uk/linguistics/research/workingpapers/volume-16/ (accessed 23 October 2014).

Heller, M. (1999) *Linguistic Minorities and Modernity.* London: Longman.

Hobsbawm, E. (1992) *Nations and Nationalism Since 1780: Programme, Myth, Reality.* Cambridge: Cambridge University Press.

Hogan-Brun, G., Mar-Molinero, C. and Stevenson, P. (2009) *Discourses on Language and Integration. Critical Perspectives on Language Testing Regimes in Europe.* Amsterdam: John Benjamins.

Hornberger, N.H. (2006) Frameworks and models in language policy and planning. In T. Ricento (ed.) *An Introduction to Language Policy: Theory and Method* (pp. 24–41). Oxford: Blackwell.

Jaffe, A. (2011) Multilingual citizenship and minority languages. In M. Martin-Jones, A. Blackledge and A. Creese (eds) *The Routledge Handbook of Multilingualism* (pp. 314–332). London: Routledge.

Jaspers, J. and Verschueren, J. (2011) Multilingual structures and agencies. *Journal of Pragmatics* 43 (5), 1157–1160.

King, L., Byrne, N., Djouadi, I., Lo Bianco, J. and Stoicheva, M. (2011) *Languages in Europe. Towards 2020. Analysis and Proposals from the LETPP Consultation and Review.* London: The Languages Company.

Kloss, H. (1977) *The American Bilingual Tradition.* Rowley, MA: Newbury House.

Kraus, P.A. (2011) The multilingual city. The cases of Helsinki and Barcelona. *Nordic Journal of Migration Research* 1 (1), 25–36.

Liddicoat, A.J. and Baldauf, R.B. (2008) Language planning in local contexts: Agents, contexts and interactions. In A.J. Liddicoat and R.B. Baldauf (eds) *Language Planning in Local Contexts* (pp. 3–17). Clevedon: Multilingual Matters.

Little, D. (2010) The linguistic integration of adult migrants: Evaluating policy and practice. Strasbourg: Language Policy Division, Council of Europe. See www.coe.int/t/dg4/linguistic/liam/Source/Events/2010/2010evaluatingpolicy_EN.pdf (accessed 23 October 2014).

Lo Bianco, J. (2008) Language planning as applied linguistics. In A. Davies and C. Elder (eds) *The Blackwell Handbook of Applied Linguistics* (pp. 738–762). Oxford: Blackwell.

Love, S. (2014) Language testing, 'integration' and subtractive multilingualism in Italy: Challenges for adult immigrant second language and literacy education. *Current Issues in Language Planning* 16 (1–2), 26–42.

Luevano-Molina, S. (ed.) (2001) *Immigrant Politics and the Public Library.* Westport, CT: Greenwood Press.

Martin-Jones, M., Blackledge A. and Creese, A. (2012) Introduction: A sociolinguistic of multilingualism for our times. In M. Martin-Jones, A. Blackledge and A. Creese (eds) *The Routledge Handbook of Multilingualism* (pp. 1–26). London: Routledge.

May, S. (2011) Language rights: The 'Cinderella' human right. *Journal of Human Rights* 10 (3), 265–289.

Meylarts, R. (2011a) Translational justice in a multilingual world: An overview of translational regimes. *Meta* 56 (4), 743–757.
Meylarts, R. (2011b) Translation policy. In Y. Gambier and L. van Doorslaer (eds) *Handbook of Translation Studies*, Vol. 2 (pp. 163–168). Amsterdam: John Benjamins.
Ministry of Science, Education and Sports (2013) Education in the language and script of national minorities. Zagreb: Croatian Ministry of Science, Education and Sports of the Republic of Croatia. See http://public.mzos.hr/Default.aspx?sec=3194 (accessed 8 November 2014).
OECD (2013) *OECD Skills Outlook 2013: First Results from the Survey of Adult Skills*. Paris: OECD Publishing. See http://dx.doi.org/10.1787/9789264204256-en (accessed 23 October 2014).
Ozolins, U. (2010) Factors that determine the provision of public service interpreting: Comparative perspectives on government motivation and language service implementation. *Journal of Specialised Translation* 14, 194–215.
Paul, R. (2013) Strategic contextualisation: Free movement, labour migration policies and the governance of foreign workers in Europe. *Policy Studies* 34 (2), 122–141.
Rindler Schjerve, R. and Vetter, E. (2012) *European Multilingualism: Current Perspectives and Challenges*. Bristol: Multilingual Matters.
Schierup, C.-U., Hansen, P. and Castles, S. (2006) *Migration, Citizenship, and the European Welfare State. A European Dilemma*. Oxford: Oxford University Press.
Steiner, N. (2009) *International Migration and Citizenship Today*. London: Routledge.
Travis, A. (2013) Eric Pickles: Councils must cut back on foreign language materials. *The Guardian*, 12 March. www.theguardian.com/politics/2013/mar/12/eric-pickles-councils-foreign-languages (accessed 23 October 2014).
UNWTO (2014) *Tourism Highlights, 2014 Edition*. Madrid: UN World Tourism Organization. See http://mkt.unwto.org/publication/unwto-tourism-highlights-2014-edition (accessed 25 October 2014).
Wee, L. (2011) *Language Without Rights*. Oxford: Oxford University Press.
Williams, L.M. (2014) Public libraries and immigrants: Influences on the degree of welcomeness. *Social Science Research Network*. See http://ssrn.com/abstract=2481392 (accessed 25 October 2014).
Wilson, C.W. L., Turner, G.H. and Perez, I. (2012) Multilingualism and public service access. In M. Martin-Jones, A. Blackledge and A. Creese (eds) *The Routledge Handbook of Multilingualism* (pp. 314–332). London: Routledge.

Chapter 5

Allen, M. (2004) Reading achievement of students in French immersion programs. *Educational Quarterly Review* 9 (4), 25–30.
Auger, N. (2013) Exploring the use of migrant languages to support learning in mainstream classrooms in France. In D. Little, C. Leung and P. Van Avermaet (eds) *Managing Diversity in Education: Languages, Policies, Pedagogies* (pp. 223–242). Bristol: Multilingual Matters.
August, D. and Shanahan, T. (eds) (2006) *Developing Literacy in Second-Language Learning. Report of the National Literacy Panel on Language-Minority Children and Youth*. Mahwah, NJ: Lawrence Erlbaum.
Baker, C. and Hornberger, N. (eds) (2001) *An Introductory Reader to the Writings of Jim Cummins*. Clevedon: Multilingual Matters.
Barnes, D. (1976) *From Communication to Curriculum*. Harmondsworth: Penguin.
Basu, R. (2011) Multiculturalism through multilingualism in schools: Emerging places of integration in Toronto. *Annals of the Association of American Geographers* 6.

Beacco, J.-C. and Byram, M. (2007) *From Linguistic Diversity to Plurilingual Education: Guide for the Development of Language Education Policies in Europe* (main version). Strasbourg: Council of Europe. See www.coe.int/t/dg4/linguistic/Guide_niveau3_EN.asp#TopOfPage (accessed 7 October 2014).

Bialystok, E. (2001) *Bilingualism in Development: Language, Literacy, and Cognition*. Cambridge: Cambridge University Press.

Bialystok, E., Luk, G. and Kwan, E. (2005) Bilingualism, biliteracy and learning to read. Interactions among languages and writing systems. *Scientific Studies of Reading* 9 (1), 43–61.

Britton, J. (1970) *Language and Learning*. London: Allen Lane.

Britton, J., Burgess, T., Martin, N., McLeod, A. and Rosen, H. (1975) *The Development of Writing Abilities (11–18)*. Basingstoke: Macmillan Education.

Bruner, J.S. (1966) *Toward a Theory of Instruction*. Cambridge, MA: Belknap Press.

Bruner, J.S. (1986) *Actual Minds, Possible Worlds*. Cambridge, MA: Harvard University Press.

Bullock, A. (1975) *A Language for Life*. London: HMSO.

Canadian Council on Learning (2009) *Educational Pathways and Academic Performance of Youth of Immigrant Origin: Comparing Montreal, Toronto, and Vancouver*. Toronto: Canadian Council on Learning. See www.ccl-cca.ca/pdfs/OtherReports/CIC-CCL-Final12aout2009EN.pdf (accessed 7 October 2014).

Coste, D., Cavalli, M., Crisan, A. and van de Ven, P.-H. (2009) *Plurlingual and Intercultural Education as a Right*. Strasbourg: Council of Europe. See www.coe.int/t/dg4/linguistic/Source/LE_texts_Source/EducPlurInter-Droit_en.pdf (accessed 7 October 2014).

Council of Europe (2001) *Common European Framework of Reference for Languages: Learning, Teaching, Assessment*. Cambridge: Cambridge University Press. See www.coe.int/t/dg4/linguistic/Source/Framework_EN.pdf (accessed 7 October 2014).

Council of Europe (2008) *Curriculum Framework for Romani*. Strasbourg: Council of Europe. See www.coe.int/t/dg4/linguistic/minorities_romani2008_EN.asp? (accessed 7 October 2014).

Council of Europe (2011) *European Language Portfolio (ELP) Principles and Guidelines, With Added Explanatory Notes*. Strasbourg: Council of Europe. See www.coe.int/t/dg4/education/elp/elp-reg/Source/Templates/ELP_Annotated_PrinciplesGuidelines_EN.pdf (accessed 7 October 2014).

Cummins, J. (1979) Cognitive/academic language proficiency, linguistic interdependence, the optimum age question and some other matters. *Working Papers on Bilingualism* 19, 197–205.

Cummins, J. (1981) The role of primary language development in promoting educational success for language minority students. In California State Department of Education (ed.) *Schooling and Language Minority Students: A Theoretical Framework*. Los Angeles, CA: Evaluation, Dissemination and Assessment Center, California State University.

Cummins, J. (1991) Conversational and academic language proficiency. *AILA Review* 8, 75–89.

Cummins, J. (2008) Total immersion or bilingual education? Findings of international research on promoting immigrant children's achievement in the primary school. In J. Ramseger and M. Wagener (eds) *Chancenungleichheit in der Grundschule, Jahrbuch Grundschulforschung*. Wiesbaden: VS Verlag für Sozialwissenschaften.

Cummins, J. (2013) Language and identity in multilingual schools: Constructing evidence-based instructional policies. In D. Little, C. Leung and P. Van Avermaet (eds) *Managing Diversity in Education: Languages, Policies, Pedagogies* (pp. 3–26). Bristol: Multilingual Matters.

Cummins, J. and Early, M. (eds) (2011) *Identity Texts: The Collaborative Creation of Power in Multilingual Schools*. London: Trentham Books.

Dam, L. (1995) *Learner Autonomy 3: From Theory to Classroom Practice.* Dublin: Authentik.
Duarte, J. and Gogolin, I. (eds) (2013) *Linguistic Superdiversity in Urban Areas: Research Approaches.* Amsterdam: John Benjamins.
European Commission (2012) *First European Survey on Language Competences. Executive Summary.* Brussels: European Commission. See www.surveylang.org/media/ExecutivesummaryoftheESLC_210612.pdf (accessed 7 October 2014).
First Peoples' Heritage, Language and Culture Council (2010) *Report on the Status of B.C. First Nations Languages.* See www.fpcc.ca/files/PDF/2010-report-on-the-status-of-bc-first-nations-languages.pdf (accessed 7 October 2014).
Genesee, F., Lindholm-Leary, K., Saunders, W.M. and Christian, D. (eds) (2006) *Educating English Language Learners: A Synthesis of Research Evidence.* Cambridge: Cambridge University Press.
Gogolin, I., Neumann, U. and Roth, H.-J. (eds) (2005) *Sprachdiagnostik bei Kindern und Jugendlichen mit Migrationshintergrund.* Münster: Waxmann.
Grommes, P. and Hu, A. (eds) (2014) *Plurilingual Education: Policies – Practices – Language Development.* Amsterdam: John Benjamins.
Jerrim, J. (2014) *Why Do East Asian Children Perform So Well in PISA? An Investigation of Western-born Children of East Asian Descent.* See https://johnjerrim.files.wordpress.com/2013/07/australia_asia_paper.pdf (accessed 9 October 2014).
Kenner, C. and Ruby, M. (2012) *Interconnecting Worlds: Teacher Partnerships for Bilingual Learning.* London: Trentham Books.
King, L., Byrne, N., Djouadj, I., Lo Bianco, J. and Stoicheva, M. (2011) *Languages in Europe: Towards 2020. Analysis and Proposals from the LETPP Consultation and Review.* London: The Languages Company. See www.letpp.eu/component/content/article/108-languages-in-europe-towards-2020 (accessed 7 October 2014).
Kirwan, D. (2013) From English Language support to plurilingual awareness. In D. Little, C. Leung and P. Van Avermaet (eds) *Managing Diversity in Education: Languages, Policies, Pedagogies* (pp. 189–203). Bristol: Multilingual Matters.
Kostopoulou, S. (2011) Developing English language support for immigrant students in Irish post-primary schools: A corpus linguistics approach. PhD thesis, University of Dublin, Trinity College.
Kostopoulou, S. (2013) A corpus-based analysis of the lexical demands that Irish post-primary subject textbooks make on immigrant students. In D. Little, C. Leung and P. Van Avermaet (eds) *Managing Diversity in Education: Languages, Policies, Pedagogies* (pp. 147–166). Bristol: Multilingual Matters.
Little, D. (2007) Language learner autonomy: Some fundamental considerations revisited. *Innovation in Language Learning and Teaching* 1 (1), 14–29.
Little, D. (2009) Learner autonomy in action: Adult immigrants learning English in Ireland. In F. Kjisik, P. Voller, N. Aoki and Y. Nakata (eds) *Mapping the Terrain of Learner Autonomy: Learning Environments, Communities and Identities* (pp. 51–85). Tampere: Tampere University Press.
London Metropolitan University (2010) *Impact of Supplementary Schools on Pupils' Attainment: An Investigation into what Factors Contribute to Educational Improvements.* London: Department for Children, Schools and Families. See http://core.ac.uk/download/pdf/4150856.pdf (accessed 17 August 2015).
Lyons, Z. (2013) Assessing the impact of English language support programme materials on post-primary language support and mainstream subject classrooms in Ireland. In D. Little, C. Leung and P. Van Avermaet (eds) *Managing Diversity in Education: Languages, Policies, Pedagogies* (pp. 167–184). Bristol: Multilingual Matters.
Madie, C. (2012) Official language bilingualism to the exclusion of multilingualism: Immigrant student perspectives on French as a second language in 'English-dominant' Canada. *Language and Intercultural Communication* 12 (1), 74–89.

Norris, M.J. (2007) *Aboriginal Languages in Canada: Emerging Trends and Perspectives on Second Language Acquisition*. Ottawa: Statistics Canada. See www.statcan.gc.ca/pub/11-008-x/2007001/pdf/9628-eng.pdf (accessed 7 October 2014).

OECD (2006) *Where Immigrant Students Succeed – A Comparative Review of Performance and Engagement in PISA 2003*. Paris: OECD. See www.oecd-ilibrary.org/education/where-immigrant-students-succeed_9789264023611-en (accessed 7 October 2014).

Ohm, U., Kuhn, C. and Funk, H. (2007) *Sprachtraining für Fachunterricht und Beruf*. Münster: Waxmann.

Reich, H.H., Roth, H.-J. and Neumann, U. (eds) (2007) *Sprachdiagnostik im Lernprozess*. Münster: Waxmann.

Rose, D. and Martin, J.R. (2012) *Learning to Write, Reading to Learn*. Sheffield and Bristol, CT: Equinox.

Sachdev, I., Giles, H. and Pauwels, A. (2012) Accommodating multilinguality. In T.K. Bhatia and W.C. Ritchie (eds) *The Handbook of Bilingualism and Multilingualism* (2nd edn) (pp. 391–416). Chichester: Wiley-Blackwell.

Schofield, J.W. and Bangs, R. (2006) Conclusions and further perspectives. In J.W. Schofield (ed.) *Migration Background, Minority-Group Membership and Academic Achievement. Research Evidence from Social, Educational and Developmental Psychology*. AKI Research Review 5. Berlin: Social Science Research Center.

Siemund, P., Gogolin, I., Schulz, M.E. and Davydova, J. (eds) (2013) *Multilingualism and Language Diversity in Urban Areas: Acquisition, Identities, Space, Education*. Amsterdam: John Benjamins.

Sierens, S. and Van Avermaet, P. (2013) Language diversity in education: Evolving multilingual education to functional multilingual learning. In D. Little, C. Leung and P. Van Avermaet (eds) *Managing Diversity in Education: Languages, Policies, Pedagogies* (pp. 204–222). Bristol: Multilingual Matters.

Chapter 6

Alexander, J.C. (2013) Struggling over the mode of incorporation: Backlash against multiculturalism in Europe. *Ethnic and Racial Studies* 36 (4), 531–556; doi:10/1080/01419 870.2012.752515.

Ali, M. (2004) *Brick Lane*. London: Black Swan.

Andelman, D.A. (2008) *A Shattered Peace: Versailles 1919 and the Price We Pay Today*. Hoboken, NJ: John Wiley.

Barber, B. (2013) *If Mayors Ruled the World: Dysfunctional Nations, Rising Cities*. New Haven, CT: Yale University Press.

BBC (2014) *Bombay Railway*. See www.bbc.co.uk/programmes/b007t30p.

BBC News (2010) Merkel says German multicultural society has failed. *BBC News*,17 January. See www.bbc.co.uk/news/world-europe-11559451 (accessed 1 December 2014).

Blanc, M. (2008) Multilingualism in the Ancient Near East. Paper presented at a Conference to Honour Professor Michel Blanc, Birkbeck College, University of London. Unpublished manuscript.

Blish, J. (1962) *A Life for the Stars*. New York: Puttnams. Extract taken from compendium version (1970) *The Novels of the Cities in Flight*. New York: Avon.

Bosetti, G. (2011) Introduction: Addressing the politics of fear. The challenge posed by pluralism to Europe. *Philosophy and Social Criticism* 37 (4), 371–382; doi:10.1177/01914 53711400998.

Chakrabarti, V. and Foster, N. (2013) *A Country of Cities: A Manifesto for an Urban America*. New York: Metropolis.

City of Melbourne (2015) *Sandridge Bridge Precinct Redevelopment*. See www.melbourne.vic. gov.au/AboutMelbourne/ProjectsandInitiatives/MajorProjects/Pages/SandridgeBridge. aspx (accessed 3 January 2015).

Council of Europe (1992) *European Charter for Regional or Minority Languages*. European Treaty Series No. 148. Strasbourg: Council of Europe.

Council of Europe (2007) *From Linguistic Diversity to Plurilingual Education: Guide for the Development of Language Education Policies in Europe*. Language Policy Division, Strasbourg: Council of Europe.

de Swaan, A. (2001) *Words of the World: The Global Language System*. Malden, MA: Polity Press.

European Commission (2008) *A Rewarding Challenge: How Language Diversity Could Strengthen Europe (Proposals from the Group of Intellectuals for Intercultural Dialogue)*. Brussels: European Commission. See http://bookshop.europa.eu/en/a-rewarding-challenge-how-language-diversity-could-strengthen-europe-pbNC3008147/ (accessed 7 October 2014).

Extra, G. and Yağmur, K. (2012) *Language Rich Europe. Trends in Policies and Practices for Multilingualism in Europe*. Cambridge: Cambridge University Press.

Glaeser, E. (2011) *Triumph of the City*. London: MacMillan.

Glaeser, E. and Gottlieb, J.D. (2009) The wealth of cities, agglomeration economies and spatial equilibrium in the United States. NBER Working Paper No. 14806. Cambridge, MA: National Bureau of Economic Research. See www.nber.org/papers/w14806.pdf (accessed 11 December 2014).

Gogolin, I. and Pries, L. (2004) Transmigration und Bildung. *Zeitschrift für Erziehungswissenschaft (ZfE)* 7 (1), 5–19.

Habermas, J. 2006. Opening up Fortress Europe: Jürgen Habermas on immigration as the key to European unity. *Signandsight.com: Let's Talk European*, 16 November. See www.signandsight.com/features/1048.html (accessed 30 April 2015).

Judt, T. (2005) *Postwar: A History of Europe since 1945*. London: Heinemann. Paperback version 2010. London: Vintage.

Katz, B. and Bradley, J. (2013) *The Metropolitan Revolution. How Cities and Metros Are Fixing our Broken Politics and Fragile Economy*. Washington, DC: Brookings Institution Press.

King, L., Byrne, N., Djouadj, I., Lo Bianco, J. and Stoicheva, M. (2011) *Languages in Europe Towards 2020. Analysis and Proposals from the LETPP Consultation and Review*. London: The Languages Company.

Lo Bianco, J. (2013) The Cosmopolis: Urban life and multilingualism. LUCIDE Seminar: The Challenges of Multilingual Urban Communities – the South East European Perspective, Varna Free University, Bulgaria, 11–12 September.

Lo Bianco, J. (2014) The Cosmopolis – historically and in the world today. Keynote talk at LUCIDE Final Conference: The Future of the Multilingual City, London School of Economics and Political Science, 3–4 September.

Lo Bianco, J., with Slaughter, Y. (2009) Second languages and Australian schooling. *Australian Education Review* 54.

Mak, G. (2004) *In Europe. Travels Through the Twentieth Century* (trans. S. Garrett). London: Vintage Books.

McMonagle S. (n.d.) *Sustaining Linguistic Diversity in the Information Age: A Survey of Minority Language Vitality on the Internet*. See www.nachhaltige.uni-hamburg.de/postdoc-kolleg/alumni/mcmonagle.html (accessed 1 December 2014).

Manent, P. (2013) *Metamorphoses of the City: On the Western Dynamic* (trans. Lepain). Cambridge, MA: Harvard University Press.

Mullen, A. and James, P. (2012) *Multilingualism in the Graeco-Roman Worlds*. Cambridge: Cambridge University Press.

Multilingual Manchester (n.d.) Multilingual Manchester website. See http://mlm.humanities.manchester.ac.uk (accessed 1 December 2014).

ONS (Office of National Statistics) (2014) *ONS 2013 Mid-year Population Estimates.* Reported in *GLA Intelligence Update 09–2014.* See www.london.gov.uk/sites/default/files/update-09-2014-2013-mye.pdf.

Orr, D. (2014) The UK's big supermarkets sowed the seeds of their own decline. *The Guardian,* 3 October. See www.theguardian.com/commentisfree/2014/oct/03/uk-big-supermarkets-sowed-seeds-own-decline (accessed 10 October 2014).

Pantel, M. (1999) Unity-in-diversity: Cultural policy and EU legitimacy. In T. Banchoff and M. Smith (eds) *Legitimacy and the European Union: The Contested Polity* (pp. 46–66). London: Routledge Taylor and Francis.

Phelps, N. (2013) *US–Habsburg Relations from 1815 to the Paris Peace Conference.* Cambridge: Cambridge University Press.

Pinker, S. (2011) *The Better Angels of Our Nature. A History of Violence and Humanity.* London: Penguin.

Sandercock, L. (1998) *Towards Cosmopolis: Planning for Multicultural Cities.* London: John Wiley.

Sandercock, L. (2003) *Cosmopolis II: Mongrel Cities in the 21st Century.* London: Continuum.

Saunders, D. (2010) *Arrival City.* London: Heinemann.

Shelley, P.B. (1826) Ozymandias. *Miscellaneous and Posthumous Poems of Percy Bysshe Shelley.* London: William Benbow.

Sparrow, A. (2014) Nigel Farage: Parts of Britain are 'like a foreign land'. *The Guardian,* 28 February. See www.theguardian.com/politics/2014/feb/28/nigel-farage-ukip-immigration-speech (accessed 2 April 2014).

Stern, H.H. (1964) We tend to forget that our educational systems had their foundations laid in an age of relatively small, independent nation states. Paper read to the International Conference on Modern Language Teaching, West Berlin. In P.H. Hoy (1977) *The Early Teaching of Modern Languages.* London: Nuffield Foundation.

Weber, E. (1976) *Peasants Into Frenchmen: The Modernization of Rural France, 1870–1914.* Stanford, CA: Stanford University Press.

Woodward, D.R. (2009) *World War 1 Almanac.* New York: Facts on File.

Index

Academic language 150, 152, 156, 175
Advertising 9, 53, 59, 66, 68
Africa 22, 23, 27, 30, 37, 39, 42, 44, 61, 75, 90, 118, 181, 184, 187, 194
Alphabet 70
Alsatian 39, 42, 61, 62, 81, 98
Antiquity 18, 23, 24, 32, 43
Arabic 25, 26, 27, 41, 42, 54, 59, 62, 71, 72, 73, 76, 133, 139, 140, 165, 168
Asylum seeking, asylum seekers 29, 117, 130, 194
Assimilation 11, 19, 31, 45, 98, 104, 118, 123, 125, 145, 146, 194, 198
Attitudes 5, 11, 25, 44, 47, 84, 93, 99, 101, 102, 103, 104, 105, 106, 111, 112, 135, 144, 153, 185, 187, 193, 196, 201, 202
Athens ix, x, 22, 23, 32, 33, 34, 38, 40, 43, 44, 45, 56, 70, 74, 91, 94, 99, 102, 108, 111, 131, 132, 133, 134, 135, 136, 140, 154, 163, 168, 170, 180, 181, 184, 186, 195
Australia ix, 5, 6, 8, 18, 21, 22, 31, 33, 37, 43, 44, 54, 117, 123, 131, 150, 153, 173, 193, 197, 201

Babel 17, 18, 26, 202
Bengali 30, 56, 165, 189
Bilingual/ism 5, 6, 19, 20, 23, 27, 31, 33, 37, 38, 39, 40, 41, 42, 43, 44, 54, 56, 57, 59, 60, 62, 63, 64, 68, 71, 79, 82, 92, 97, 102, 106, 123, 129, 135, 137, 138, 140, 143, 155, 164, 165, 168, 169, 173, 188, 201
Bosnian 82
Bulgaria 25, 30, 33, 34, 38, 74, 103, 122, 154, 170
Bulgarian (language) 33, 34, 51, 68, 69, 103, 122, 154, 163

Business 10, 53, 56, 68, 69, 158, 168, 187, 188

Canada ix, 5, 6, 8, 18, 21, 31, 32, 40, 41, 43, 44, 45, 63, 98, 99, 109, 117, 123, 131, 135, 150, 153, 162, 168, 173, 197
Capitalism 21
Chinese 10, 27, 30, 32, 37, 38, 43, 45, 54, 62, 65, 140, 141, 165, 168, 189
Citizenship 11, 44, 100, 116, 117, 118, 120, 124, 135
Cityscape 1, 6, 28, 31, 46, 47, 48, 51, 52, 53, 54, 58, 60, 62, 63, 65, 70, 73, 80, 86, 93, 196, 199, 200, 202
Civic institutions 8, 13, 114, 123, 127, 129
Code-mixing, code-switching 60, 77, 174
Colonialism, colonisation 19, 21, 25, 43, 120, 123
Cosmopolis 185, 187, 192, 198, 199
Cosmopolitanism 66, 83, 181
Council of Europe 9, 39, 125, 158, 169, 170, 171, 173, 198
  Common European Framework of Reference for Languages (CEFR) 124, 148, 150, 169, 170, 171
  European Charter for Regional and Minority Languages 98
  European Language Portfolio 170, 175
  Framework Convention for the Protection of National Minorities 98
  Languages of Schooling project 156
Croatia 38, 70, 122, 161, 170
Croatian (language) 8, 38, 42, 68, 154 161,
Cyprus 37, 38

Danish 34, 35, 163
Dialect/s 24, 26, 27, 42, 88, 92, 105, 175

Index 219

Diplomacy 66, 99
Dublin ix, x, 5, 14, 22, 23, 35, 36, 37, 42, 43, 45, 46, 47, 49, 50, 52, 54, 55, 58, 62, 63, 64, 65, 69, 73, 74, 75, 80, 81, 88, 90, 91, 99, 101, 102, 103, 106, 107, 129, 131, 132, 139, 141, 154, 155, 156, 160, 163, 165, 167, 168, 170
Dutch (language) 25, 49, 50, 53, 57, 58, 69, 77, 78, 79, 98, 103, 104, 131, 163, 167

Economy 30, 34, 36, 44, 47, 118, 145, 185, 191
Economic crisis, recession 33, 45, 134, 155, 157, 193
   Fiscal austerity 145
Education, educational sphere 6, 11, 13, 31, 36, 43, 44, 45, 46, 63, 97, 98, 103, 105, 117, 118, 119, 120, 121, 123, 135, 142–176, 180, 185, 188, 189, 194, 199
   Adult education ix, 135, 200
   Bilingual education 161, 164, 169
   CLIL 169, 175
   Complementary schools 6, 30, 121, 162
   Curricula 30, 121, 148, 150, 151, 152, 156, 158, 159, 162, 163, 164, 169, 172, 175
   Education policy 9, 82, 121, 141, 149, 171
   Educational exchange 19, 101
   Exams 156, 161, 163
   Foreign language teaching and learning 13, 101, 121, 148, 150, 155, 158, 161, 163, 168, 169, 170, 172, 175
   Heritage-language education 160, 161, 162
   Immersion schooling 155, 160, 161
   Intercultural education 163
   Language of schooling 13, 148, 150, 152, 153, 154, 155, 157, 158, 163, 169, 174, 175
   Language support 148, 150, 154, 155, 156, 158, 159
   Mother-tongue education 34, 82, 122, 138
   Multilingual/plurilingual education 45, 56, 138, 158, 167, 174, 175, 200, 201
   Pre-school, Kindergarten 122, 158, 161, 168, 169
   Primary education, schools 6, 74, 102, 155, 158, 160, 161, 163, 167, 168, 169
   Post-primary/Secondary education, schools 6, 74, 155, 156, 158, 160, 161, 168, 169, 187
   Teachers 31, 136, 151, 152, 154, 155, 156, 161, 162, 163, 165, 167, 168, 169, 170, 175
   Vocational training 158, 159
Emigration x, 23, 27, 32, 33, 35, 37, 38, 41, 134, 186
Emotions 74, 95, 98, 101, 103, 111, 113
Empire 16, 19, 20, 23, 42, 43, 181, 182, 183, 197, 199
   Austro-Hungarian Empire, Habsburg Empire 20, 38, 42, 43, 149, 183
   British Empire 29, 35
   Dutch Empire 25
   Ottoman Empire 20, 33, 42, 43, 149, 183, 187
   Roman Empire 19, 20, 24, 42, 182
   Russian Empire 20, 36
   Spanish Empire 26
Employment 25, 26, 39, 40, 99, 103, 104, 196
England 20, 65, 98, 150, 162, 170
English (language) 8, 21, 25, 26, 27, 28, 30, 31, 32, 33, 34, 35, 36, 37, 38, 39, 40, 41, 42, 43, 44, 45, 46, 49, 50, 51, 53, 56, 57, 58, 59, 60, 62, 63, 64, 65, 66, 67, 68, 69, 70, 72, 74, 75, 76, 77, 79, 80, 81, 82, 90, 98, 102, 118, 128, 129, 130, 131, 132, 133, 134, 136, 139, 141, 143, 145, 150, 153, 154, 155, 156, 157, 160, 162, 163, 164, 165, 168, 169, 173, 174, 186, 189, 191
   English as a lingua franca 2, 43, 80, 81, 132
   English as an additional language 156, 166, 168
   English for Speakers of Other Languages (ESOL) 135
   English language support 154, 155, 156
   Multicultural London English 77, 78, 79
Entrepreneurs 29, 55
Essekerisch 38, 68, 98
Ethnicity/ethnicities 2, 4, 8, 22, 56, 95, 103, 104, 155, 199
Europe ix, 2, 5, 6, 11, 17, 18, 19, 20, 21, 22, 23, 24, 27, 29, 30, 31, 33, 34, 35, 36, 37, 39, 40, 43, 44, 45, 48, 58, 66, 75, 76, 81, 88, 90, 97, 99, 100, 101, 117, 118, 123, 124, 154, 172, 181, 182, 183, 184, 185, 191, 193, 194, 197, 199, 202
European Economic Area 37
European institutions 39, 44, 60, 121

European Union (EU) 8, 16, 21, 22, 23, 24, 30, 34, 36, 37, 38, 42, 43, 45, 88, 90, 99, 100, 104, 116, 117, 120, 121, 125, 163, 169, 172, 173, 174, 184, 185
   European/EU citizenship 100, 116, 121, 125
   European Commission 169, 172, 173, 174, 185
   European Council 169
   European Parliament 39, 75
   EU Lifelong Learning Programme ix
Exclusion 1, 12, 19, 48, 76, 104, 105, 118, 125, 140, 145, 146, 194, 198

Festivals, celebrations 6, 106, 107, 108, 127, 137, 138, 140, 188
France 9, 26, 29, 31, 39, 60, 66, 68, 97, 98, 99, 100, 101, 144, 162, 167, 170, 182
Freedom of movement 88, 100
French (language) 8, 20, 21, 25, 30, 31, 32, 37, 40, 41, 42, 43, 45, 50, 53, 54, 56, 61, 62, 63, 68, 75, 79, 80, 81, 82, 97, 98, 106, 120, 128, 129, 136, 139, 144, 149, 160, 162, 165, 166, 168, 169, 173, 182, 183, 189

German (language) 3, 8, 25, 27, 30, 38, 39, 42, 43, 45, 50, 51, 56, 58, 59, 60, 62, 66, 73, 76, 80, 82, 120, 128, 129, 144, 155, 161, 167, 168, 169, 189
Germany 20, 27, 28, 33, 39, 50, 60, 76, 98, 100, 156, 160, 193
Globalisation 2, 5, 8, 16, 21, 22, 42, 51, 66, 116, 184, 185, 193, 196, 197, 198
Governance 2, 7, 9, 40, 127
Graffiti 48, 54, 65, 67, 70, 71
Greece 32, 33, 37, 134, 135, 138, 170, 182
Greek (language) 19, 20, 37, 42, 56, 70, 132, 135, 136, 162, 163,
Guest workers 25, 99
Gujarati 29, 165, 173

Hamburg ix, x, 3, 5, 9, 23, 27, 28, 42, 43, 44, 45, 46, 58, 59, 60, 65, 66, 67, 76, 77, 80, 82, 83, 88, 90, 91, 92, 94, 96, 97, 98, 99, 100, 101, 106, 107, 111, 117, 120, 131, 132, 135, 136, 137, 138, 139, 143, 149, 154, 155, 158, 159, 160, 167, 168, 196, 197, 200
Hebrew 19, 26, 34, 161

Home languages 6, 13, 60, 106, 135, 143, 148, 150, 152, 153, 154, 155, 158, 161, 162, 163, 164, 165, 167, 174, 175
Host language 6, 77, 106
Hungarian (language) 38, 39, 68, 81, 82, 161, 163

Identity ix, 4, 5, 31, 39, 42, 60, 61, 77, 79, 81, 84, 85, 86, 87, 92, 94, 95, 97, 100, 101, 102, 103, 104, 105, 108, 109, 110, 111, 112, 113, 126, 158, 164, 167, 171, 172, 180, 183, 184, 187, 191, 198, 199, 200
Indigenous peoples, languages 21, 31, 43, 46, 120, 123
   Aboriginal people, languages 30, 31, 98, 134, 160, 161
   First Nations 32, 160
Immigration/Immigrants ix, x, 4, 6, 8, 11, 19, 21, 23, 25, 26, 27, 29, 30, 31, 32, 33, 34, 35, 36, 37, 38, 39, 40, 41, 42, 43, 44, 45, 46, 54, 55, 56, 63, 75, 77, 82, 88, 90, 91, 97, 99, 104, 108, 111, 116, 117, 118, 120, 123, 124, 130, 132, 135, 136, 137, 140, 141, 143, 145
Inclusion ix, 6, 75, 116, 137
Integration 4, 19, 25, 30, 37, 43, 45, 76, 97, 106, 114, 116, 117, 118, 119, 120, 124, 125, 126, 127, 130, 135, 136, 137, 145, 146, 152, 153, 154, 155, 156, 163, 172, 192
Intercultural awareness 170
Intercultural dialogue x, 75
Interpreting/interpretation ix, 4, 6, 13, 114, 119, 127, 128, 129, 130, 131, 132, 133, 134, 141, 200
Ireland 21, 35, 36, 37, 43, 44, 55, 62, 63, 64, 65, 69, 70, 74, 104, 129, 154, 157, 160, 168
Irish (Gaelic) language 29, 35, 36, 37, 43, 47, 62, 63, 64, 65, 74, 75, 81, 103, 104, 129, 139, 141, 154, 160, 165, 166, 168
Italian (language) 20, 23, 24, 30, 32, 37, 41, 55, 56, 58, 60, 72, 112, 124, 128, 165, 168, 169, 173
Italy 20, 24, 30, 66, 112, 120, 124, 138, 162

Japanese 30, 49, 50, 57, 72, 128, 168, 190

Korean 96, 128, 130, 190
Kurdish 76, 82, 139, 189

Labour/labourers 2, 6, 27, 28, 30, 35, 60, 91, 99, 116, 117, 145
Language acquisition 4, 25, 116, 118, 119, 123, 124, 127, 135, 136, 137, 138, 149, 152, 166, 173, 175
Language endangerment 21
Language hierarchies 30, 43, 102, 118, 143, 145
Language learning ix, 6, 13, 33, 76, 114, 121, 124, 125, 127, 135, 136, 137, 158, 165, 166, 168, 169, 170, 171, 173, 175
Language planning 36, 116, 125, 126
Language policy/policies 6, 8, 13, 31, 38, 44, 45, 64, 65, 81, 93, 114, 115, 116, 119, 120, 122, 141, 169, 185
Language revitalisation 31, 65
Language rights 121, 122, 123, 126, 129
Language shift 10
Language testing 124, 125, 136
Latin 19, 20, 24, 26, 38
Legislation, law(s) 6, 19, 53, 54, 64, 68, 81, 82, 98, 121, 122, 124, 125, 129, 134, 182, 200
Limassol ix, 5, 23, 33, 37, 38, 42, 43, 44, 45, 79, 88, 90, 106, 111, 131, 132, 143, 149, 154, 163, 183
Lingua franca 2, 24, 43, 80, 81, 118, 131, 132
Linguistic landscape 24, 38, 49, 51, 53, 62, 63, 65, 66, 69, 73, 80, 83, 91, 99
Linguistic soundscape 48, 73, 76
Literacy 135, 136, 137, 148, 150, 153, 157, 158, 162, 163, 164
London ix, 3, 5, 22, 23, 29, 30, 41, 42, 43, 44, 45, 46, 52, 56, 57, 60, 75, 76, 77, 78, 79, 83, 87, 88, 89, 90, 91, 92, 93, 94, 96, 99, 101, 109, 111, 120, 128, 129, 131, 132, 133, 134, 135, 136, 138, 141, 143, 145, 149, 154, 155, 157, 162, 165, 168, 170, 173, 180, 181, 184, 190, 191, 192, 193, 195, 202

Madrid ix, x, 23, 26, 27, 42, 43, 44, 81, 88, 90, 91, 92, 94, 99, 101, 102, 109, 111, 128, 129, 131, 132, 133, 136, 143, 149, 154, 155, 163, 169, 170, 184
Media 4, 6, 24, 44, 45, 46, 75, 76, 79, 100, 127, 140, 196

Books 18, 21, 50, 127, 140, 141, 156, 157
Newspapers 3, 56, 145, 173
Radio 46, 68, 73, 74, 75, 76, 122
Social media 2, 3, 22, 105
Television 46, 68, 73, 74, 122
Websites 7, 55, 56, 57, 64, 73, 129, 132, 141, 157, 160, 188
Mega-cities 1
Melbourne ix, 5, 23, 30, 31, 32, 33, 42, 43, 44, 45, 46, 54, 55, 75, 91, 92, 99, 101, 129, 131, 138, 149, 162, 189, 191, 192, 200
Middle East 19, 37, 42, 44, 58, 90, 187
Migration/migrants x, 2, 4, 5, 6, 19, 24, 25, 27, 28, 29, 30, 31, 33, 35, 37, 40, 41, 42, 45, 55, 58, 60, 63, 75, 76, 77, 82, 88, 90, 91, 92, 97, 98, 99, 100, 103, 105, 106, 116, 117, 118, 119, 121, 124, 125, 129, 132, 135, 136, 138, 139, 140, 155, 158, 159, 182, 185, 186, 196, 197, 198
Mobility 2, 4, 6, 8, 11, 16, 21, 24, 38, 42, 83, 84, 87, 88, 99, 100, 101, 110, 116, 118, 124, 125, 153, 169, 181, 193, 197, 199
Monolingual/ism 5, 9, 10, 17, 19, 21, 27, 34, 42, 43, 44, 45, 46, 53, 58, 60, 65, 66, 69, 72, 92, 93, 95, 96, 97, 105, 106, 122, 130, 145, 146, 155, 170, 172, 178, 182, 183, 188, 201
Montreal ix, 5, 23, 32, 40, 41, 42, 53, 54, 68, 79, 81, 88, 90, 101, 106, 108, 109, 120, 129, 149, 162, 168
Multiculturalism 11, 24, 33, 134, 193, 194
Multiethnolects 48, 76, 77, 78, 79
Multinational companies 36, 63, 66, 181

National minorities 98, 122, 126, 183, 187
Nationalism 16, 20, 120, 178, 183, 187, 193, 201
Nation building 110, 120, 183
Netherlands 24, 27, 29, 76, 79, 163, 170
Non-governmental organisations (NGOs) 115, 121, 125, 135, 136, 195
Norway 34, 35, 99, 136
Norwegian 34, 71, 72, 79

OECD 136, 137, 153, 155, 156
Osijek ix, x, 8, 23, 38, 39, 42, 43, 50, 51, 66, 67, 68, 70, 81, 82, 88, 90, 91, 92, 94, 98, 103, 107, 122, 132, 137, 140, 141, 149, 154, 161, 163, 168, 169, 170, 183, 184
Oslo ix, 5, 12, 23, 34, 35, 70, 71, 72, 73, 79, 82, 111, 131, 135, 136, 140, 170, 186
Ottawa ix, 23, 31, 32, 40, 42, 108, 109, 149, 154, 189

Plebeian multilingualism 25, 44, 143
Plurilingual/ism 9, 13, 16, 17, 22, 24, 26, 31, 42, 45, 46, 47, 60, 93, 102, 140, 142, 143, 148, 149, 150, 158, 159, 162, 170, 171, 172, 173, 174, 175, 176, 185, 187, 188, 191, 199, 200, 201, 202
Polis 1, 11
Polish (language) 29, 37, 42, 45, 69, 140, 163, 165, 173,
Population growth 2
Portuguese 20, 30, 75, 128, 163, 165, 173
Poverty 1, 33, 105, 153
Prestigious multilingualism 11, 25, 44, 83, 103, 104, 121, 143
Private sphere 32, 70, 73, 105, 106, 188
Public sphere 6, 37, 54, 63, 81, 82, 103, 105, 119, 137, 189
  Daycare 158
  Health services/healthcare ix, x, 6, 45, 75, 130, 131, 132, 133, 134, 185, 200
  Libraries 72, 140, 141, 145, 158
  Municipalities 6, 33, 56, 58, 91, 149
  Police 69, 131
  Public transport 6, 28, 57, 58, 74, 80, 128
  Social services ix, 97, 200
Punjabi 43, 173

Racism 33, 112, 135, 140, 145
Refugees 27, 35, 36, 40, 42, 76, 99, 100, 136, 138, 181
Religion, 1, 6, 19, 20, 22, 24, 27, 29, 36, 45, 46, 76, 103, 104, 106, 139
Religious activities 189, 198
  Islam 28, 40, 104, 139
  Roman Catholic Church 20, 24
Repertoires 4, 5, 9, 12, 13, 48, 60, 77, 79, 96, 102, 104, 105, 108, 110, 114, 140, 143, 148, 150, 154, 162, 165, 170, 171, 173, 187

Roma/Romany, Romani/Romanes 33, 34, 42, 43, 76, 82, 161
Romanian 20, 27, 37, 163
Rome ix, x, 13, 18, 22, 23, 24, 41, 43, 44, 56, 75, 88, 90, 91, 94, 99, 101, 102, 109, 111, 112, 129, 131, 132, 136, 138, 139, 140, 141, 182
Russian 37, 38, 42, 44, 69, 128, 140, 168, 169

Sami 34, 82
Serbian (language) 8, 38, 75, 82, 103, 123, 161
Signs, signage 6, 13, 26, 28, 29, 48, 49, 50, 52, 53, 54, 55, 56, 57, 58, 59, 60, 61, 62, 63, 64, 65, 66, 68, 69, 70, 71, 72, 74, 80, 81, 82, 89, 94, 141, 188
Sign Languages 74, 75
Slovakian 161, 163
Social cohesion 11, 176, 201
Sofia ix, 14, 23, 33, 34, 38, 42, 43, 45, 74, 86, 88, 92, 93, 94, 98, 111, 129, 132, 141, 168, 169, 170, 182
Spain 24, 27, 133, 162, 170
Spanish (language) 8, 20, 30, 41, 44, 45, 50, 54, 56, 58, 60, 128, 136, 140, 154, 155, 163, 164, 165, 168, 169, 173
  Castilian 21, 26
Strasbourg ix, 9, 23, 39, 40, 42, 43, 44, 51, 58, 60, 61, 62, 65, 66, 68, 81, 89, 90, 91, 93, 94, 97, 98, 100, 101, 106, 108, 120, 129, 131, 135, 139, 141, 144, 162, 168, 169, 170, 184
Stratification 104, 118, 145
Street art 53, 56, 70
Super-diversity/hyper-diversity 22, 46
Swedish 35, 66, 163

Technology, 2, 3, 5, 21, 181
  Communication technology
Toronto ix, 23, 31, 32, 41, 42, 45, 46, 47, 55, 56, 90, 98, 99, 108, 129, 130, 131, 134, 135, 136, 149, 153, 154, 161, 162
Tourism, tourists 6, 24, 25, 26, 38, 41, 44, 48, 50, 52, 53, 55, 56, 57, 58, 62, 63, 64, 65, 66, 80, 92, 100, 101, 102, 109, 110, 111, 128, 185, 189, 198
Trade 1, 19, 27, 29, 35, 37, 42, 51, 52, 55, 66, 68, 99, 169, 185, 188

Trade unions 136
Translation ix, 2, 4, 6, 13, 20, 41, 64, 68, 69, 114, 119, 121, 122, 123, 127, 129, 130, 131, 132, 133, 134, 139, 141, 154, 166
Trilingual/ism 20, 129
Turkish (language) 25, 29, 30, 34, 37, 42, 59, 60, 62, 76, 80, 82, 104, 132, 144, 161, 165, 167, 168, 189

UK 29, 30, 31, 32, 37, 43, 45, 70, 90, 100, 134, 170
Unemployment 153
Unilingual/ism 31, 41, 42, 54, 68, 69, 134
University/Universities ix, 1, 24, 39, 45, 101, 118, 140, 155, 156, 158, 159, 160, 162, 163, 168, 173, 185
Urbanisation 46, 181
Urbanism 2, 3, 4, 5, 54, 87, 181, 199
Urban studies 1, 4, 100
Urdu 30, 140, 165, 166

Utrecht ix, x, 5, 23, 24, 25, 41, 43, 44, 45, 46, 49, 50, 51, 57, 58, 69, 70, 76, 77, 78, 81, 88, 90, 91, 92, 94, 98, 99, 103, 104, 111, 131, 137, 138, 141, 142, 143, 163, 167, 168, 169, 170, 191, 196, 200

Varna ix, x, 5, 23, 25, 26, 38, 41, 42, 43, 44, 45, 50, 51, 68, 70, 81, 92, 98, 103, 111, 122, 129, 132, 141, 149, 154, 161, 168, 169, 170
Vancouver ix, 5, 10, 23, 32, 41, 43, 46, 90, 108, 109, 120, 129, 138, 149, 153, 154, 160, 161, 165, 173
Volunteer/voluntary organisations 33, 106, 131, 136

Wealth 1, 22, 35

Xenophobia 33, 118, 124, 140, 145, 193, 198

Yiddish 32, 38, 40

For Product Safety Concerns and Information please contact our EU Authorised Representative:

Easy Access System Europe

Mustamäe tee 50

10621 Tallinn

Estonia

gpsr.requests@easproject.com